Emerging Extended Reality Technologies For Industry 4.0

Scrivener Publishing
100 Cummings Center, Suite 541J
Beverly, MA 01915-6106

Publishers at Scrivener
Martin Scrivener (martin@scrivenerpublishing.com)
Phillip Carmical (pcarmical@scrivenerpublishing.com)

Emerging Extended Reality Technologies For Industry 4.0

Early Experiences with Conception, Design, Implementation, Evaluation and Deployment

Jolanda G. Tromp

State University of New York, Oswego, New York, USA

Dac-Nhuong Le

Haiphong University, Haiphong, Vietnam

Chung Van Le

Duy Tan University, Danang, Vietnam

Scrivener
Publishing

WILEY

This edition first published 2020 by John Wiley & Sons, Inc., 111 River Street, Hoboken, NJ 07030, USA and Scrivener Publishing LLC, 100 Cummings Center, Suite 541J, Beverly, MA 01915, USA
© 2020 Scrivener Publishing LLC
For more information about Scrivener publications please visit www.scrivenerpublishing.com.

Wiley Global Headquarters
111 River Street, Hoboken, NJ 07030, USA

For details of our global editorial offices, customer services, and more information about Wiley products visit us at www.wiley.com.

Limit of Liability/Disclaimer of Warranty
While the publisher and authors have used their best efforts in preparing this work, they make no representations or warranties with respect to the accuracy or completeness of the contents of this work and specifically disclaim all warranties, including without limitation any implied warranties of merchantability or fitness for a particular purpose. No warranty may be created or extended by sales representatives, written sales materials, or promotional statements for this work. The fact that an organization, website, or product is referred to in this work as a citation and/or potential source of further information does not mean that the publisher and authors endorse the information or services the organization, website, or product may provide or recommendations it may make. This work is sold with the understanding that the publisher is not engaged in rendering professional services. The advice and strategies contained herein may not be suitable for your situation. You should consult with a specialist where appropriate. Neither the publisher nor authors shall be liable for any loss of profit or any other commercial damages, including but not limited to special, incidental, consequential, or other damages. Further, readers should be aware that websites listed in this work may have changed or disappeared between when this work was written and when it is read.

Library of Congress Cataloging-in-Publication Data

ISBN 978-1-119-65463-6

Cover image: Pixabay.Com
Cover design by Russell Richardson

Set in size of 11pt and Minion Pro by Manila Typesetting Company, Makati, Philippines

Contents

Part I Extended Reality Education

Part II Internet Of Things

Part III Mobile Technology

6   Human Factors for E-Health Training System: UX Testing for XR Anatomy Training App ... **81**

Zhushun Timothy Cai, Oliver Medonza, Kristen Ray, Chung Van Le,
Damian Schofield, Jolanda Tromp

Part IV   Towards Digital Twins and Robotics

7   Augmented Reality at Heritage Sites: Technological Advances and Embodied Spatially Minded Interactions ... **101**

Lesley Johnston, Romy Galloway, Jordan John Trench, Matthieu Poyade,
Jolanda Tromp, Hoang Thi My

Part VI Towards Cognitive Computing

List of Figures

List of Tables

Foreword

The 5th International Conference on Communication, Management and Information Technology (ICCMIT'19)[1] was jointly organized in Vienna, Austria, on March 26-28, 2019,, by the Universal Society of Applied Research, Prague, Czech Republic, in collaboration with the University of Denver, Colorado, United States of America. The main objective of this conference, which has been running yearly since 2015, was to bring together researchers, societies, new technology experts, and manufacturing professionals interested or already involved in R&D with new technologies and innovative ideas at any scale and create a community spirit and learn from each other. The aim of this yearly conference is to facilitate sharing of research, ideas, and lessons learned by international researchers and explore collaborations to begin working towards achieving the highest standards of ICT. One of the major overall themes of the conference is Industry 4.0 and smart citizens, smart cities, smart factories, etc. These recent and innovative Industry 4.0 technologies are prototypes for the next generation of 21st century production systems. Advancement of information technologies and their convergence with operational technologies paves the way for an evolution of production systems. To remain competitive in the market, enterprises want to utilize these technological advancements in order to solve current challenges and serve customers in new ways which were not imagined before. In order to provide new services and products quickly, new methods and business models are needed. In order to exploit these new technologies they have to be introduced at manufacturing level.

The Fourth Industrial Revolution is emerging and evolving at an exponential rather than linear pace and disrupting almost every industry in every country around the globe. These changes are signaling the transformation of entire systems of production, management, and governance. Industry 4.0 will impact our business, and those businesses which are prepared are already implementing changes to adapt to a future where smart machines will allow them to escalate their business success. The participants of the ICCMIT'19 conference deeply discussed their diverse views on Industry 4.0 based on their expertise, and the major topics of discussion related to the digital divide, how academic institutions can support and advance the digital transformation, how to organize human/robot interactions in the digital transformation era, and how to lead the digital transformation of manufacturing companies. During the conference, researchers and practitioners exchanged their

---

[1]https://www.iccmitconference.net/

experiences with the different types of 21st century smart methods of monitoring and operating engineering, analytics and servicing activities, including the impacts of automation
and smart sensing for the improvement of the quality and accuracy of the entire product or
service supply chain.

Ibrahiem M. M. El Emary, PhD
Professor of Computer Science and Systems
Faculty of Arts and Humanities, King Abdulaziz University, Jeddah, Saudi Arabia
Organizer of ICCMIT 2019

Introduction

Introduction to Key Industry 4.0 Technologies

The broad adoption of seventeen sustainable development goals has strongly emphasized using new emergent technologies for creating new solutions for our 21st century problems. This also calls for new business models and the reassessment of the current modes of government and manufacturing. This will require a global collaborative effort to work out how to employ new technologies to find these solutions, leading to a "Digital Revolution." The United Nations has identified key sustainable development goals (SDGs) to transform our world that should be part of the Digital Revolution.[1] These goals are listed below and in Figure I.1.

- No Poverty
- Zero Hunger
- Good Health and Well-Being
- Quality Education
- Gender Equality
- Clean Water and Sanitation
- Affordable and Clean Energy
- Decent Work and Economic Growth
- Industry, Innovation and Infrastructure
- Reduced Inequality
- Sustainable Cities and Communities
- Responsible Consumption and Production
- Climate Action
- Life below Water
- Life on Land
- Peace, Justice and Strong Institutions
- Partnerships to Achieve the Goal

The convergence of associated emerging technologies in the form of the Internet of Things along with Artificial Intelligence will create large-scale intelligent networks. In addition, Machine Learning (ML) will facilitate the emergence of a worldwide Internet of Smart Things. These combinations of Artificial Intelligence and the Internet of Things can be called an Artificial Intelligence supported Internet of Things (AIIoT). The networks that implement these converged technologies will be the first major events of the Digital Revolution.

---

[1]https://www.un.org/development/desa/disabilities/envision2030.html

It marks the time when users begin to see how vendor components and smart systems implement frictionless economics across integrated Smart Cities.

The exponential growth of AIIoT is based on the numerous configurations of new, smaller, more affordable networked sensors that can communicate with each other and potentially with all other sensors and processes in the supply chain. The configurations and implementation of the networked sensors and the data analytics for business intelligence need to be tailor-made to the requirements of human users, including the entire value chain and supply chain. The estimated 26 million software developers at the end of 2019 is predicted to grow to more than 27 million by 2023. Clearly, new approaches will need to be developed to assure that system professionals are compensated at a level that assures there will be an adequate supply of skilled workers.[2]

Figure I.1 Seventeen sustainable development goals.

The smooth implementation of automation across a number of industries relies on the coming together of stakeholders. Early successes will translate into rapid adoption and provide the foundation for later intelligent applications. There is a need for international standards in order to facilitate an efficient global collaboration. A number of stakeholders will be involved in collaborative efforts to make this happen. At a minimum these groups will include the following:

- *Government:* Although governments are not developing the technology, the responsibility for AIIoT systems to meet the needs of society is their purview. In performing this role they can facilitate communication between the various stakeholders and make sure that each voice is heard and collaboration ensures the successful operation of a Smart City and a caring society. It is expected that a government agency is appointed to oversee the implementation processes for AIIoT adoption.
- *National Laboratories:* Although governments ensure equal access to stakeholders, they will need to rely on the expertise of national laboratories to

---

[2]http://worldslargestlesson.globalgoals.org#the-goals

oversee the complex technical issues that will arise as large systems are assembled and tested. Furthermore, the experts of the Digital Revolution will be called on to identify needs of both the automated systems and their business users and end users. These smart field labs can provide system-level tools for monitoring and diagnostics and modeling and simulations services once component digital twins are populated into the system models. Another role for the labs will be to assist stakeholders in the development of curriculum that will assure that AIIoT professionals are available for system development and implementation. This may include assistance in developing explainable AI, scheme extraction algorithms and ML analytics.

- *Vendors:* Many AIIoT system components have already been developed and tested against industrial procedures and standards. The integration across public communities will lead to new types of issues that were not foreseen. Public-private partnerships are encouraged because they combine public sector needs with private sector technology and innovation.
- *Users:* Typically, there will be a core of early adopter companies and others will begin integration at a later time. There is a need to make sure that regardless of when companies begin and independent of their system type of size, that the resources are there to help them in their efforts.
- *Educators:* The development of curriculum, driven by inputs from the national labs, will assure that all required AIIoT topics are covered for targeted skills. Educators may also be called on to provide certifications based on testing developed by other agencies. It is likely that new cognitive computing systems will be used to rapidly access large libraries of data analytics. New curriculum components will be needed to support this addition. This is also an opportunity to identify student innovators that can aid in new development paradigms.

Voicing Concerns

Communication between stakeholders is key to realizing the benefits of AIIoT. To facilitate a global conversation forum, there should be a framework for communication that permits conversations in all directions and is capable of addressing any issue. Experts with system-level experience are needed, who can draw on their experiences to avoid pitfalls and minimize risks. The framework may take the form of conferences, meetups or website forums. Moderators working closely with system experts can address issues that are raised by participants. It is important that a solid foundation is put in place that will support additional innovations that will be added at a later date.

The new digital economy is a paradigm shift, towards a data marketplace with many diverse data producers who need a distributed brokering system; a ledger, with seamless insurance and logistics, big data analytics and self-learning systems. The technologies that enable the new digital economy paradigm shift are interconnected, overlapping and converging.

These emergent AIIoT Industry 4.0 pillars currently are: Extended Reality (XR: virtual reality, augmented reality, mixed reality and other new forms still under development) development and deployment education, Sensors, Internet of Things (IoT) and Cybersecurity, Mobile Technologies and Cloud Computing, Machine-to-Machine Communication and Digital Twins, Blockchain, Big Data Analytics, Cognitive Computing, and 3D Printing, among others.

The sections in this book are organized according to these various branches of the emergent technologies and the chapters address the evolving research that paves the way and enables solutions for smart cities and smart global solutions. Each chapter provides a time-stamp of current activities towards the paradigm shift and provides the necessary vision statements and use-case descriptions that help steer the adoption of smart city components. These vision statements will be translated into directives or regulations to be enacted by stakeholders. This involves a sequence of examinations and reviews by each participating company. The best general sequence follows the following processes or similar ones:

- *Policy Statements*: Regulations are distilled to individual directives. These are first reviewed by the national laboratories, perhaps working in a sandbox developed in conversations with vendors.
- *Vetting*: Once preliminary reviews have been completed the policy statements are provided to local governments for review against their needs. Issues that arise can be communicated with others or a digital regulatory agency. Local governments may also implement their own sandboxes that focus on their specifically unique environment.
- *Buy-In*: Once participants have tested and acknowledged the usefulness and performance of a policy statement, the parent policy regulation can be put into effect.
- *Compliance*: Full testing may be used to make sure that regulations perform across the smart city system. During this phase system data compliance and risk analysis reports can be used to address system issues.

The early AIIoT participants will be strategically placed to exponentially grow their productivity through AI and ML analysis and optimization. The superior products and services will rapidly reduce the market demand for other products and services that are outdated and lack functionality or quality, and such operations would systematically shut down due to inefficiency and high costs. Those who are already on the underdeveloped side of the digital divide will increasingly be more rapidly pushed out of competition. The configurations and implementation of the networked sensors and the data analytics for business intelligence need to be tailor-made to the requirements of the human users, and the business and value chains. Human needs for a prosperous, healthy, happy, safe, sustainable environment, are the main drivers for change and innovation. Successful international and intercultural respectful solutions for 21st century global issues can be built, using emergent technologies in novel ways. It is therefore necessarily a human-centered innovation design and development process.

Dr. Jolanda G. Tromp
Director of Center for Visualization and Simulation
Duy Tan University, Da Nang, Vietnam

John Bottoms
CEO FirstStar Systems
Boston, Massachusetts, USA

Preface

In Industry 4.0, extended reality (XR) technologies, such as virtual reality (VR) and augmented reality (AR), are creating location-aware applications to interact with smart objects and smart processes via cloud computing strategies enabled with artificial intelligence (AI) and the Internet of Things (IoT). Factories and processes can be automated and machines can be enabled with self-monitoring capabilities. Smart objects are given the ability to analyze and communicate with each other and their human coworkers, delivering the opportunity for much smoother processes, and freeing up workers for other tasks. Industry 4.0-enabled smart objects can be monitored, designed, tested and controlled via their digital twins, and these processes and controls are visualized in VR/AR. The Industry 4.0 technologies provide powerful, largely unexplored application areas that will revolutionize the way we work, collaborate and live our lives. It is important to understand the opportunities and impacts of the new technologies and the effects from a production, safety and societal point of view.

This book presents empirical research results from user-centered qualitative and quantitative experiments on these new applications, and facilitates a discussion forum to explore the latest trends in XR applications for Industry 4.0. Additional contributions were collected via a public call to raise the number and quality of the chapters to the highest standard.

The selected best papers in this book are from the International Conference on Communication, Management and Information (ICCMIT'19), www.icmit.net (International Conference on Communication, Management and Information, 26-28 March 2019, Vienna, Austria) plus an open call for contributions showcasing the state-of-the-art of these new technologies and applications in terms of design challenges, evaluations and long-term use implications.

As we have entered the Industrial Revolution 4.0, XR applications, in combination with AI/IoT technologies, are fundamentally changing the way we work and live, generally referred to as Industry 4.0 or IR 4.0. Developments in these fields are very important because the novel combinations of these technologies can help improve and save lives, improve the work and collaboration processes and create smart objects in smart systems and smart cities. This in turn has far-reaching effects for educational, organizational, economic and social improvements to the way we work, teach, learn and care for ourselves and each other.

This book aims to combine the early explorations and discussions of Industry 4.0 key features that need to be addressed on a global scale:

- The latest trends in new XR Industry 4.0 application developments.
- Powerful, largely unexplored application areas that will revolutionize the way we work and live.

- Combinations of XR technologies with artificial intelligence (AI) and the Internet of Things (IoT), showcasing the effect this has on Industry 4.0.
- Practical use cases and evaluations of new XR technologies and applications that can help improve work processes and the way we live our lives.
- Overview of the economic, psychological, educational and organizational impacts of the new XR applications on the way we work, teach, learn and collaborate in Industry 4.0 use cases.
- Overview of the design, evaluation and long-term use implications for the development, assessment and use of XR applications.

Dac-Nhuong Le, PhD
Associate Professor of Computer Science
Deputy Head, Faculty of Information Technology
Hai Phong University, Hai Phong, Vietnam

Acknowledgments

First of all, I would like to thank the authors for contributing their excellent chapters to this book. Without their contributions, this book would not have been possible. Thanks to all my colleagues and friends for sharing my happiness at the start of this project and following up with their encouragement when it seemed too difficult to complete.

I would like to acknowledge and thank the most important people in my life, my father, my mother and my partner, for their support. This book has been a long-cherished dream of mine which would not have been turned into reality without the support and love of these amazing people, who encouraged me despite my not giving them the proper time and attention. I am also grateful to my best friends for their blessings, unconditional love, patience and encouragement.

Dac-Nhuong Le, PhD
Associate Professor of Computer Science
Deputy Head, Faculty of Information Technology
Hai Phong University, Hai Phong, Vietnam

Acronyms

5G	The next (5th) Generation
AI	Artificial Intelligence
AIIOT	Artificial Intelligence and Internet of Things
ADWIN	Adaptive Windowing
ADT	Active Drawing Time
AES	Advanced Encryption Standard
API	Application Programming Interface
AR	Augmented Reality
AUE2	Accuracy Updated Ensemble
AWS	Amazon Web Services
ASQ	After-Scenario Questionnaire
AGV	Automated Guided Vehicle
BPMN	Business Process Management Notation
B2B	Business-to-Business
B2C	Business-to-Consumer
B2G	Business-to-Government
B2E	Business-to-Employee
CA	Cellular Automaton
C2C	Consumer-to-Consumer
C2G	Consumer-to-Government
CoP	Communities of Practice
CRM	Customer Relationship Management
CPU	Central Processing Unit
CalTo	Calibration Timeouts
CR	Common Rail
CMD	Charge Motion Design
CRI	CR Rail Injector
CVS	Center of Visualization and Simulation
DDM	Drift Detection Method
DNS	Domain Name System
DaaM	Drawing as a Matrix
DST	Drawing Start Time
DET	Drawing End Time

DAnim	Drawing Animation
DWM	Dynamic Weighted Majority
DWCDS	Double-Window-Based Classification Algorithm
DSM	Data Stream Mining
EFT	Electronic Funds Transfer
EDI	Electronic Data Interchange
E2E	Employee-to-Employee
EIPM	Enterprise Innovation Processes Management
EDDM	Early Drift Detection Method
FPDD	Fisher Proportions Drift Detector
FTDD	Fisher Test Drift Detector
FSDD	Fisher Square Drift Detector
FFS	Fuel Feed System
FHDDM	Fast Hoeffding Drift Detection Method
GUI	Graphical User Interface
GUID	Global Unique Identification
GTM	Google Transactions Model
GPS	Global Positioning System
GIS	Geographic Information System
GPRS	General Packet Radio Service
HTTP	Hypertext Transfer Protocol
HTML	Hypertext Markup Language
HCI	Human Computer Interaction
HMD	Head-Mounted Display
HVAC	Heating, Ventilating, and Air Conditioning
ICT	Information and Communications Technology
IoT	Internet of Things
IP	Internet Protocol
IPv6	Internet Protocol version 6
IT	Information Technology
ISO	International Organization for Standardization
iLRN	Immersive Learning Research Network
LO	Learning Object
LoWPAN	Low-Power Wireless Personal Area Networks
LMS	Learning Management Systems
LPG	Liquefied Petroleum Gas
LPWAN	Low Power WANs
MOS	Mean Opinion Score
MOA	Massive Online Analysis

MQ6	LPG Gas Sensor
MDDM	McDiarmid Drift Detection Method
MRI	Magnetic Resonance Imaging
ML	Machine Learning
M2M	Machine to Machine
MPI	Message Passing Interface
NLP	Natural Language Processing
NB	Naive Bayes
OLS	Ordinary Least Squares
OS	Operating System
OpenGL	Open Graphics Library
OT	Operational Technology
ISO	International Organization for Standardization
PKI	Public Key Infrastructure
PHP	Hypertext Preprocessor
PC	Personal Computer
P2P	Peer to Peer
PLS	Partial Least Squares
PESQ	Perceptual Evaluation Speech Quality
PIR	Passive Infrared Sensor
PL	Paired Learner
PSSUQ	Post-Study System Usability Questionnaire
PLC	Powerline Connections
QS	Queuing System
QGD	Quasigasdynamic
RTW	Response Time Window
RS	Real Student
RFID	Radio Frequency Identification
RSSI	Received Signal Strength Indication
RDDM	Reactive Drift Detection Method
RC	Rivest Cipher
RefD	Reference Drawing
SAC	Strict Avalanche Criterion
SABI	Simple Algorithm for Boredom Identification
SAMOA	Scalable Advanced Massive Online Analysis
SEM	Structural Equation Modeling
SEO	Search Engine Optimization
SDM	Server Data Model
SIT	Secure IoT
SLA	Service Level Agreement

SME	Small and Medium-Sized Enterprise
SMS	Short Message Service
SNA	Social Network Analysis
SNR	Signal-to-Noise Ratio
SSL	Secure Sockets Layer
SQL	Structured Query Language
STEPD	Statistical Test of Equal Proportions
TCR	Task Completion Rate
TOT	Time on Task
TSL	Transport Layer Security
TCP	Transmission Control Protocol
TiAPI	TELECI input from Application Programming Interface
ToAPI	TELECI output to Application Programming Interface
ToITC	TELECI input from Initial Test Component
ToITC	TELECI output to Initial Test Component
TiPSC	TELECI input from Preliminary Survey Component
ToPSC	TELECI output to Preliminary Survey Component
TixAPI	TELECI input from Experience API
ThT	Threshold Time
TEA	Tiny Encryption Algorithm
URL	Uniform Resource Locator
UX/UI	User Experience/User Interface
UX	User Experience
UI	User Interaction
VR	Virtual Reality
VFDT	Very Fast Decision Tree
W3C	World Wide Web Consortium
WSN	Wireless Sensor Network
XRDC	eXtended Reality Developer Conference
XR	Extended Reality
XSS	Cross-Site Scripting
XML	Extensible Markup Language

PART I

EXTENDED REALITY EDUCATION

The stakeholders in the AIIoT simulation-based optimization of planning, processing and delivery of operations, are the following three human user groups: human society, human operators, and human developers of the systems. Based on the exponential growth and all-pervasiveness of the AIIoT technologies that are embedded throughout our processes and will be driving our systems, it is rapidly clearly becoming more urgent to prepare a labor force with the required digital skills at all levels of education and training in order to be able to harness and benefit from the digital AIIoT transformations.

New job categories will arise with tasks that require technical capabilities and soft skills – essential human skills to manage the errors and problem solving that machines cannot handle. Governments and companies must plan to accelerate the creation of industrial engineering jobs dedicated to 3D modeling, 3D simulations, big data analytics, ML, robotics and development and customization of integrations of AIIoT-driven simulations and robotics solutions. Chapter 1 presents the results from an international survey regarding the use of XR technologies in the classroom to deliver classes, to teach the development of XR technologies and to research XR technologies, and a summary of the lessons learned.

There is a global need for skilled engineers and operators in order to research, build, test, deploy and maintain these new AIIoT-driven products, services, machines and platforms. To achieve positive economics for investment, robots must replace humans on the work floor, rather than support them. Routine manual activities can become fully automated. Routine and non-routine human activities will change, and the share of non-routine activities will increase for the human operator. Manual work will shift towards non-routine tasks, which means that workers must acquire more advanced skills. Chapter 2 presents a use-case study of a XR e-Health, e-Learning application for teaching anatomy, showing how disruptive new technologies can be to traditional education and accelerating opportunities for learning.

- Chapter 1: Mixed Reality Use in Higher Education: Results from an International Survey

- Chapter 2: Using 3D Simulation in Medical Education

CHAPTER 1

MIXED REALITY USE IN HIGHER EDUCATION: RESULTS FROM AN INTERNATIONAL SURVEY

J. Riman[1], N. Winters[2], J. Zelenak[3], I. Yucel[4], J. G. Tromp[5,*]

[1] SUNY Fashion Institute of Technology, New York, New York, USA

[2] SUNY Delhi College of Technology, Delhi, New York, USA

[3] University at Albany - State University of New York, Albany, New York, USA

[4] SUNY Polytechnic Institute, Utica, New York, USA

[5] Duy Tan University, Da Nang, Vietnam

*Corresponding author: jolanda.tromp@duytan.edu.vn

Abstract

Respondents identified some challenges in implementing mixed reality in their work with a majority reporting student reluctance, faculty reluctance, and lack of infrastructure and hardware as significant challenges. There was a significant reduction in perceived value added by the research respondents. Poor user experience, difficult to use hardware and software, and lack of educational content were among the lowest ranked challenges.

Keywords: Mixed reality, survey, community of practice

1.1   Introduction

Mixed reality (MR) is comprised of augmented reality (AR), virtual reality (VR) and arguably, 360-degree video. AR and VR are in use in numerous commercial applications from Pokemon GO to the *New York Times*. These tools have serious implications for higher education in areas that include virtual labs, student engagement, and student success and retention [2-5]. The State University of New York (SUNY) FACT[2] Mixed Reality Task Group was charged with exploring the use of Mixed Realities in the higher education setting and analyze the opportunities they offer to enhance the teaching, learning, and professional development experiences of students and faculty using paths of inquiry [1] such as: What are the opportunities for these emergent tools to be integrated into higher education outcomes? What training, tools and hardware are needed to initiate and support integration into teaching and learning? Describe the learning curve to optimize course and degree outcomes. Is there enough research and experience to frame the potential benefits of these tools in fully online, hybrid and conventional modalities?

Additionally, the task group sought to recruit collaborators from SUNY and beyond (faculty, instructional designers, content and product manufacturers) who have subject matter expertise and experience with the goal of augmenting and expanding teaching and learning opportunities that can be sustained as a community of practice (CoP). Effective strategies for creating and sustaining a CoP were researched and a special group was created to explore the tools and methods being developed to support course and degree outcomes and lay the groundwork for a CoP.

The task group met a total of 20 times throughout the 2017-2018 academic year and consisted of 18 initial members. The task group developed a survey to investigate the current uses of MR in higher education and research. The survey was circulated internationally. The results are reported here.

1.2   Organizational Framework

The following organizational framework was created to coordinate the work of the task group:

- *Action* research with volunteer faculty, instructional designers and students.

- *Teaching*: What can/should we do now, in the near or distant future in the education space?

- *Learner*: How will learners of all ages use these tools in and out of the learning space?

- *New Skills*: How will these new skills change certificate and degree program requirements?

- *Content Creation*: Tools to create content to meet specific needs; Open source and proprietary.

- *Career Skills*: How will these tools impact the workplace? Worker skills that will be in demand.

- *Sustainability*: What is required to keep these tools up to date?

- Examine the emerging cost barrier/benefit to explore the feasibility of deployment and training in each modality.

Initially, we divided the task group into two segments (Figure 1.1). First, a group dedicated to exploring primary research and related tools and methods. Second, a group focused on the acquisition of secondary sources that would serve as a library in support of our efforts, which would ultimately be a living resource for all who are interested.

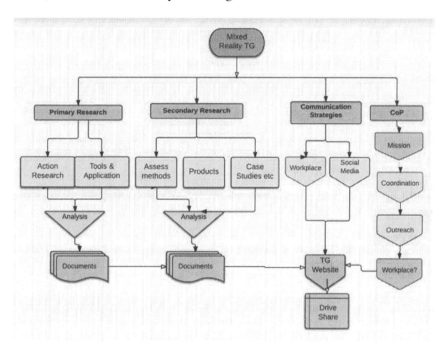

Figure 1.1   Task group projected workflow.

A Zotero group was created and populated with writing and resources, for instance [6-15], amongst many others (Figure 1.2).

We soon realized that the content was becoming obsolete shortly after being published. It also became evident that the whole taxonomy in mixed realities was rapidly changing, making organizational strategies time-consuming if not daunting. At this point the group paused to reflect on the best path, deciding to first focus on the active use of mixed reality tools in the teaching and research spaces. This allowed us to collect data from early adopters whose experiences would inform our strategy. Later in the process we revisited the secondary research, communication and community development.

1.3   Online Survey About MR Usage

The task group developed an online survey to investigate the current uses of mixed realities (MR) in higher education and research. The survey was circulated internationally and within SUNY. A total of 123 respondents completed the survey. The survey consisted of open-ended questions about the use and the challenges for teachers and students, in

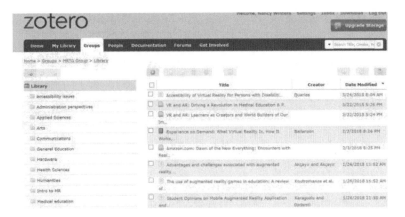

Figure 1.2 Detail from Zotero group.

terms of using MR in the classroom and for research, and also collected information about the hardware and software currently in use. The results are summarized in the following sections.

1.4 Results

Of the 123 respondents, 35% (43) are currently using some form of MR tools in the classroom. Of the remaining 80, only six stated they planned to use MR in the future, 20 said they had no intentions of using these technologies, and 46 felt that they may consider it in the future. Most of the respondents were in the role of faculty (61%), followed by researcher (22%), and instructional design/support (17%). There were no librarians. Fifty-eight percent of respondents were from a SUNY campus.

Fifty-eight percent of respondents are currently employed by a SUNY school covering the following campuses: University at Albany,[1] Binghamton University,[2] University at Buffalo[3], SUNY Delhi[4], SUNY Downstate Medical Center,[5] Empire State College,[6] Fashion Institute of Technology,[7] Finger Lakes Community College,[8] SUNY Geneseo,[9] Maritime College,[10] SUNY Old Westbury,[11] SUNY Oneonta,[12] SUNY Plattsburgh,[13]

[1] https://www.albany.edu
[2] https://www.binghamton.edu
[3] www.buffalo.edu
[4] https://www.delhi.edu
[5] https://www.downstate.edu
[6] https://www.esc.edu
[7] https://www.fitnyc.edu
[8] https://www.flcc.edu
[9] https://www.geneseo.edu
[10] https://www.sunymaritime.ed
[11] https://www.oldwestbury.edu
[12] https://suny.oneonta.edu
[13] https://www.plattsburgh.edu

SUNY Potsdam,[14] Purchase College,[15] Stony Brook University,[16] SUNY Polytechnic,[17] and SUNY Ulster.[18] Non-SUNY representation (42%) includes Canada, UK, Germany, Ireland, Massachusetts, Colorado, Italy, New Zealand, Scotland, California, and Australia.

MR is being used successfully in classrooms and in research. Respondents identified some challenges in implementing MR in their work with a majority reporting student reluctance, faculty reluctance, and lack of infrastructure and hardware as significant challenges. In narrative form, several faculty respondents expressed concern over perceived value of this technology. However, there was a significant reduction in perceived value concerns by the research respondents. Poor user experience, difficult to use hardware and software, and lack of educational content were the least identified challenges identified by respondents.

When looking at the lowest ranking challenges it's clear that respondents think there is high quality educational content available but that a lack of infrastructure, hardware and software exists, potentially adding to their reluctance to use MR experiences in the higher education classroom.

Specific examples of current use in the classroom include: At SUNY Plattsburgh and SUNY Delhi, nursing faculty currently use several virtual reality simulations via external vendors such as vSim, SimPractice, and Shadow Health. These types of simulations are used to increase safety in the clinical environment and are mostly used as independent lab homework outside of the classroom. Similarly, at SUNY Ulster, nursing faculty are using an electronic health record through Evolve for simulation experiences.

Those that are researchers in MR have interests in multiple areas. For example, at SUNY Polytechnic, one researcher is using VR to study anatomy with Vive. Another researcher at this college researches the use of MR in education and game design.

At the outset our goals were very broad and the development and use of mixed realities in education is still in its infancy. As a task group we found we were exploring the beginnings of a new evolutionary stage in the synthesis of teaching with technology. Our group was a mix of people currently researching and those who are interested in learning more. The former represents the majority of teaching faculty, many who are skeptical about the value of these new tools. As you will see in the survey results there are many perceived and imagined barriers to success. Other significant outcomes are described below.

- *FACT*[2] *Symposium*: Virtual Immersive Pedagogy is planned for November 9th 2018 to be held at SUNY Admin in the Zimpher Boardroom. This one day event has a call out for presenters and will feature an exposition where speakers will share their work in a hands-on environment.

- *CIT VR Expedition*: Presentation on the use of VR in some teaching settings. Led by UB Professor Richard Lamb and co-sponsored with CrossWater. Attendees were briefed on current examples and given a set of Google Cardboard to experiment with. This event was held twice during the conference.

- The Zotero Group was created and populated with materials which will serve as a prototype for future efforts.

[14] https://www.potsdam.edu
[15] https://www.purchase.ed
[16] https://www.stonybrook.edu
[17] https://sunypoly.edu
[18] https://www.sunyulster.edu

- *A Community of Practitioners*: A Workplace Group has been created and was softly launched in June 2017. The upcoming symposium will host the formal launch. This is a multi-company group which is open to all of SUNY and can also accommodate non-SUNY participants with a manual enrollment plan.

1.4.1 Use in Classrooms

At Maritime College, the Marine Transportation Department is using this technology to teach vessel operations in their Bridge Resource Management course. The full mission bridge simulator is used to simulate the vessel in different scenarios.

At SUNY Potsdam, software such as View-Master VR, Richie's Plank Experience, Google Earth VR, and Tilt Brush are used in their Teaching and Learning with Simulations and Games course. Right now, it is mostly being used as an extracurricular activity to allow students to experience the "presence" and spatial relationship that this technology gives. One student developed a Google Cardboard lesson wherein the class explored the ruins in Athens.

At SUNY Plattsburgh and SUNY Delhi, nursing faculty currently use several virtual reality simulations via external vendors such as vSim, SimPractice, and Shadow Health. These types of simulations are used to increase safety in the clinical environment and are mostly used as independent lab homework outside of the classroom. Similarly, at SUNY Ulster, nursing faculty are using an electronic health record through Evolve for simulation experiences.

At SUNY Old Westbury, the New Media in Action course is using Aurasma for augmented reality projects. This is done with creative 360-degree videos. They are assessing student learning using rubrics. Faculty teaching Wave Motion and Methods and Materials of Teaching Science use Vernier, Backyard Brains, Wolfram Mathematica, and PhEt Interactive Simulations for classroom discussion and experimental tasks.

At SUNY Geneseo, the Introduction to Museum Studies course is using Google Street View, Expeditions, and Unity. In addition, they use 360-degree videos projected up on a planetarium dome. They are using this technology to give virtual tours, for immersive psychology experiments, and for capturing remote locations and experiences.

Purchase College is incorporating 360-degree video experiences into advanced video classes using Adobe Premiere, 360fly, Theta S, and other phone applications. Another faculty is teaching Unity 3D in a New Directions in Virtual Spaces course. In this course, several of the senior students are using Vive to complete their final project.

At Empire State College, one faculty member reports using virtual reality in the online classroom using OpenSimulator/Second Life. It is used mostly for virtual-reality meetings, classroom experiences, poster sessions, and student presentations. Students also develop their own projects using 360-degree cameras and open source software using Kitely.

At the University of Massachusetts, Music Department faculty are using Ambeo A-B, Ambeo Orbit, and React VR in their Audio Theory courses to create engaging educational experiences.

At the University of Colorado, faculty in the Music and Entertainment Department are using Google Cardboard with Reaper, Pro Tools, and FB360 in their Introduction to Sound Design course to give an overview of psychoacoustics.

At the Fashion Institute of Technology, Instructional Design/Support use Google Cardboard and Tiltbrush for faculty development and experimentation. Tiltbush was used in the Anatomy for Artists course, where it was used to draw muscles and their attachments onto a 3D rendering of a human skeleton.

In California, instructional design/support has been aided by integration of several free or low cost ($2.99-$29.99) MR software options into many different courses (astronomy, gaming, neurosciences, electrodynamics, optics and lasers, nursing, engineering, journalism, media and technology, photography, visual communications, and media).

Outside of the US, in Ireland, faculty of computer science departments are integrating MR into their Interactive Media, Digital Humanities, and IT courses, specifically by using UE4, Unity, WebGL, Three.js, and WebVR/XR. They are using this technology to teach VR/AR/MR systems development. They are researching multimodal interaction and user measurement in VR/AR/MR.

In the UK, some game engines (Unity and Unreal) and applications (Virtual Battlespace 3, Elite: Dangerous, Google Tilt Brush, Google Blocks, Flight Simulator X, Project CARS) are used in their Department of Defense and Security. They use the technology to show students that the right technology must be used to solve particular issues.

In Italy, faculty of Psychology of Technology courses are having students develop VR experiences using Unity and InstaVR.

In New Zealand, faculty teaching medical imaging have replaced the usual simulation experiences with VR experiences related to patient positioning.

In Canada, faculty are researching the use of 360 Storytelling for journalism. And, in the School of Media and Design, faculty are using Rumii and Unreal Engine 4 to teach students how to make basic VR games and hold VR conferences for collaboration. Faculty at another Canadian college are using custom content solutions to teach anatomy and physiology.

1.4.2 Challenges

Respondents reported the challenges of using MR in the classroom (see Figure 1.3). The highest ranking challenges included student and faculty reluctance, and insufficient infrastructure and hardware. The lowest ranking challenges included difficulty of use and lack of content.

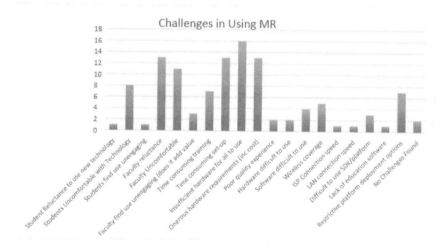

Figure 1.3   Respondents reported the challenges of using MR in the classroom.

1.4.3 Examples of Research in Action

Those that are researchers in MR have interests in multiple areas. These areas are best described in terms of their scope and perspective on MR. The first area of focus is the development of hardware and peripherals to improve the immersion of the participant. The second is in the development of tools to create content in MR. Finally, the last area of research is in the use of MR in a variety of contexts.

The majority of the research seen at SUNY institutions is focused on this third perspective. Researchers at university research centers see the opportunity the recent reduced cost of MR has for professional and educational purposes. Below are some examples from our survey of the work being done at SUNY and other higher education institutions.

For example, at SUNY Polytechnic, an IITG grant is investigating commercially available VR solutions in a case study. The study utilized Organon VR software to help students study anatomy with the HTC Vive headset. They are expanding from this case study to create a more generic augmented reality learning space, where instructors will be able to create lesson plans around 3D objects that can be seen on multiple interfaces. Another researcher at SUNY Poly is investigating the use of MR in physics education.

At SUNY Oneonta, one study described the use of Second Life as a concert venue, as well as augmented reality in the chemistry laboratory.

In Canada, a researcher is interested in the psychological impact of "perceived" environmental immersion in the areas of medical/health/treatment, training, simulation, visualization, entertainment/gaming, and epigenomic mapping. Funding was reported as the biggest challenge.

In the UK, a researcher is focused on digital publication using Mixed Autodesk Suite, Blender, Adobe Suites, and Unreal. The biggest challenges reported were onerous hardware requirements, and difficulty in using both hardware and software. Another researcher is interested in the use of MR in clinical simulations, rehabilitation, and mental health. Having insufficient hardware for all students is a major concern. In yet another college, a researcher is interested in the use of VR/AR/MR in defense, healthcare, heritage, outreach, and public engagement.

In Germany, the use of VR/AR for companies, enveloping concepts of applications, and new forms of journalistic storytelling is an area of research interest. This researcher is using HoloLens, Vive, and Google Cardboard.

In Australia, a behavior change researcher is interested in using MR to encourage nonviolence in young males. This researcher is using Unity, Oculus Rift, and Samsung Gear VR.

1.4.4 Hardware and Software for Use in Classrooms and Research

Interestingly, while Magic Leap was still the least used hardware for researchers (11%), both Vive (67%) and Oculus Rift (67%) were used more often than Google Cardboard (56%) in this group. Other hardware used included PlayStation VR,[19] Windows Mixed Reality,[20] Meta 2, Vive Focus,[21] Samsung Odyssey,[22] PSVR, Manus,[23] and Senso Gloves.[24]

---

[19]https://www.playstation.com
[20]https://www.microsoft.com/en-us/windows/windows-mixed-reality
[21]https://www.vive.com/
[22]https://www.samsung.com/us/computing/hmd/windows-mixed-reality
[23]https://manus-vr.com/
[24]https://senso.me/

For classroom use, Google Cardboard is currently being used by many of the participants (41%), likely due to its inexpensive costs. Magic Leap was the least used hardware (4%). Other hardware included HoloLens (15%), Vive (33%), Oculus Rift (33%), and Samsung Gear VR (26%). Several respondents added some additional hardware that they are currently using: Full Mission Bridge Simulator, virtual reality simulations via external vendors (Elsevier, Lippincott, Shadow Health, Laerdal), VSN Mobil V.360 Panoramic VR, 360-degree video projected onto planetarium dome, Sennheiser Ambeo,[25] MetaVR,[26] HoloLens, Gear 360, PrioVR,[27] GoPro Fusion,[28] Insta360 Pro, 360fly, Theta S,[29] Google Daydream,[30] Microsoft MR headset,[31] Vernier,[32] Backyard Brains.[33] For an overview of the software used in the classroom and by the researchers, see Table 1.1.

Table 1.1   Software in use for classrooms and research.

Simulator Specific	Viewmaster VR	Richie's Plank Experience
Google Earth VR	Tilt Brush	vSim
SimPractice	Shadow Health	Aurasma for Augmented Reality
Google Street View	Expeditions	Unity
HoloLens	UE4	Unity
WebGL	Three.js	WebVR/XR
Ambeo A-B	Ambeo Orbit	React VR
Unity	Unreal Apps (Virtual Battlespace 3)	Google Blocks
Flight Simulator X	Project CARS	Reaper
Pro Tools	FB360	InstaVR
Premiere Pro	Oculus	Gear 360
Adobe, Blackboard, Zoom	Virtual environments – Open Simulator, Second Life	Anatomy and Physiology – custom content solutions
Bespoke	EHR from Evolve	Adobe Premiere
Kitely open source virtual reality software	Vernier	Backyard Brains
Wolfram Mathematica	PhEt Interactive Simulations	VR Museum of Fine Art
Engage	Metaverse Construction Kit	Verto Studio 3D for HoloLens
Surgeek Virtual Surgeon	Apollo 11	Paint:Lab
Speech Trainer	Universe Sandbox and Start Chart	The Body VR
Nano One	Stanford Ocean Acidification Experiment	Calcflow
The Lab	AHS Fearless VR Experience	Gnomes & Goblins
Space Tours VR	Stonehenge VR	Facebook Spaces
GoPro Fusion Studio	Rumii	Unreal Engine 4

---

[25] https://en-us.sennheiser.com/ambeo-soundbar
[26] https://www.metavr.com/
[27] https://yostlabs.com/priovr/
[28] https://gopro.com/
[29] https://theta360.com/
[30] https://arvr.google.com/daydream/
[31] https://www.microsoft.com/en-us/store/collections/VRandMixedrealityheadsets
[32] Vernier
[33] https://backyardbrains.com/

1.4.5   Challenges Described by Researcher Respondents

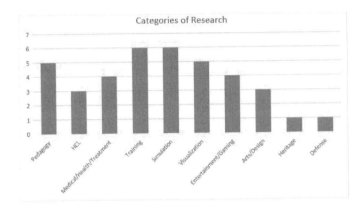

Figure 1.4   Research categories for which respondents reported use of MR.

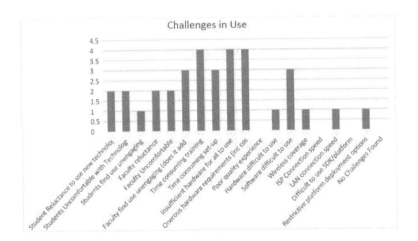

Figure 1.5   Challenges in use of MR for researchers.

Researcher reported costs and use value has the highest ranked challenges, and ranked poor quality experience and difficult to use platform as the lowest challenges.

1.4.6   Anecdotal Responses about Challenges

As part of our charge to understand if VR is viable for use in SUNY classrooms, we asked our participants to tell us what challenges they saw to the adoption of MR. The question was in a short answer format and the responses were coded to the following categories, see Table 1.2.

Table 1.2   Anecdotal responses about challenges.

Code/category of response	Matching responses
Not sure how to integrate into teaching	10
Funding and/or support (including need to update computers on campus)	9
Not sure if university plans to use	3
Feels they are already doing simulations	3
Does not feel that curriculum would be enhanced in any way	1
Investigating the viability	1
Needs to be easy to use	1
Might use for nontraditional lab experiences	1
Would like to use for game design in Unity using VR perspective to explain 3D using two lenses	1
Concerned about accessibility	1
Would like to develop AR models to overlay some field sites visited in Geology	1

Many of the responses express a concern that MR is still too expensive or that the technology is unproven. Studies such as this one, the mixed reality symposium, and other exhibitions such as games for change and XRDC (eXtended Reality Developer Conference) will be showcasing the possibilities of the technology and hopefully will begin to change the anxiety around its use in the classroom.

At this juncture, the cost of MR will mean that its use will most likely focus on areas with proven savings over alternative learning tools or in areas where we see market growth. This implies we will see a focus on more healthcare and entertainment applications in the near future.

1.5   Conclusion

Mixed reality tools present educators with a great opportunity to enter the arena while it is still possible to influence the outcomes and grow. While there are many challenges associated with the development and implementation of new technologies, the potential gains are enormous as interactivity and experiential learning shift to a new level of complexity. Entry barriers include the cost and time needed to train faculty and staff to support teaching with AR and VR products. Faculty resistance to new technology is also a factor given the demands of effective teaching and the time needed to learn new methods. There have been some efforts at SUNY to introduce faculty to new products. In 2016 a SUNY-wide pilot offered faculty the opportunity to try Labster lab modules for a 1 month period. (Labster is an online lab available in desktop simulation and in VR form.) More than 130 faculty members participated, 33 of which filled out a post-pilot survey. The responses were heavily skewed against adoption, with just 17% in favor of adopting the Labster virtual lab product for their courses. Since that time Labster and many other products have evolved and improved, meaning that the past impressions are not a predictor in this case. However, those that tested an early version of the product may retain their negative perspective.

Progress has been made, as evidenced by commitments made by other institutions outside of SUNY. This spring, Drexel University purchased a campus-wide license to deploy Labster for its science courses. On May 9, 2018, it was announced that Google has teamed up with Labster to create a VR laboratory, which means that colleges and universities will be able to offer fully online, remote courses such as biology. That same month, Labster presented at the FACT[2] Conference on Instruction and Technology, where attendees were invited to sample the VR lab experience. SUNY might want to revisit the use of virtual labs in the sciences in support of online and blended learning.

Equipment costs continue to decline; however, hardware, especially headgear, currently has a projected life of 18 months before newer models render older products obsolete, keeping costs high. VR content designed for education is still in the early stages especially for virtual reality products; however, augmented reality creation is less costly and easier to produce. Augmented reality tools are increasingly used for self-guided tours, scavenger hunts and for providing detailed instructions on the safe use of equipment in a lab or workshop. Tools to create content are also rapidly evolving, gradually making the creation of AR/VR content more accessible to those who are not deeply knowledgeable about coding or user experience design. As the complexities are reduced, accessibility to create, customize and deploy improve the environment for faculty to develop courses that employ new mixed reality tools for the creation of curriculum.

Aside from the survey results, the outcomes of the FACT[2] Mixed Reality Task Group activities can be summarized as follows:

1. An open community of practice (CoP VR) was formed to continuously explore, collaborate and share its findings as a resource to the SUNY system.

2. A communication strategy was developed to actively provide information (using a FACT[2] website), with quarterly summative reporting to the FACT[2] Council.

3. A repository of content that includes: past reports, case studies, resources and an active list of AR/VR resources that would be regularly updated, evaluated, reviewed, and changed as the technology evolves.

4. Partnerships with colleges and groups like COTE, CPD and others to share information and to be a persistent resource for all stakeholders.

5. Present and discuss issues at major events like the SUNY CIT and FACT[2] Symposium, the VR First network, the VRAR Association and conferences such as the Immersive Learning Research Network (iLRN) Conference.

6. Recommendations and next steps:

   - Create a VR/emerging technology track in the IITG grants targeted to fund efforts that link new mixed reality technologies to effective content creation, development, training and teaching practices.

   - Foster interaction between researchers, stakeholders, and educators. A SUNY-wide initiative to develop a very robust community of practice that encourages the sharing of research, teaching and learning working with mixed realities products using Workplace. The premise of this CoP was explored at the FACT[2] Symposium, November 9th, 2018, Albany, New York, USA.

   - Fund a SUNY-wide emerging technology demo space in coordination with CPD and FACT[2]. This event-oriented space would be where researchers and teachers share their efforts and results. This could be embedded within the CoP.

   - Develop/foster open source solutions for the creation and deployment of mixed reality products that dovetail with the values and benefits of OER. In part this avenue of inquiry will be pursued as part of the goals set forth in the new FACT[2] Task Group on Open Pedagogy.

- Partner with innovators within and outside SUNY that share our interest in open education strategies and resources. A team devoted to partnerships with educators, content developers, hardware developers and service providers may provide important connections that may lead to a faster pace of innovation and adoption within the SUNY network.

ACKNOWLEDGMENTS

This research was conducted by a group of volunteers from the State University of New York, at various locations. The work was coordinated by Jeffrey Riman, with collaboration from the other authors and John Locke, Amanda Hollister, Michael Reale, Lauren Williams, Richard Lamb and John Kane.

REFERENCES

1. Riman, J.: Mixed Reality Task Group Final Report 2018. Presented at Conference of Instruction and Learning (CIT2018), Albany, State University of New York, USA (2018).

2. Cobb S., Nichols S., Ramsey A. and Wilson J.R (1999). Virtual reality-induced symptoms and effects (VRISE), *Presence: Teleoperators & Virtual Environments*, April 1999, 8(2), 169-186.

3. Dede, C., Salzman, M. C., & Loftin, R. B. (1996). The development of a virtual world for learning newtonian mechanics. In P. Brusilovsky, P. Kommers, & N. Streitz, (Eds.). *Multimedia, Hypermedia, and Virtual Reality*, (pp. 87-106). Berlin: Springer/Verlag.

4. Duffy, T. M., & Jonassen, D. H. (1992). *Constructivism and the Technology of Instruction: A Conversation*. Hillsdale N.J.: Lawrence Erlbaum.

5. Feldman, A., & Acredolo, L. (1979). The effect of active versus passive exploration on memory for spatial location in children. *Child Development*, 50, 698-704.

6. Taxn, G., & Naeve, A. (2002). A system for exploring open issues in VR-based education. *Computers & Graphics*, 26(4), 593-598.

7. Abidi, M., El-Tamimi, A., & Al-Ahmari, A. (2012). Virtual reality: Next generation tool for distance education. *International Journal of Advanced Science and Engineering Technology*, 2(2), 95-100.

8. Sampaio, A. Z., Ferreira, M. M., Rosrio, D. P., & Martins, O. P. (2010). 3D and VR models in Civil Engineering education: Construction, rehabilitation and maintenance. *Automation in Construction*, 19(7), 819-828.

9. Dvidekova, M., Mjartan, M., & Gregus, M. (2017). Utilization of virtual reality in education of employees in slovakia. *Procedia Computer Science*, 113, 253-260.

10. Ahlberg, G., Enochsson, L., Gallagher, A. G., Hedman, L., Hogman, C., McClusky III, D. A., ... & Arvidsson, D. (2007). Proficiency-based virtual reality training significantly reduces the error rate for residents during their first 10 laparoscopic cholecystectomies. *The American Journal of Surgery*, 193(6), 797-804.

11. Kaufmann, H., & Schmalstieg, D. (2002, July). Mathematics and geometry education with collaborative augmented reality. In *ACM SIGGRAPH 2002 Conference Abstracts and Applications* (pp. 37-41). ACM.

12. Merchant, Z., Goetz, E. T., Cifuentes, L., Keeney-Kennicutt, W., & Davis, T. J. (2014). Effectiveness of virtual reality-based instruction on students' learning outcomes in K-12 and higher education: A meta-analysis. *Computers & Education*, 70, 29-40.

13. Shin, D., Yoon, E. S., Lee, K. Y., & Lee, E. S. (2002). A web-based, interactive virtual laboratory system for unit operations and process systems engineering education: issues, design and implementation. *Computers & Chemical Engineering*, 26(2), 319-330.

14. Engum, S. A., Jeffries, P., & Fisher, L. (2003). Intravenous catheter training system: computer-based education versus traditional learning methods. *The American Journal of Surgery*, 186(1), 67-74.

15. Chen, C. J., Toh, S. C., & Fauzy, W. M. (2004). The theoretical framework for designing desktop virtual reality-based learning environments. *Journal of Interactive Learning Research*, 15(2), 147-167.

CHAPTER 2

APPLYING 3D VIRTUAL REALITY TECHNOLOGY FOR HUMAN BODY SIMULATION TO TEACHING, LEARNING AND STUDYING ACTIVITIES

Le Van Chung,[1,*] Gia Nhu Nguyen,[1,*], Tung Sanh Nguyen,[2] Tri Huu Nguyen,[2] Dac-Nhuong Le[3,*]

[1] Duy Tan University, Da Nang, Vietnam

[2] Hue University of Medicine and Pharmacy

[3] Hai Phong University, Hai Phong, Vietnam

*Corresponding authors: levanchung@duytan.edu.vn; nguyengianhu@duytan.edu.vn; nhuongld@dhhp.edu.vn

Abstract

Universities realize the importance of the new experience-based method of education that allows students to study and learn through real practice that completely enhances their abilities before graduating. For teaching, learning, and research purposes, universities need to provide and carry out realistic training relating to actual real use cases for practicing. This is especially necessary for medical students studying anatomy, since there are very few real human cadavers available for practicing. The aim of the simulation system presented here is to accurately simulate a visual representation of the human body in the ratio of 1:1 with fully represented systems of the organs, and provide the ability to interact directly with each of them in 3D by using 3D virtual reality technology. The system supports and serves teaching, learning and researching activities related to aspects of health science in order to acquire career goals and provides the ability to work in a dynamic and changeable world.

Keywords: Virtual reality, anatomy, 3D simulation, human body, medical training

2.1 Introduction

According to an analysis report of the Vietnamese Ministry of Education and Training, more than 50 universities, 42 colleges and 49 vocational schools set up medical departments in the year 2016-17 [1]. In the departmental curriculum, surgery skills are considered mandatory. Although these skills are required learning, there have been some stones (such as unavailability of equipment and human bodies) along the road to learning and implementing them [2].

Anatomy [3-6] is a fundamental subject among other clinical subjects in medicine. Students cannot understand cell structure of tissues, organs (histology), the growth of individuals (embryology) as well as functions of organs (physiology), etc. As readers of textual descriptions [7], they don't have much information about the form and structures of organs. Similarly, for other clinical training, the trainee doctor must acquire anatomical knowledge to examine organs and efficiently diagnose disease and provide treatment. Traditionally, learning anatomy [8-10] required learners to practice on human cadavers. However, according to the survey, only 10% of training departments have human cadavers available to practice on. Therefore, most of the students study anatomy using plastic models, photos, 2D sketches, templates or foreign software.

Foreign software does not simulate the full body features of the Vietnamese, which leads to inaccuracy in learning anatomy for Vietnamese students. At present, there is no medical anatomy training software in Vietnam that includes the body structures with full 3D simulations [11-13] of all organs and organic systems consistent with scientific data, fully interactive and with animated simulations [14-16] of body movements, with the ability to run on a diverse range of technology platforms. So, the challenge is to find a more efficient and less costly way to approach the subject of anatomy training with culturally and ethnic correct features and forms. The aim of the application is to use 3D virtual reality [17-20] to simulate the human body complete with all human body organic systems, i.e., the skeletal, muscular, circulatory, nervous, respiratory, digestive, and reproductive systems, and glands and lymph nodes, with realistic anatomical details that most closely resemble the human body. In this chapter, we present the application of 3D computer-generated graphics with virtual reality and augmented reality technology, to create a complete model of the human body, which students can interact with in a variety of ways. All medical anatomy information is displayed on the models of organs and systems, where even very small anatomical details can be viewed with uniform scientific data sets, which can be exactly tailored to target the needs of learners who can be students, lecturers, researchers or medical practitioners.

2.2 Related Works

Many researchers have proposed different kinds of studies to improve the learning of anatomy with the aid of virtual reality (VR), augmented reality (AR) and 3D simulation. Codd [21] proposed human interaction with a three-dimensional (3D) VR computer model of a human forearm in the category of a musculoskeletal system. The main aim of this model is to evaluate the comparison of anatomy teaching between the proposed model and the traditional methods. Three different groups are categorized and results are analyzed through the statistical parameters namely, mean score and F (feedback question) value. Results shown that VR teaching is more reliable and increases student motivation. To improve anatomy learning the authors [22-25] presented three-dimensional (3D) virtualization methods that act as a learning tool. These virtualization techniques are based on the Web, desktop application as well as VR and used different parts of the human body. The 3D method results clearly show that learning anatomy from these models is more effective than the traditional way. Ferrer-Torregrosa *et al.* [25] developed a tool called "ARBOOK" based on augmented reality (AR) for learning lower limb anatomy. For ARBOOK evaluation, a questionnaire of three blocks was performed based on the Delphi method. For the experimentation part, 211 students were selected from seven public and private Spanish universities. The outcome shows that AR technology is more suitable as compared to other anatomy learning methods. An interactive and personalized AR-based system [27-28] has been developed to promote better learning of the anatomy. The authors called this system a "Magic Mirror" which provides real-time results or in-site virtualization of the user's body. Moreover, this system is equipped with an RGB-D sensor which allows tracking the motion of the human body in front of a screen. The system is being tested by 7 clinicians and 72 students that further split into two different studies. Kucuk [28] proposed an AR application called "Blackbook" which is based on the neuroanatomy. Multiple tools were utilized to develop this application such as cognitive load scale and a MANOVA (multivariate analysis of variance) test used for data collection and data analysis respectively. There were 70 undergraduate students who participated in this experiment.

In the above studies, researchers mainly focused on the anatomy of one human body part using 3D simulation and VR. In this chapter, we develop a 3D application for the full human body, including the muscular, nervous and endocrine systems, which is compatible with VR glasses. Moreover, this application supports two different languages such as English and Vietnamese.

2.3   3D Human Body Simulation System

The anatomy simulation system is based on OpenGL (Open Graphics Library)[1] tools to simulate the parts modeled in the virtual reality 3D environment, and Blender[2] software was used to model the limbs. Details are drawn from anatomical imagery material. Simulation of the human anatomy system is implemented on interactive 3D virtual reality technology including all organ systems in the human body such as skeletal system, muscular system, circulatory system, nervous system, respiratory system..., digestive system, excretory and genital system, glands and lymph nodes. The parameters used in the simulation process are evaluated and assessed by anatomy professors at key schools and hospitals, evaluating the accuracy of every detail in the organ systems [29, 30].

2.3.1   The Simulated Human Anatomy Systems

Full simulation of the human anatomy system with anatomical landmarks on 3D models is shown in Table 2.1.

---

[1]https://www.opengl.org/
[2]https://www.blender.org/

Table 2.1   Organ systems in the human body.

No.	Organ systems	Illustration	No.	Organ systems	Illustration
1.	Skeletal system - ligament (589 models: 317 skeletal models, 272 ligament models)		5	Muscular system (510 models)	
2.	Respiratory system (6 models)		6	Digestive system (41 models)	
3.	Cardio-vascular system (1517 models: 1472 arterial and venous models, 45 cardiac models)		7	Nervous system (1028 models: 989 neural models, 39 brain models) Excretory & genital system (20 models)	
4.	Excretory & genital system (20 models)		8	Endocrine system (glands and lymph nodes include 191 models: 11 glands, 180 lymph node models).	

Diversity of anatomical presentation: Anatomical details, anatomical mold, anatomical region, anatomical group, anatomical area, and anatomical system.

2.3.2 Simulated Activities and Movements

The system allows simulation of activities and movements like:

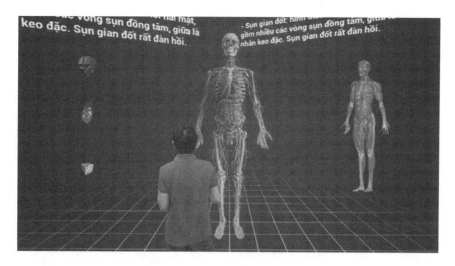

Figure 2.1   Human body simulation.

▪ Shoulder movement, elbow movement, wrist movement, finger movement, hip movement, knee movement, ankle movement, neck movement, lower jaw movement, spine movement.

▪ Shoulder group movement, elbow muscle movement, arm muscle movement, back and hand muscles movement, back muscle group movement, rib lift group movement, abdominal muscle movement, pelvic group movements, thigh muscle movements, knee and elbow muscle movements, ankle group movements, hip and foot muscle movements, facial muscles movements, chewing muscle group movements, eye group muscle movement, ear muscle group movement (see Figure 2.2).

Figure 2.2   Simulated jaw and limb activity.

▪ Activity of the heart, heart valves, ventricles, atria, coronary group.

▪ Motor activity signals controlling muscle groups.

▪ Respiratory activity and volume expansion of lungs, airflow movement.

▪ Activity of the digestive system with the contraction of the stomach and the transport of food in the system, the operation of glands in the system.

- Excretion and renal activity.

- Some gland activity in the body, and some lymph node function (see Figure 2.3).

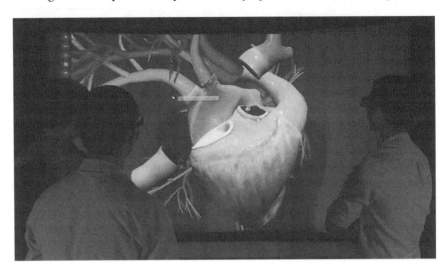

Figure 2.3   Simulation of the heart and circulatory system.

The marker method supports viewing and remembering anatomical characteristics of organs:

- Pin marking (pins, 568 details for some muscles that have their own anatomical identification point; heart organ, brain organ).

- Marked by color zones (287 color areas of anatomy; for the skull, the cartilage of the convex bridge, the skeletal muscle, brain organ).

- Drawing on the surface (for bones, muscles, heart organ, brain organ, organs, glands) (see Figure 2.4).

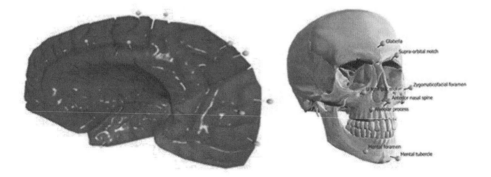

Figure 2.4   The process of marking and remembering anatomical points.

- 3D control features: Rotate, hide, show, transparent, remove, move, brighten.

- Object selection feature: Select one object, select multiple objects, select anatomical group (130 standard sample groups are available).

- Feature that allows option to create a group: Option to create a group inside system, option to create different groups.

- Devices that interact and view: Interact on a computer, interact on an Android or iOS device and interact on a VR device (see Figure 2.5).

Figure 2.5   Users interact with the system via computer, mobile device and VR device.

- Search for 3D images, and allow the extraction of related data sets.

- Intelligent data access according to anatomical relationship.

- Establish the structure of lectures, standard lessons.

- Allow self-created lessons, lectures.

- Supported languages include: Vietnamese-Latin, English-Latin.

2.3.3   Evaluation of the System

The work of applying 3D virtual reality technology creates a complete human body, allows users to interact in a variety of ways on the model objects of organs, systems, even small details, and provides a unified set of scientific data aimed at learners who are students, lecturers, researchers or doctors.

The system constructs the entire virtual human anatomy system, with more than 3924 details simulating organs, organ systems (skeletal system, muscle system, blood and heart system, nervous system and brain, respiratory system, digestive system, excretory and genital system, glands and lymph nodes) in the human body. Anatomical details are simulated in complete accordance with the characteristics of the anatomy and anatomical characteristics of Vietnamese people.

The correctness of the data science, and the shape and location of all details on models have been tested and checked on anatomical objects by surgeons and professors specializing in surgery. With this software, teachers and learners can completely build their own lesson structures and case study scenarios that are suitable for each individual and serve different purposes.

The software helps learners visualize each organ in specific anatomical detail and interact (rotate, hide, show, move; see the name, scientific name, brief description of detailed surgical solutions, marking the surface of an organ in a variety of ways, animation, motion, transmission, search, enumeration, etc.) with diverse anatomical details such as anatomical markers, sites, objects, groups, and systems (which cannot be performed on an anatomical picture or model), see Figure 2.6.

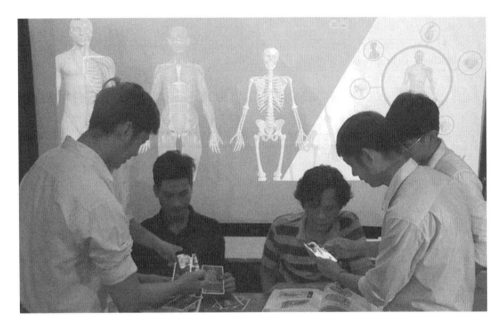

Figure 2.6   Study group interacting via AR-enabled smartphones.

About interactive methods:

- Interactive system in which users can directly carry out tasks in the 3D space via 3D projectors, 3D glasses, or through VR (virtual reality) glasses such as Oculus Rift, Gear VR, HoloLens, HTC Vive, navigation devices and touch.

- Interactive system in which users can carry out tasks via computers (Windows, Mac, Linux) or via smartphones and tablets (Android or iOS operating systems).

- Systems with the ability to simultaneously control all components such as images, audio, video, according to personal capacity and preference. Students can experience interacting with each 3D object. In lectures, by a combination of stereo 3D simulations or by evolutions, depending on the control skills of students. More importantly, it is from these experiences that students gain specific experience in anatomy and body composition.

The system provides an interface that allows the user to manipulate and view images of parts of the skeletal system, respiratory system, nervous system, and circulatory system at different angles and enables searching for information through sample information.

2.4   Discussion of Future Work

Currently, there are many companies in the world developing and building virtual body projects projects, such as InnerBody,[3] Healthline Media,[4] Visible Body,[5] Khan Academy,[6] etc., the most prominent of which is Human Anatomy Atlas.[7] However, most are designed to simulate those in the Western world and English is the language, which is a major barrier to Vietnamese students accessing foreign lectures [5-10].

The cost of foreign products is relatively expensive and not customized when designing according to a specific case study, costing much to customize or upgrade.

Using the software on multiple device platforms helps save on procurement costs, maintenance costs for models, pictures, and templates.

The anatomical relationship-based lookup function combined with accurate scientific data helps reduce the time it takes to search for, aggregate, and compare significant data information.

The application of body simulations in doctors' training courses, skills training courses, and training for hospital systems will bring about remarkably professional efficiency (easy access, large amount of knowledge), and significant reduction in training costs (printing many types of documents, practicing on the body many times, needing many new bodies to ensure proficiency).

These products are perfectly suitable for deployment in medical training facilities and hospitals. At the same time, they are a useful tool for hospitals in vocational training for newly graduated doctors and improving skills of lower level staff. The products completely overcome the traditional ways of learning, bringing significant learning and research effects.

Products can be expanded and developed for preclinical simulation projects or endoscopic simulation projects to help students get vocational training while still in school.

In hospitals, in order to treat patients with peace of mind and understanding, doctors use software to advise patients and explain their illness, especially in cases of orthopedic trauma.

These systems will continue to expand and develop in the future in many directions, such as:

- Interact with models through virtual surgery equipment, virtual endoscopy, virtual parameters measurement, treatment with virtual patients, etc.

- Simulate common and special pathologies unique to Vietnam and Asia.

- Help diagnose images better. When medical staff scan X-ray images into the system, they automatically build up 3D models for easy diagnosis by doctors.

- Simulate and predict diseases from scanning MRI scans, thereby making early predictions of the pathology to have a reasonable prevention.

- Simulate conditions, such as myocardial infarction, anterior disk locus, broken limbs, appendicitis, etc., and the effect that a drug has on the patient's body upon being taken and their resistance to it.

---

[3] www.innerbody.com
[4] https://www.healthline.com
[5] https://www.visiblebody.com
[6] https://www.khanacademy.org
[7] https://www.visiblebody.com/anatomy-and-physiology-apps/human-anatomy-atlas

2.5 Conclusion

Application of this software to training has the following advantages:

- Reduces the frequency of using human and animal carcasses.

- Learners easily remember more anatomical details than before when they learned through models, pictures, and templates.

- Users can create case studies by themselves, which increases self-study with more data to compare and brings autonomy to learning, therefore freedom from stereotyping.

- Using the software on many device platforms helps to save shopping costs, and maintenance costs of models, pictures, and templates.

- An anatomical relationship-based lookup function combined with accurate scientific data sets greatly reduces time searching for, aggregating and comparing significant data information.

- The application in doctor training courses, skills training courses, and training for hospital systems will bring about remarkably professional efficiency (easily accessible, large amount of knowledge), significant reduction of time spent on training (printing many types of documents, practicing on the body many times, needing many new bodies to ensure proficiency).

- 3D models can be extracted from the software in order to print 3D models at half the price, and above all, customize the printing of 3D models of the body to suit the needs of each school.

In Vietnam today, the construction of software applications in the health sector is still a limited open area, with no appropriate investment. Similarly, simulation applications in disease diagnosis or vocational training of schools and health centers are few. This is really the problem posed for universities, software developers and hospitals. The Ministry of Health needs to work together with software developers to create high-value interdisciplinary applied products for school training as well as skills training in health facilities. With our products, we will approach these issues easily, at low cost and bring high efficiency. The product is the foundation for developing medical simulation projects, proceeding to developing technology for remote medical examination and treatment (telemedicine).

REFERENCES

1. Fan, A. P., Tran, D. T., Kosik, R. O., Mandell, G. A., Hsu, H. S., & Chen, Y. S. (2012). Medical education in Vietnam. *Medical Teacher*, 34(2), 103-107.

2. Arnold, P., & Farrell, M. J. (2003). Embodiment and spatial behavior in virtual environments: comments on Durlach *et al.* (2000). *Presence: Teleoperators & Virtual Environments*, 12(6), 658-662.

3. Garg, A., Norman, G. R., Spero, L., & Maheshwari, P. (1999). Do virtual computer models hinder anatomy learning?. *Academic Medicine*, 74(10 Suppl), S87-9.

4. Wilson, D. B., & Wilson, W. J. (1983). *Human Anatomy*. New York: Oxford University Press.

5. Ajita, R., & Singh, Y. I. (2007). Body donation and its relevance in anatomy learning: a review. *J Anat Soc India*, 56(1), 44-47.

6. Craig, J. A., Perkins, J., & Netter, F. H. (2002). Atlas of Neuroanatomy and Neurophysiology: Selections from the Netter Collection of Medical Illustrations. Icon Custom Communications.

7. Do Nang Toan, Pham Tan Nam, Tran Thanh Hiep, Trinh Hien Anh, An approach for creating 3-dimensional models, in Proceeding of the National Conference on Some Selected Issues on ICT, Haiphong 25-27/08/2005

8. Laird, J. E., Rosenbloom, P. S., & Newell, A. (1986). Chunking in Soar: The anatomy of a general learning mechanism. *Machine Learning*, 1(1), 11-46.

9. Preece, D., Williams, S. B., Lam, R., & Weller, R. (2013). Let's get physical: advantages of a physical model over 3D computer models and textbooks in learning imaging anatomy. *Anatomical Sciences Education*, 6(4), 216-224.

10. Azer, S. A., & Azer, S. (2016). 3D anatomy models and impact on learning: a review of the quality of the literature. *Health Professions Education*, 2(2), 80-98.

11. Van De Graaff, K. M. (2002). *Human Anatomy* (pp. 93-113). New York, NY, USA: McGraw-Hill.

12. Garg, Geoff Norman, Lawrence Spero, Ian Taylor, A. (1999). Learning anatomy: do new computer models improve spatial understanding?. *Medical Teacher*, 21(5), 519-522.

13. Akpan, J. P., & Andre, T. (2000). Using a computer simulation before dissection to help students learn anatomy. *Journal of Computers in Mathematics and Science Teaching*, 19(3), 297-313.

14. Mathiowetz, V., Yu, C. H., & QuakeRapp, C. (2016). Comparison of a gross anatomy laboratory to online anatomy software for teaching anatomy. *Anatomical Sciences Education*, 9(1), 52-59.

15. Cevidanes, L. H., Tucker, S., Styner, M., Kim, H., Chapuis, J., Reyes, M., ... & Jaskolka, M. (2010). Three-dimensional surgical simulation. *American Journal of Orthodontics and Dentofacial Orthopedics*, 138(3), 361-371.

16. Trinh Xuan Dan, Do Nang Toan (2010), Nghien cuu phat trien he thong thuc tai ao mo phong du lieu bo xuong truc nguoi viet nam truong thanh phuc vu cho viec giang day va tra cuu, *Tap chi Khoa hc cong nghe*, 89 (01/2): 117-121.

17. Allen J, Brown L, Duff C, Nesbitt P & Hepner A (2013) Development and evaluation of a teaching and learning approach in cross-cultural care and antidiscrimination in university nursing students. *Nurse Education Today* 33, 1592-1598.

18. Netter, F. H. (2017). *Atlas of Human Anatomy E-Book: including NetterReference.com Access with Full Downloadable Image Bank*. Elsevier Health Sciences.

19. Nicholson, D. T., Chalk, C., Funnell, W. R. J., & Daniel, S. J. (2006). Can virtual reality improve anatomy education? A randomised controlled study of a computer-generated three-dimensional anatomical ear model. *Medical Education*, 40(11), 1081-1087.

20. Codd, A. M., & Choudhury, B. (2011). Virtual reality anatomy: Is it comparable with traditional methods in the teaching of human forearm musculoskeletal anatomy? *Anatomical sciences education*, 4(3), 119-125.

21. Petersson, H., Sinkvist, D., Wang, C., & Smedby, O. (2009). Webbased interactive 3D visualization as a tool for improved anatomy learning. *Anatomical Science Education*, 2(2), 61-68.

22. Siln, C., Wirell, S., Kvist, J., Nylander, E., & Smedby, O. (2008). Advanced 3D visualization in student-centred medical education. *Medical Teacher*, 30(5), e115-e124.

23. Nicholson, D. T., Chalk, C., Funnell, W. R. J., & Daniel, S. J. (2006). Can virtual reality improve anatomy education? A randomised controlled study of a computergenerated threedimensional anatomical ear model. *Medical Education*, 40(11), 1081-1087.

24. Yeung, J. C., Fung, K., & Wilson, T. D. (2011). Development of a computerassisted cranial nerve simulation from the visible human dataset. *Anatomical Sciences Education*, 4(2), 92-97.

25. Ferrer-Torregrosa, J., Torralba, J., Jimenez, M. A., Garca, S., & Barcia, J. M. (2015). AR-BOOK: Development and assessment of a tool based on augmented reality for anatomy. *Journal of Science Education and Technology*, 24(1), 119-124.

26. Ma, M., Fallavollita, P., Seelbach, I., Von Der Heide, A. M., Euler, E., Waschke, J., & Navab, N. (2016). Personalized augmented reality for anatomy education. *Clinical Anatomy*, 29(4), 446-453.

27. Blum, T., Kleeberger, V., Bichlmeier, C., & Navab, N. (2012, March). mirracle: An augmented reality magic mirror system for anatomy education. In *2012 IEEE Virtual Reality Workshops (VRW)* (pp. 115-116). IEEE.

28. Kucuk, S., Kapakin, S., & Gokta, Y. (2016). Learning anatomy via mobile augmented reality: effects on achievement and cognitive load. *Anatomical Sciences Education*, 9(5), 411-421.

29. Le, D. N., Van Le, C., Tromp, J. G., & Nguyen, G. N. (Eds.). (2018). *Emerging Technologies for Health and Medicine: Virtual Reality, Augmented Reality, Artificial Intelligence, Internet of Things, Robotics, Industry 4.0*. John Wiley & Sons.

30. Tromp, J., Le, C., Le, B., & Le, D. N. (2018). Massively multi-user online social virtual reality systems: ethical issues and risks for long-term use. In *Social Networks Science: Design, Implementation, Security, and Challenges* (pp. 131-149). Springer, Cham.

PART II

INTERNET OF THINGS

The Industry 4.0-enabled Internet of Things facilitates machine-to-machine (M2M) communication and collaboration technology, connecting machines to each other without human input or interference via low-power wide-area networks (LPWANs), wireless sensors, in networks, with computers and serial connections and power-line connections (PLCs). The computers run machine learning (ML) software, creating AI-powered systems that automatically learn and improve via apps that can access data and use it to learn. There are currently four major application areas: 1) Manufacturing, 2) Smart Home apps, Platforms and Remote Control HVAC, 3) Healthcare, 4) Smart Utility Management. There are many automation and data management challenges to overcome. Chapter 3 presents a social innovation M2M sensor technology use case for safely tracking moving vehicles.

The internet of things (IoT) creates a huge amount of data which in turn creates a data marketplace. The data producers are manifold: people, products, processes, buildings, automobiles, healthcare systems, logistics equipment, plant floor equipment, environment monitoring systems, etc. Traditionally the machine operation network has consisted of a separate network for operational technology (OT), which is now in the process of converging with the information technology (IT) network. This introduces considerable risk to critical OT software. For instance, monitoring and controlling physical devices (such as pumps and valves) which previously ran in their own secure environment, are now connected to the broader network, creating an easy target for hackers. Chapter 4 presents an IoT security scenario and speech encryption methodology and use case.

- Chapter 3: A Safety Tracking and Sensor System for School Busses in Saudi Arabia.

- Chapter 4: An Algorithm of Lightweight Encryption Applied to Quantified Speech-Secure IoT.

CHAPTER 3

A SAFETY TRACKING AND SENSOR SYSTEM FOR SCHOOL BUSES IN SAUDI ARABIA

SAMAH ABBAS,[1] HAJAR MOHAMMED,[1] LAILA ALMALKI[2] MARYAM HASSAN,[2] MARAM MECCAWY[2,*]

[1]Management Information Systems Department, Faculty of Economics and Administration, King Abdulaziz University, Jeddah, Saudi Arabia

[2]Information Systems Department, Faculty of Computing and Information Technology, King Abdulaziz University, Jeddah, Saudi Arabia

*Corresponding author: mmeccawy@kau.edu.sa

Abstract

Technology can facilitate the daily transport of students to and from schools. There are a number of information technology systems that support the transportation of students, but the most important aspect is to ensure students' safety. This is especially necessary due to the increasing number of accidents related to forgotten students who fall asleep inside school buses. Such incidents may result in asphyxiation or death. This chapter presents a system that helps to reduce the number of incidents of students being forgotten inside school buses by enabling parents to track their children. It includes installing a sensor system in school buses to protect the students during their daily journeys to and from their school by utilizing IoT technologies.

Keywords: Tracking system, sensor, tracking school buses, temperature sensor, GPS, IoT

3.1   Introduction

Technology has found wider use in ensuring our safety and protection in the form of surveillance cameras installed in public places such as in schools for protection and prevention of accidents, crime, and disasters. Recently, technology has come to be used to solve several critical issues in the educational environment, especially the problem of providing the students' safe transportation to and from their schools every day; a matter about which the parents of the students feel very much concerned.

There is a continuing series of painful accidents caused by the lack of care by drivers in ensuring that all the students who board buses actually get to their schools. Some students fall asleep on the school bus and do not accompany their classmates to school. They can be forgotten inside the bus for hours [1]. The child left alone inside the bus may develop an anxiety disorder involving constant tension and fear, which may affect the child's future psychological state. A major concern is that the child may develop claustrophobia (the phobia of closed places). Also, the child may suffocate, which may harm the child's health by causing injury or diseases such as asthma, and, in critical cases, may even cause death. Recently, there was an incident in Saudi Arabia where a second-grade student was forgotten while he was sleeping in the back seat for many hours which resulted in death from asphyxiation [2]. There was another tragic accident in 2010 in which a four-year-old girl died inside the school bus in another Arab state [3]. Therefore, systems based on sensing and tracking technologies can be used in school buses to prevent such accidents [2].

There is a need for a tracking and sensor system that combines GIS, GPS, and SMS, which can be implemented as a mobile application for school buses. In this study, the researchers explored the need for a tracking and sensor system in the school buses of Saudi Arabia and suggest a combination system that can be applied in the mobile devices of drivers, parents, and schools.

3.2   Related Work

The intense interest around the world in creating effective ways of using technology to ensure that the students who fall asleep or otherwise get trapped inside school buses are not forgotten there and suffer an accidental death by asphyxiation is illustrated by the numerous studies on this topic. Some of the studies are on using technologies to develop methods for tracking the school children to ensure their safety on board the school bus. For instance, the study by Shinde *et al.* [4] proposed a system using an embedded Linux board and android method for providing a real-time system to track and monitor the school bus; and an additional LPG MQ6 gas leakage sensor and temperature sensor to detect and prevent a fire hazard inside the school bus.

However, some studies focused on providing a system just for tracking children when they go to school. For example, a study by Ghareeb *et al.* [5] was about developing a smart bus system that would notify the parents, the school, and the drivers. The system, in addition to allowing parents to notify the school if their child would not be attending school on a certain day, would enable parents to track the bus on the GPS in real time using an android mobile application. In addition, two of the studies focused on providing a tracking method for students by using radio frequency identification (RFID) technology. One of them combined RFID with a global positioning system (GPS), which is a satellite-based navigation system that is used in determining an object's position on Earth [6].

The RFID and GPS systems were linked with the general packet radio service (GPRS) that connects to the application in order to notify the parents. Yet another used the two different tags of RFID (readers of which are installed on the school bus and the receiver implemented by using a specific card). This card would be placed in the student's school-bag for recording events and logging data such as the date and time the student enters and leaves the bus. All of the data is saved directly on the server and also sent to the parents. This integrated system provided a solution for monitoring children while on their way to and from school by school bus without the driver's intervention [7, 8]. In our opinion, using the card for detection is a good method unless a student forgets to place the card in the schoolbag. Other solutions were suggested such as a study proposed by Habadi and AbuAbdullah for a system for a smart and safe school bus. It used sensors to monitor the increase in carbon dioxide level in the bus. If it increased beyond a certain limit, the system would open a window to prevent the injury or death of the student by asphyxiation.

In Saudi Arabia, we found a lack of procedures for ensuring the safety of students traveling on school buses. Hence, the lack of awareness about technology that can provide safety and protection for the students inside the buses. The school bus drivers in Saudi Arabia are not familiar with technology and they do not use it most of the time. Hence, it is essential to implement such systems and instruct bus drivers, parents, and school administrators about their use to provide safety and protection for students who use school buses.

The government of Saudi Arabia is working with consulting companies to implement some projects for scheduling or tracking school buses and students [9]. A study by two students at Taibah University [10] proposed a mobile Android application suitable for tracking buses of Taibah University, their routing, and scheduling. The system could be useful for the bus drivers and the students of the university. This application provided GIS, GPS, notification system (SMS & GSM), arrival time, and dynamic maps. Another study suggested a smart bus system to optimize the bus routes, pick up and drop off points for students and notification and feedback system from excused or absent students for the students of Taif University [11]. Although there is a lack of technology for tracking school buses in Saudi Arabia, there are some technologies that are used in the Hajj buses for tracking and controlling the pilgrims such as the study by Abdessemed [12]. This study proposed using an RFID-based system, which connected with the pilgrims' buses for supervising, tracking and controlling the pilgrims and their buses.

However, there is still a need for a tracking and sensor system for school buses, which combines GIS, GPS, and SMS and is suitable for implementation as a mobile application. In the study presented below, the researchers explore the requirements of a tracking and sensor system in the school buses in Saudi Arabia and suggest a composite system that can be implemented on the mobile devices of parents, drivers and schools. The question here is how to provide safety and protection, especially for young children who travel to and from home and school on school buses. How can we minimize the possibility of suffocation or death inside the school bus? How can the system be made simple and easy to use?

3.3 Data Gathering Phase

To study and explore the research problem, we gathered the information from our target sample. In this study, we used qualitative and quantitative research methods for collecting data to discover the real situation of the school buses in Saudi Arabia. The questionnaires were distributed to parents and school administrators. Individual interviews of school bus drivers were used as sources of data/information from our sample of private schools and educational institutions. This included kindergartens, elementary, intermediate and secondary schools that provide bus service to their students. The objectives of using the questionnaire were:

(a) To assess the current situation of the school buses in Saudi Arabia.

(b) To measure the needs of the parents to track their children when they ride the school bus.

(c) To assess the importance of providing protection for the students inside the school bus.

(d) To gain more future users for the system we would produce from the sample.

(f) To gather more information for better understanding our research problem and to identify our system requirements.

3.3.1 Questionnaire

Our questionnaire was distributed electronically to reach as many participants among our target sample as possible. We made two questionnaires, one for school administration and the other for students' parents. First, we asked the participants a common question about the grade level of children using school buses. The subsequent questions focused on the importance of facilitating the safe movement of students between schools and their houses. The response from the school administrators was as following:

> Almost 66% of schools provided student transportation service by bus while 34% did not. In addition, 60% of schools did not have a supervisor in the bus responsible for ensuring safe entry and exit of the students while 40% did. That means there is a safety issue regarding school buses in Saudi Arabia. In addition, we asked school administrators, "What are the security and safety systems currently available on the bus to protect the students?" The results show 39% have a fire alarm system, and 6% have a system to prevent suffocation. However, an alarming 63% gave such answers as, "There is no safety system in the buses," "I don't know if there is a safety system in buses," and "No, I do not know that such systems exist for buses."

On the other hand, we asked the parents, "How do you usually keep track of your children's arrival at school?". The responses showed that 47% of parents tracked their children's arrival at school in special circumstances by contacting the school, 63% said they contacted the driver or the supervisor, 38% said they did not track their child's arrival at school.

We received other responses such as: "I have my own driver," or "I put a camera in the car and drive them myself." The fact that a high percentage, which was 63%, of parents, contacted the bus driver in special circumstances showed the need for including the bus driver in our proposed tracking system, as shown in Figure 3.1.

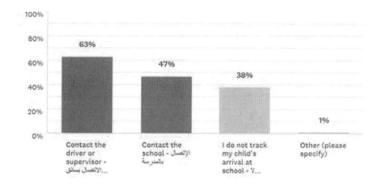

Figure 3.1   Ways to track children as they travel to and from school.

Based on widespread use of mobile applications in all areas, around 88% preferred using the mobile application that enabled tracking the bus while 12% did not prefer it. Finally, we asked the parents about the systems they want to be implemented in the school buses and gave them the choice of several. "Fire alarm system" was chosen by 29%, "A sensor system to prevent student detention inside the bus" was the choice of a very high 87%, "Tracking system for the bus" was the highest choice with 92%, and "System to prevent suffocation" was supported by 47%, as shown in Figure 3.2.

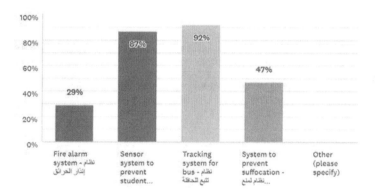

Figure 3.2   Systems parents want implemented in school buses.

3.3.2 Driver Interviews

We interviewed eight school bus drivers from different levels (kindergarten, elementary, intermediate, and high school) of private schools in different cities in Saudi Arabia.

The aim of these interviews was to collect specific information for explaining the real difficulties and problems facing school bus drivers in Saudi schools. Also, to measure and assess the ability of the drivers to act positively and manage emergency situations, such as student's suffocation or a fire inside the bus, to ensure the safety and protection of the bus passengers, that is, the school students. The responses of the bus drivers strongly indicated the need for sensor systems that can send notifications (alerting messages) to the bus driver's mobile phone in real time if a student is forgotten and stranded inside a bus.

Furthermore, all the interviewees preferred checking the bus personally to ensure that no student remained on the bus. Some of the bus drivers preferred to have a supervisor supervise the students on the school bus. Their rejection of the system was caused by difficulties that they faced in using mobile phone applications such as registering in the app, etc. Some of them may not trust the accuracy of the system, especially when it came to relying on the system to alert them about a missing student.

For getting more requirements for our proposed system, we interviewed two of the parents and school administrators. The parents strongly supported our proposed system that would help them track their children. Also, the school administrators saw that it was important to have a system that provided safety and protection for their students when they used the school buses, particularly as the system could also provide them information about the absent students.

3.4   The Proposed Safety Tracking and Sensor School Bus System

The main objectives of the proposed safety tracking and sensor school bus system are as follows:

(1) Ensuring that all the students who got on the bus got off the bus when they reached the schools or their homes.

(2) Ensuring that the driver was alerted to the presence of a sleeping student on the bus, and to relieve the parents' anxiety about their children by including them in the system to follow their children.

This proposed system is developed as a mobile application that connects the school bus driver, the student's parents, and the school. This application would allow them to track the student using GPS during their journey on the school bus. Moreover, the system will notify the parents about the arrival of the bus from the school five minutes ahead of the time. It will enable the parents to inform the bus driver about the student's absence from the school. Therefore, the driver does not have to pick up the student, thus saving time. To ensure safety, a passive infrared sensor (PIR) has been added to the design, which is a non-contact temperature sensor that includes a sensing element that interacts with its own temperature, which varies as it absorbs or emits heat by radiation [13-15]. This PIR sensor is used to detect the temperature of a student's body inside the bus from a remote location. This sensor will work when the school bus stops at its station at the school. If the heat of a student's body is sensed inside the bus, the system will send a continuous voice alarm message to the driver until the driver checks inside the bus. Thus, a student's life could be saved. The system also includes electronic supervision in real time rather than the traditional way of appointing a person to supervise the students inside the bus. Furthermore, since the proposed system is a mobile app it will provide usability and mobility at any time. Also, the school can use the information that will be recorded in the system to know the number of absent students each day.

3.4.1 System Analysis and Design

As shown in Figure 3.3, our safety tracking and sensor school bus system is comprised of four actors. They are the school, the school bus driver, the parents, and the application. The first three actors have the following functional and non-functional requirements.

The functional requirements in our safety tracking and sensor school bus system are divided into two parts. First, for parent, driver, and school, which consists of registering in the application, log in/log out, getting a notification (sensor and tracking), checking absence records of each student, and getting the bus location, including updates of the location and distance from the location of the person seeking the information. Second, for the application, which consists of getting the current location, sending a notification (sensor and tracking), and sending the location.

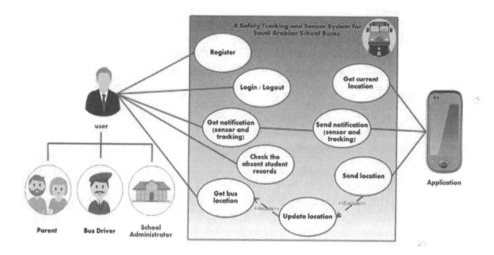

Figure 3.3   School bus tracking sensor system use case.

In general, the software of our safety tracking and sensor system has three main components. First, the tracking system with the server that is provided by GPS (vehicle tracking system) using Google Maps. The second component is the GPRS/GSM service used to support the communication between the GPS system and a safety tracking and sensor application and database cloud servers. The third component depends on passive infrared (PIR), which is one of the infrared systems to detect heat radiated from a body. The required sensor installed inside the school bus will be linked by a program in Java programming language with our proposed application system that should be installed on the mobile phone of parents, drivers, and school administrators. When the bus driver stops the school bus at the bus station, the PIR sensor will start searching for the presence of a human body. If there is a student left inside the bus, the PIR will sound an alarm to alert the bus driver, at the same time sending an alert on the driver's mobile through the application. Moreover, the system will send a notification to the student's parent five minutes before the bus arrives at a student's home.

The following diagram shown in Figure 3.4 clearly shows how our safety tracking and sensor system would work.

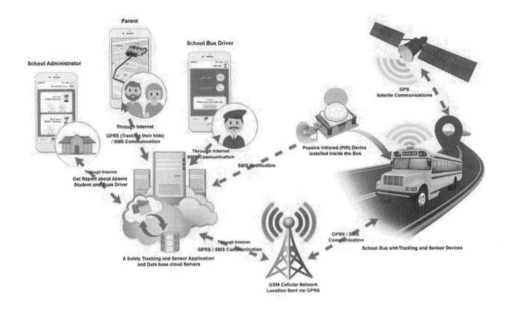

Figure 3.4 Diagram of safety tracking and sensor system.

3.4.2 User Interface Design

The safety tracking and sensor school bus system begins with the login/sign up page (see Figure 3.5). First, before the user can log in the user should sign in to the system, unless the user has previously signed in. In which case the user should directly login.

Figure 3.5 Sign up/sign in page.

The user should select his mission, driver, parent or school administrator. For example, if the user were a parent, the system will display a page that would allow the user to enter his information such as name, email address and phone number. After the user fills in the complete information, the system will confirm registration by sending a verification code to the user's mobile device, and when the user reenters the verification code correctly, the system creates the user's account. The bus driver and school administrator can sign up in the system in the same way as the parent. The bus driver should enter the required information like name, phone number, and bus number, and then confirm his/her registration. Similarly, the school administrator should complete his/her information and then confirm his/her registration.

The home page of parent interface has four sections: track the bus, inform the bus driver about the child's absence from school, call the bus driver, and add new bus driver if the driver changed. Figure 3.6 shows us how parents can inform the bus driver about the student's absence. The parent can track the bus location by clicking on the "tracking bus" button, and then the parent would be able to see the current bus location, as shown in Figure 3.6.

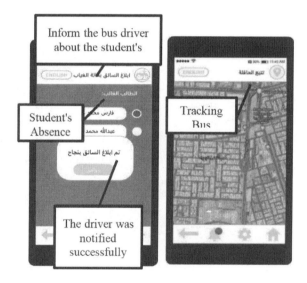

Figure 3.6   Informing the bus driver and tracking the bus.

The bottom bar has four buttons that allow the user to access the home page easily or change the settings and follow up on the new bus alerts or log out. Moreover, the system will allow the parents to inform the bus driver if their children will be absent from the school, and also provide for making a call to the bus driver. In addition, if the driver is changed, the parent will be able to add the new driver driving their children by searching for the phone number of the new bus driver, as shown in Figure 3.7.

Figure 3.7   Add bus driver.

Notice that the new driver must have an account in the system in order to be assigned by the parent as the new driver who will be driving their children's school bus.

Figure 3.8 represents the home page of the school bus driver. It has two sections: show absent students and call the students' parents. When the user (bus driver) clicks on the absent students' button, the system will restore all the information about absent students provided by the respective absent students' parents. The system will also send an SMS alert directly to the bus driver when the parents select the absent button on their interface. The system will inform the bus driver through an SMS alert if there is a student forgotten inside the bus. The school bus driver will receive this alerting message when the sensor installed inside the bus detects the body heat of a person inside the bus. Therefore, this is the main feature of the system. The lower bar has the same functions as the parent interface.

Figure 3.8   Bus driver.

The home page of the school administrator involves a list of bus drivers of the school and the facility for calling the drivers. The school administrator can follow up on the absent students and store this record, as shown in Figure 3.9. Therefore, this list of school bus drivers will help inform the school about the absent students in each school bus on each day.

Figure 3.9   School administrator.

The development of our mobile application is based on the Android platform using multiple software programs, starting with using Java and XML of Android Studio to create the mobile application for the parent, bus, and school. Then, using XAMPP to run APACHE and SQL servers and using MYSQL for our system database. In addition, we use PHP for server-side programming and connecting Android Studio with a database. The monitoring and tracking system will be updated and stored in the servers built in the Cloud. For alerting, the application will notify the parent if the bus driver will not come and the parent can send information about their children's absence. Our proposed system was simulated to test usability and design satisfaction. The testing and results of this simulation are presented in the next section.

3.5 Testing and Results

For evaluating the effectiveness of the simulated school bus safety tracking and sensor system, usability testing was conducted on 150 people in the three schools in Jeddah, where the test sample included school administrators, teachers who have children and bus drivers. They were asked about the fictional and nonfictional requirement of the application: ease of using the application, clarity in registration steps, navigating between the application screens, and ease of communication. We asked the bus drivers about the accuracy of the system when the system sent a notification about an absent student. The test results found that 65% of the users were satisfied; the users liked the interface design and did not notice any difficulties in navigating between screens. According to the parents' answers, using the application was easy, and made them feel comfortable and assured about their children's safety when they started to track them using the GPS tracking system. Moreover, the bus drivers had a good impression of the sensor integrated into the mobile application when the PIR sensor was implemented inside the bus, which enables them to receive the notification about forgetting student inside the bus. In general, the users were satisfied with the system's usability, interaction, accuracy and security features.

3.6   Discussion and Limitation

The previous studies mentioned in the literature review section showed the importance of the system for ensuring the safety of children using school buses in Saudi Arabia, especially the safety of young schoolchildren. The safety tracking and sensor school bus system helps to reassure parents about their children through the ability to track the bus location accurately by using GPS. The system enables the school to supervise the drivers and to follow up with the attendance records of students. Furthermore, it enables drivers to keep track of students left on the bus due to the efficient operation of the sensor and issuance of accurate alerts in the mobile application. These functions can contribute to reducing the cases of students forgotten on buses and reduce the number of injuries and deaths by suffocation inside the bus. Despite the positive results, there are some obstacles that schools may face when using the system:

(1) Acquiring and installing the PIR sensors in school buses is costly and complex.

(2) Some drivers, given their age or limited IT skills, may resist using the new technology.

3.7   Conclusions and Future Work

Using emerging technology is possible not only for facilitating the process of education itself but also for providing the most comfort and safety possible for students and parents. This work was conducted to improve the transport services provided to the students in Saudi Arabia's schools. For this, the safety tracking and sensor system for school buses was designed and developed using a software application. This proposed system provides a way for parents to track their children during their daily journeys to and from school using GPS, and notifies them before the arrival of the bus at their doorstep. The application also notifies the school bus driver about absentee students. In addition, the system informs the bus driver through an SMS alert if there is a forgotten student inside the bus detected by the PIR sensor in the bus. The experiment results showed the positive impact of the system and provided a better understanding of the needs of those using school buses. Future work including a full implementation of the sensor system will be achieved and tested. Therefore, we suggest the application of the tracking and sensor system in all the schools of Saudi Arabia to achieve a high level of safety, security, and comfort for students and their families.

REFERENCES

1. Katims, L. (2011). High-tech school bus teaches students on the road. *The Education Digest*, 77(2), 50.

2. https://sabq.org/Xs7cmK. [Accessed: 23-Dec-2018].

3. Toumi, H. Four-year-old girl left alone in school bus dies. Availableat: http://gulfnews.com/news/gulf/qatar/four-yearold-girl-left-alone-in-school-bus-dies-1.628394 [Accessed: 07-Oct-2018].

4. Shinde, P. A., Mane, Y. B., & Tarange, P. H. (2015, March). Real time vehicle monitoring and tracking system based on embedded Linux board and android application. In 2015 *International Conference on Circuits, Power and Computing Technologies* [ICCPCT-2015] (pp. 1-7). IEEE.

5. Ghareeb, M., Bazzi, A., Abdul-Nabi, S., & Ibrahim, Z. A. A. (2018). Towards smarter city: clever school transportation system. *Analog Integrated Circuits and Signal Processing*, 96(2), 261-268.

6. "GPS (Global Positioning System) Definition." [Online]. Available: https://techterms.com/definition/gps. [Accessed: 09-Oct-2018].

7. Habadi, A. A., & AbuAbdullah, Y. S. (2018, April). Intelligent Safety School Buses System Using RFID and Carbon Dioxide Detection. In 2018 1st *International Conference on Computer Applications & Information Security* (ICCAIS) (pp. 1-7). IEEE.

8. Shaaban, K., Bekkali, A., Hamida, E. B., & Kadri, A. (2013). Smart Tracking system for school buses using passive RFID technology to enhance child safety. *Journal of Traffic and Logistics Engineering*, 1(2), 191-196.

9. S. Furniss (2015). "Edulog's Technology Helps Get Saudi Arabian Girls to School, Provides 130+ Jobs in Missoula," Montana High Tech Business Alliance, 04-Jun-2015.

10. Ahmed, A., Al-Mutiri, W., & Nada, E. (2017). University Buses Routing and Tracking System, *Int. J. Comput. Sci. Inf. Technol.*, 9(1), 95-104..

11. Assery, F., Alajmy, M., & Albagory, Y. (2018). Smart bus transportation system for fast arrival time to the girls campus at Taif University. *International Journal of Applied Engineering Research*, 13(10), 8022-8025.

12. Abdessemed, F. (2011, October). An integrated system for tracking and control pilgrims shuttle buses. In *2011 14th International IEEE Conference on Intelligent Transportation Systems (ITSC)* (pp. 384-389). IEEE.

13. Urban, G. (2016). Jacob Fraden: Handbook of modern sensors: physics, designs, and applications. *Analytical and Bioanalytical Chemistry*, 408(21), 5667-5668.

14. Puar, V. H., Bhatt, C. M., Hoang, D. M., & Le, D. N. (2018). Communication in Internet of Things. In *Information Systems Design and Intelligent Applications* (pp. 272-281). Springer, Singapore.

15. Le, D. N., Bhatt, C., & Madhukar, M. (Eds.). (2019). *Security Designs for the Cloud, IoT, and Social Networking*. John Wiley & Sons.

CHAPTER 4

A LIGHTWEIGHT ENCRYPTION ALGORITHM APPLIED TO A QUANTIZED SPEECH IMAGE FOR SECURE INTERNET OF THINGS

MOURAD TALBI

Laboratory of Semiconductors, Nanostructures and Advanced Technology; Center of Research and Technologies of Energy of Borj Cedria, Tunis, Tunisia
Corresponding author: talbi1969@yahoo.fr

Abstract

The IoT (internet of things) is a promising technology of the future. It is expected to connect billions of devices. The increasing amount of communication is expected to generate mountains of data and the data security can be threatened. The devices in the architecture are smaller in size and low powered. Generally, classical encryption schemes are computationally expensive due to their complexity, which requires numerous rounds of encryption, essentially wasting the constrained energy of the gadgets. A less complex algorithm, though, may compromise the desired integrity. In this work, we apply a lightweight encryption algorithm termed secure IoT (SIT) to a quantized speech image for a secure internet of things. It is a 64-bit block cipher and needs a 64-bit key for data encryption. This quantized speech image is constructed by first quantizing a speech signal and then splitting the quantized signal into frames, which are the different columns of this quantized speech image. Simulation results show that the algorithm provides substantial security.

Keywords: Encryption, quantized speech image, internet of things, security

4.1   Introduction

In the last few years, the internet of things (IoT) has become an emerging domain of research and practical implementation. The IoT is a model including ordinary entities with the ability to sense and communicate with corresponding devices employing the internet [1]. Since the broadband internet is actually accessible to any user and its cost of connectivity is also being reduced, more sensors and gadgets are getting connected to it [2]. Such conditions are providing appropriate ground for IoT growth. Because of our desire to approach any object from anywhere in the world, many research works are focusing on the complexities around the IoT [3].

The sophisticated sensors and chips are embedded in the physical things surrounding us, each transmitting valuable data. The sharing process of such a large amount of data begins with the devices themselves, which should securely communicate with the IoT platform. The latter integrates the data from many devices and applies analytic computations to share the most valuable data with the applications. The IoT is taking the mobile network, conventional internet and sensor network to another level, as everything will be connected to the internet. A matter of concern that should be kept in mind when working on emerging issues related to data integrity, confidentiality and authenticity is guaranteed security and privacy of the user's account [4, 5].

4.2   Applications of IoT

With the revolution in telecommunication, we need more and more devices connected to the internet. Many devices, such as personal computers, smartphones, tablets, laptops, smart TVs, video game consoles, and even refrigerators and air conditioners, have the ability to communicate with each other via the internet. This trend is extending outwards and it is estimated that by the year 2020 there will be over 50 billion objects connected to the internet [6]. This estimates that for each person in the world there will be 6.6 objects online [1]. The world will be blanketed with millions of sensors gathering information from physical objects and will upload it to the internet. It is suggested that IoT application is still at an early stage, although it is beginning to evolve fast [7, 8]. An overview of the use of IoT in building an automation system is given in [9]. In [10], it is suggested that a variety of industries have a growing interest in IoT use.

Different IoT applications in healthcare industries are presented in [11, 12] and the development opportunities in healthcare brought in by IoT will be huge [13]. It is predicted that IoT will contribute to making mining production safer [14], in addition to making it possible to forecast disasters. It is expected that IoT will transform transportation systems and automobile services [15]. Since more physical objects will be equipped with sensors and RFID tags, transportation companies will be able to track and monitor an object's movements from origin to destination [16]. Consequently, IoT also shows promising behavior in the logistics industry. With many applications eyeing the adaptation of technology with the intentions of contributing to economic growth, healthcare, transportation and a better life style for the public, IoT should provide adequate security for user data to encourage the adaptation process [1].

4.3   Security Challenges in IoT

To adopt the internet of things (IoT) technology, it is important to build the confidence among the users about its security and privacy so that it will not cause any grave threat to their data integrity, authority and confidentiality. The IoT is intrinsically vulnerable to a variety of security threats, and if the necessary security measures aren't taken there will be a threat of information leaking or could prove damaging to the economy [17, 18]. Such threats can be considered as one of the main hindrances to the internet of things [19, 20], which is very open to attacks [21, 22], due to the arguments that there is a possibility of physical attack on its components since they remain unsupervised for long periods of time. Secondly, eavesdropping is very simple and this is due to the wireless communication medium [1].

Lastly, the constituents of IoT bear low competency in terms of energy with which they are operated and also in terms of computational capability. The implementation of conventional computationally expensive security algorithms will result in the hindrance of the performance of the energy-constrained devices. Finally, the IoT constituents bear low competency in terms of computational ability as well as in terms of the energy with which they are operated [1].

It is predicted that a substantial amount of data is predicted to be generated while IoT is employed for monitoring purposes and is vital to conserve data unification [23]. Specifically, data authentication and integrity are matters of concern. From a high level perspective, the internet of things consists of three components, namely middleware, hardware and presentation [1]. Hardware consists of actuators and sensors, the middleware provides storage and calculating tools, and the presentation provides the interpretation tools accessible on diverse platforms. Since it isn't possible to process the data collected from billions of sensors, context-aware middleware solutions are proposed to help a sensor decide the most important data for processing [24]. The IoT architecture doesn't inherently provide enough margin for accomplishing the essential actions involved in the authentication process and data integrity. The devices in the IoT, such as RFID, are questionable for achieving the fundamental requirements of the authentication process that includes constant communication with the servers and exchange messages with nodes [5].

In secure systems the data confidentiality is maintained and it is ensured that during the process of message exchange the data retains its originality and no alteration is unseen by the system. Since the IoT is composed of many small devices such as RFIDs which remain unattended for extended times, it is easier for the adversary to access the data stored in the memory [25]. For providing immunity against Sybil attacks in RFID tags, received signal strength indication (RSSI)-based methodologies are employed (see [26-29]). A great number of solutions have been introduced for the wireless sensor networks which consider the sensor as an internet part connected via nodes [30]. Though, in the IoT the sensor nodes themselves are considered as the internet nodes, making the authentication process even more significant. The data integrity also becomes vital and needs special attention in order to retain its reliability [5].

4.4   Cryptographic Algorithms for IoT

The requirements for lightweight cryptography have been extensively discussed [31, 32], and the shortcomings of the IoT in terms of constrained devices are highlighted. In fact, there are some lightweight cryptography schemes that do not continuously use security-efficiency trade-offs. Amongst the block cipher, stream cipher and hash functions, the block ciphers have been proven to have significantly better performances. A novel block cipher called mCrypton is proposed in [33]. The cipher comes with the options of 128, 96 and 64 bits key size. The architecture of this algorithm is followed by Crypton [34], although the functions of each component are simplified to enhance its performance for the constrained hardware.

In [35], the successor of Hummingbird-1 [36] was proposed as Hummingbird-2 (HB-2). With 128 bits of key and a 64 bit initialization vector, Hummingbird-2 is tested to stay unaffected by all previously known attacks [5]. However, the cryptanalysis of HB-2 [37] highlights the algorithm weaknesses and whether the initial key can be recovered. Different legacy encryption algorithms were studied in [38]. Among those algorithms, we have RC4, RC5 and IDEA and their energy consumption was measured. They calculated the computational cost of the RC4 [39], IDEA [40] and RC5 ciphers on diverse platforms, although a variety of existing algorithms were omitted during this study.

RC5 (Rivest cipher),[1] TEA (tiny encryption algorithm) [41] and Skipjack [42] algorithms have been implemented on MICA2 hardware platform [43]. For determining the energy consumption and memory use of the ciphers, MICA2 was configured in single mote. Some block ciphers, including RC5, Skipjack, AES (advanced encryption standard) [44] and XXTEA [45], have been implemented [46], and the energy consumption and execution time is determined. The results show that in the AES algorithm, the key size has great impact on the encryption phases, decryption and key setup. RC5 provides diversified parameters; i-e key size, number of rounds and word size can be altered. Various combinations have been performed that show when the word size increases, it took a longer time to execute [5].

As the key setup phase is not required in Skipjack and XXTEA, they drew less energy but their security strength is not as much as RC5 and AES [5]. The Simon and Speck lightweight block ciphers were proposed [47] in order to have optimal results in software and hardware respectively [5]. Both ciphers offer a range of key size and width, although at least 22 numbers of round are needed to perform enough encryption. Though the Simon is based on low multiplication complexity, the total number of needed mathematical operation is quite high [48, 49].

4.5   The Proposed Algorithm

In this work, we apply a lightweight encryption algorithm [5] to a quantized speech image for a secure internet of things. The application of this algorithm is argumented by the fact that we need to send confidential data between several devices with high level security. A lightweight encryption algorithm [5] can be implemented in simple devices which don't require powerful processors,

Figure 4.1 illustrates the construction of a quantized speech image.

---

[1] https://tools.ietf.org/html/rfc2040

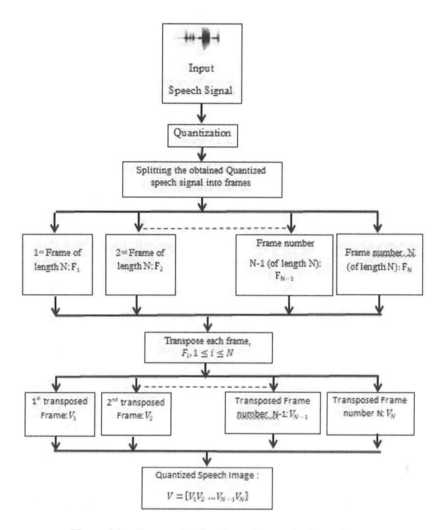

Figure 4.1   Construction flowchart of a quantized speech image.

According to this figure, the different steps of this construction are given as follow:

1. Quantization of the input speech signal,

2. Splitting the obtained quantized speech signal into frames where each of them is of length N. These frames are in number of N and are noted as follow: $F_i, i \leq i \leq N$,

3. Transpose each of these frames $F_i, i \leq i \leq N$ in order to obtain the different columns $V_i, i \leq i \leq N$ of this quantized speech image, $V = [V_1 V_2 \cdots V_{N-1} V_N]$.

Figure 4.2 shows the flowchart of the proposed encryption/decryption technique applied to the quantized speech image for secure internet of things.

As shown in Figure 4.2, a lightweight encryption algorithm proposed in [5], is applied to the quantized speech image in order to obtain the encrypted image. After that, the lightweight decryption algorithm [5] is applied to the encrypted image in order to have the decrypted image. Then, the reconstruction of the quantized speech signal is performed and finally the de-quantization is applied to this signal in order to obtain the output speech signal, which represents the confidential data.

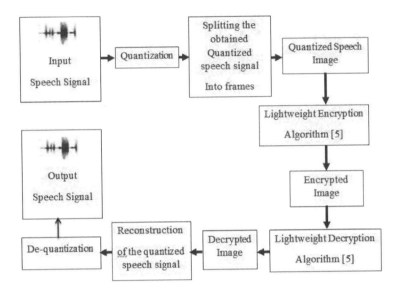

Figure 4.2 Flowchart of the proposed encryption technique applied to the quantized speech image for secure internet of things.

4.6 Experimental Setup

Since in this work we have applied the lightweight encryption algorithm proposed in [5], the same evaluation criterion are used in this work as in [5]. Furthermore, we have used the PESQ (perceptual evaluation speech quality) and the SNR (signal-to-noise ratio) in order to evaluate the perceptual quality of the reconstructed or output speech signal of the proposed Encryption/Decryption system (Figure 4.2). The evaluation criteria used in this work, are detailed as follows [5, 50]:

- *Key Sensitivity*: An algorithm of encryption should be sensitive to the key. It means that it should not retrieve the original data when the key has even a minute difference from the original key. Avalanche test is employed to evaluate the amount of alterations that occurred in the cipher text by changing one bit of the key or plain text. According to strict avalanche criterion (SAC) [5], when 50% of the bits are changed due to one-bit change, the test is considered to be perfect. To visually observe this effect, we decrypt the image with a key that has a difference of only one bit from the correct key.

- *Execution Time*: One of the fundamental parameters for the algorithm evaluation is the amount of time that it takes for encoding and decoding a particular data. The algorithm proposed in [5] is designed for the IoT environment and should consume minimal time and provide substantial security [5].

- *Memory Utilization*: Memory utilization is a principal concern in resource-constrained IoT devices. An encryption algorithm is composed of some computational rounds that may occupy significant memory, making it inappropriate to be used in IoT. Consequently, the proposed technique is evaluated in terms of its memory utilization. Smaller memory amount engagement will be favorable for its deployment in IoT.

- *Image Histogram*: A method for observing the visual effect of the cipher is to encrypt an image with the proposed algorithm and view the randomness it produces in the image. For evaluating the generated randomness, the image histogram is computed. After encryption, a uniform histogram depicts appreciable security.

- *Image Entropy*: The encryption algorithm adds extra information to the data so that it makes it difficult for the intruder to differentiate between the original information and the one added by the algorithm. The information amount is measured in terms of entropy, consequently it can be said that the higher the entropy the better the security algorithm performance. For measuring the entropy (H) for an image, equation (4.1) is applied on the intensity (I) values and $P(I_i)$ is the intensity value probability I_i.

$$H(I) = -\sum_{i=1}^{2^B} P(I_i)log_B(P(I_i)) \tag{4.1}$$

- *Correlation*: The correlation between two values represents a statistical relationship that depicts the dependency of one value on another. Data points that hold substantial dependency have a significant correlation value. A good cipher is expected to eliminate the dependency of the cipher text from the original message [5]. Consequently, no information can be extracted from the cipher alone and no relationship can be drawn between cipher text and the plain text [5]. Shannon has explained this criterion in his communication theory of secrecy systems [5].

In this experiment, we calculated the correlation coefficient for original and encrypted images. The correlation coefficient Υ is computed by employing equation (4.2). For an ideal cipher case Υ has to be equal to 0 and in the worst case Υ will be equal to 1.

$$\Upsilon_{x,y} = \frac{cov(x,y)}{\sqrt{D(x)}\sqrt{D(y}} \tag{4.2}$$

where $D(y)$, $D(x)$ and $cov(x,y)$ are respectively the variances and covariance of the variables y and x.

The spread of values or variance of any single dimension random variable can be computed by employing equation (4.3).

$$D(x) = \frac{1}{N}\sum_{i=1}^{N}(x_i - E(x))^2 \tag{4.3}$$

where $D(x)$ represents the variance variable x.

The covariance between two random variables x and y, $cov(x,y)$, is expressed as follows:

$$cov(x,y) = \frac{1}{N}\sum_{i=1}^{N}(x_i - E(x))(y_i - E(y)) \tag{4.4}$$

In equations (4.3) and (4.4), the quantities $E(x)$ and $E(y)$ represent the expected values of the random variables y and x respectively. These expectations are computed by using the following formula:

$$E(y) = \frac{1}{N} \sum_{i=1}^{N} x_i \tag{4.5}$$

where

- N is the total number of pixels in the image and is equal to $row \times col$;

- x is a vector having N as length; and

- x_i represents the ith intensity values of the original image.

- Perceptual evaluation of speech quality (PESQ): The perceptual evaluation of speech quality (PESQ) algorithm is an objective quality measure that is approved as the ITU-T recommendation P.862.[2] It is a tool of objective measurement conceived to predict the results of a subjective mean opinion score (MOS) test. It was proved [50] that the PESQ is more reliable and correlated better with MOS than the traditional objective speech measures.

- Signal-to-noise ratio (SNR): It is expressed in decibels as follow:

$$SNR_{dB} = 10 \cdot \log_{10} \left(\frac{\sum_{n=0}^{N-1} s^2(n)}{\sum_{n=0}^{N-1} (\hat{s}(n) - s(n))^2} \right) \tag{4.6}$$

where $s(n)$ and $\hat{s}(n)$ are samples of the original and the processed signals respectively.

4.7   Results and Discussion

According to [5] the algorithm simulation is made in order to perform the standard tests, including avalanche and image entropy and histogram on Intel Core i7-3770@3.40 GHz processor employing MATLAB.[3] For evaluating the performance in the real IoT environment, Muhammad Usman *et al.* Implemented the algorithm on ATmega328-based Arduino Uno board as well. The memory utilization and execution time of their proposed algorithm [5] were observed. In [5], the execution time was found to be respectively 0.188 millisconds for encryption and 0.187 milliseconds for decryption respectively, the algorithm proposed in [5] employs the 22 bytes of memory on the ATmega328 platform. As previously mentioned, in this work, we use the same encryption/decryption algorithms proposed in [5].

The encryption algorithm proposed in [5] was compared with other algorithms implemented on hardware, as shown in Table 4.1 [5].

---

[2]https://www.itu.int/rec/T-REC-P
[3]https://www.mathworks.com

Table 4.1   Results for hardware implementations.

CIPHER	DEVICE	Block Size	Key Size	Code Size	RAM	Cycles (ene)	Cycles (dec)
AES	AVR	64	128	1570	-	2739	3579
HIGHT	AVR	64	128	5672	-	2964	2964
IDEA	AVR	64	80	596	-	2700	15393
KATAN	AVR	64	80	338	18	72063	88525
KLEIN	AVR	64	80	1268	18	6095	7658
PRESENT	AVR	64	128	1000	18	11342	13599
TEA	AVR	64	128	648	24	7408	7539
PRINCE	AVR	64	128	1574	24	3253	3293
SKIPJACK	Power TOSSIM	64	80	5230	328	17390	-
RC5	Power TOSSIM	64	128	3288	72	70700	-
SIT	ATmega328	64	64	826	22	3006	2984

Key and block sizes are in bits whereas RAM and code size are in bytes. The cycles include key expansions along with both encryption and decryption [5].

The avalanche test of the algorithm shows that a single bit change in key or plain text brings around 49% change in the cipher bits, which is close to the ideal 50% change. The results in [5] show that the precise decryption is possible merely when the correct key is employed for decrypting the encrypted image. When the incorrect key is employed, the image remains non-recognizable. For a visual demonstration of the avalanche test, compared to the original key, the wrong key has a difference of just a bit; the algorithm strength can be perceived from this result.

Figure 4.3   Image encrypted/decrypted.

In order to perform histogram and entropy tests, this work used the speech signal `original1.wav` illustrated in Figure 4.4.

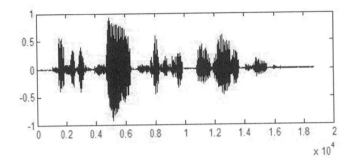

Figure 4.4   Original speech signal.

According to the results listed in Table 4.2, we can note that the entropy of the encrypted image is greater than the original image.

Table 4.2   Results for correlation and entropy.

Speech Signal	Size of the Quantized Speech Image	Correlation		Entropy		SNR (dB)	PESQ
		Original Quantized Speech Image	Encrypted Quantized Speech Image	Original Quantized Speech Image	Encrypted Quantized Speech Image	SNR of the Reconstructed Speech signal	PESQ of the Reconstructed Speech signal
'original1. wav'	220x220	0.9952	0.0255	2.7560	6.4783	33.9532	3.9794
Total encryption time (in seconds)							
27.753251							

The correlation comparison in Figure 4.9 illustrates the contrast between the original and the encrypted data. In this work, the original data is the quantized speech image. This image is highly correlated and retains a high value for the correlation coefficient. However, the encrypted image doesn't seem to have any correlation.

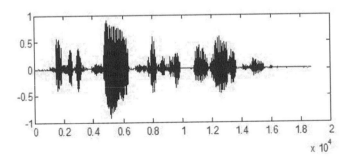

Figure 4.5   Reconstructed speech signal after decryption and dequantization.

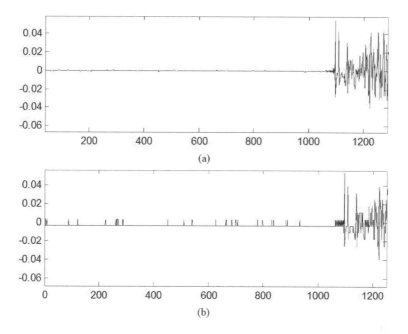

Figure 4.6 (a) The beginning of the original speech signal (zoomed); (b) the same region of the reconstructed speech signal after decryption and dequantization (zoomed).

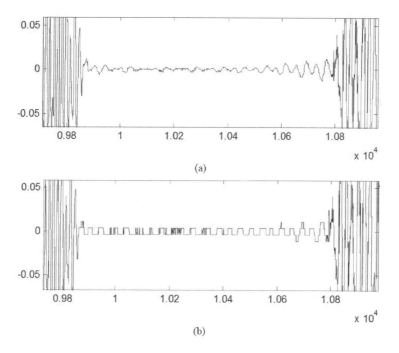

Figure 4.7 (a) The middle of the original speech signal (zoomed); (b) the same region of the reconstructed speech signal after decryption and dequantization (zoomed).

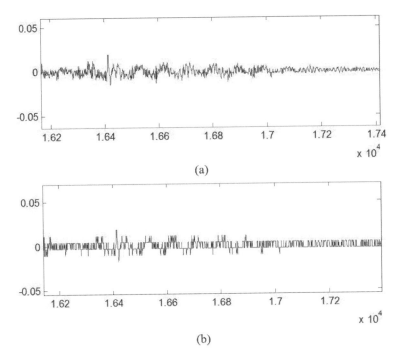

(a)

(b)

Figure 4.8   (a) The end of the original speech signal (zoomed); (b) the same region of the reconstructed speech signal after decryption and dequantization (zoomed).

Figures 4.6 to 4.10 clearly show the difference between the reconstructed speech signal and the original speech one obtained after decryption and dequantization. This difference is due to speech quantization/dequantization.

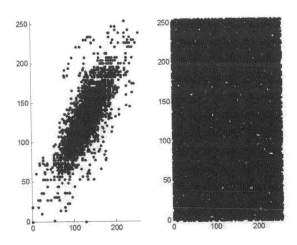

Figure 4.9   Correlation comparison.

The reconstructed speech signal has very good perceptual quality and refers to the results obtained from SNR and PESQ computations (Table 4.2).

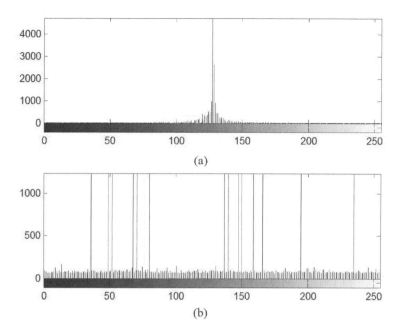

Figure 4.10   (a) Histogram of the original speech quantized image; (b) Histogram of the encrypted speech quantized image.

In the results of the histograms (Figure 4.10) for the encrypted and original images, the almost uniform distribution of intensities after the encryption is an indication of desired security.

4.8 Conclusion

In the near future, the IoT will be an essential part of our daily lives. A great number of energy-constrained devices and sensors will continuously be communicating with each other, the security of which must not be compromised. For this reason, a lightweight security algorithm is applied to a quantized speech image for secure IoT. This quantized speech image is constructed by first quantizing a speech signal and then splitting the quantized signal into frames which constitute the different columns of this quantized speech image. The simulations show promising results, making the algorithm a suitable candidate to be adopted in IoT applications.

Acknowledgment

We would like to thank all those who contributed in some way to this work which was supported by CRTEn (Center for Research and Energy Technologies of Borj Cedria, Tunis) and the Ministry of Higher Education and Scientific Research.

REFERENCES

1. Gubbi, J., Buyya, R., Marusic, S., & Palaniswami, M. (2013). Internet of Things (IoT): A vision, architectural elements, and future directions. *Future generation computer systems*, 29(7), 1645-1660.

2. Want, R., & Dustdar, S. (2015). Activating the Internet of Things [Guest editors' introduction]. *Computer*, 48(9), 16-20.

3. Romero-Mariona, J., Hallman, R., Kline, M., San Miguel, J., Major, M., & Kerr, L. (2016). Security in the industrial internet of things - the C-SEC approach. In *Proceedings of the International Conference on Internet of Things and Big Data (IoTBD 2016)* (pp. 421-428), SCITEPRESS.

4. Suo, H., Wan, J., Zou, C., & Liu, J. (2012, March). Security in the internet of things: a review. In *2012 International Conference on Computer Science and Electronics Engineering* (Vol. 3, pp. 648-651). IEEE.

5. Usman, M., Ahmed, I., Aslam, M. I., Khan, S., & Shah, U. A. (2017). SIT: a lightweight encryption algorithm for secure internet of things. *International Journal of Advanced Computer Science and Applications*, Vol. 8, No. 1, 2017.

6. Airehrour, D., Gutierrez, J., & Ray, S. K. (2016). Secure routing for internet of things: A survey. *Journal of Network and Computer Applications*, 66, 198-213.

7. Miorandi, D., Sicari, S., De Pellegrini, F., & Chlamtac, I. (2012). Internet of things: Vision, applications and research challenges. *Ad Hoc Networks*, 10(7), 1497-1516.

8. Da Xu, L. (2011). Enterprise systems: state-of-the-art and future trends. *IEEE Transactions on Industrial Informatics*, 7(4), 630-640.

9. Zhao, P., Peffer, T., Narayanamurthy, R., Fierro, G., Raftery, P., Kaam, S., & Kim, J. (2016). Getting into the zone: how the internet of things can improve energy efficiency and demand response in a commercial building. *Proceedings of ACEEE Summer Study on Energy Efficiency in Buildings*. Pacific Grove, CA. August 21-26. 12 pp.

10. Li, Y., Hou, M., Liu, H., & Liu, Y. (2012). Towards a theoretical framework of strategic decision, supporting capability and information sharing under the context of Internet of Things. *Information Technology and Management*, 13(4), 205-216.

11. Pang, Z., Chen, Q., Tian, J., Zheng, L., & Dubrova, E. (2013, January). Ecosystem analysis in the design of open platform-based in-home healthcare terminals towards the internet-of-things. In *2013 15th International Conference on Advanced Communications Technology (ICACT)* (pp. 529-534). IEEE.

12. Misra, S., Maheswaran, M., & Hashmi, S. (2017). *Security Challenges and Approaches in Internet of Things*. Cham: Springer International Publishing.

13. Domingo, M. C. (2012). An overview of the Internet of Things for people with disabilities. *Journal of Network and Computer Applications*, 35(2), 584-596.

14. W. Qiuping, Z. Shunbing, and D. Chunquan (2011). Study on key technologies of internet of things perceiving mine, *Procedia Engineering*, vol. 26, pp. 2326-2333.

15. Zhou, H., Liu, B., & Wang, D. (2012). Design and research of urban intelligent transportation system based on the internet of things. In *Internet of Things* (pp. 572-580). Springer, Berlin, Heidelberg.

16. Karakostas, B. (2013). A DNS architecture for the internet of things: A case study in transport logistics. *Procedia Computer Science*, 19, 594-601.

17. Ban, H. J., Choi, J., & Kang, N. (2016). Fine-grained support of security services for resource constrained internet of things. *International Journal of Distributed Sensor Networks*, 12(5), 7824686.

18. Khan, S., Ebrahim, M., & Khan, K. A. (2015, February). Performance evaluation of secure force symmetric key algorithm. In *Proceedings of International Multi-Topic Conference* (IMTIC).

19. Wang, P., Chaudhry, S., Li, L., Li, S., Tryfonas, T., & Li, H. (2016). The Internet of Things: a security point of view. *Internet Research*, 26(2), 337-359..

20. Ebrahim, M., Khan, S., & Khalid, U. (2014). Security risk analysis in peer 2 peer system; an approach towards surmounting security challenges. arXiv preprint arXiv:1404.5123.

21. Simplicio Jr, M. A., Silva, M. V., Alves, R. C., & Shibata, T. K. (2017). Lightweight and escrow-less authenticated key agreement for the internet of things. *Computer Communications*, 98, 43-51.

22. Atzori, L., Iera, A., & Morabito, G. (2010). The internet of things: A survey. *Computer Networks*, 54(15), 2787-2805.

23. Xie, F., & Chen, H. (2016). An efficient and robust data integrity verification algorithm based on context sensitive. *International Journal of Security and Its Applications*, 10(4), 33-40.

24. Wang, S., Zhang, Z., Ye, Z., Wang, X., Lin, X., & Chen, S. (2013). Application of environmental internet of things on water quality management of urban scenic river. *International Journal of Sustainable Development & World Ecology*, 20(3), 216-222.

25. Karygiannis, T., Eydt, B., Barber, G., Bunn, L., & Phillips, T. (2007). Guidelines for securing radio frequency identification (RFID) systems. *NIST Special Publication*, 80, 1-154.

26. Wang, J., Yang, G., Sun, Y., & Chen, S. (2007, September). Sybil attack detection based on RSSI for wireless sensor network. In *2007 International Conference on Wireless Communications, Networking and Mobile Computing* (pp. 2684-2687). IEEE.

27. Lv, S., Wang, X., Zhao, X., & Zhou, X. (2008, December). Detecting the sybil attack cooperatively in wireless sensor networks. In *2008 International Conference on Computational Intelligence and Security* (Vol. 1, pp. 442-446). IEEE.

28. Chen, Y., Yang, J., Trappe, W., & Martin, R. P. (2010). Detecting and localizing identity-based attacks in wireless and sensor networks. *IEEE Transactions on Vehicular Technology*, 59(5), 2418-2434.

29. Chen, S., Yang, G., & Chen, S. (2010, April). A security routing mechanism against Sybil attack for wireless sensor networks. In *2010 International Conference on Communications and Mobile Computing* (Vol. 1, pp. 142-146). IEEE.

30. Eschenauer, L., & Gligor, V. D. (2002, November). A key-management scheme for distributed sensor networks. In *Proceedings of the 9th ACM conference on Computer and communications security* (pp. 41-47). ACM.

31. Katagi, M., & Moriai, S. (2008). Lightweight cryptography for the internet of things. *Sony Corporation*, 7-10.

32. Ebrahim, M., Khan, S., & Mohani, S. S. U. H. (2014). Peer-to-peer network simulators: an analytical review. arXiv preprint arXiv:1405.0400.

33. Lim, C. H., & Korkishko, T. (2005, August). mCrypton-a lightweight block cipher for security of low-cost RFID tags and sensors. In *International Workshop on Information Security Applications* (pp. 243-258). Springer, Berlin, Heidelberg.

34. Lim, C. H. (1998). *CRYPTON: A new 128-bit block cipher*. NIsT AEs Proposal.

35. Engels, D., Saarinen, M. J. O., Schweitzer, P., & Smith, E. M. (2011, June). The Hummingbird-2 lightweight authenticated encryption algorithm. In *International Workshop on Radio Frequency Identification: Security and Privacy Issues* (pp. 19-31). Springer, Berlin, Heidelberg.

36. Engels, D., Fan, X., Gong, G., Hu, H., & Smith, E. M. (2009). Ultra-lightweight cryptography for low-cost RFID tags: Hummingbird algorithm and protocol. *Centre for Applied Cryptographic Research (CACR) Technical Reports*, 29.

37. Zhang, K., Ding, L., & Guan, J. (2012). Cryptanalysis of hummingbird-2. *Cryptology ePrint Archive, Report* 2012/207.

38. Ganesan, P., Venugopalan, R., Peddabachagari, P., Dean, A., Mueller, F., & Sichitiu, M. (2003, September). Analyzing and modeling encryption overhead for sensor network nodes. In *Proceedings of the 2nd ACM International Conference on Wireless Sensor Networks and Applications* (pp. 151-159). ACM.

39. Schneier, B. (2007). *Applied Cryptography: Protocols, Algorithms, and Source Code C.* John Wiley & Sons.

40. Lai, X. (1992). On the design and security of block ciphers (Doctoral dissertation, ETH Zurich).

41. Wheeler, D. J., & Needham, R. M. (1994, December). TEA, a tiny encryption algorithm. In *International Workshop on Fast Software Encryption* (pp. 363-366). Springer, Berlin, Heidelberg.

42. Brickell, E. F., Denning, D. E., Kent, S. T., Maher, D. P., & Tuchman, W. (1993). SKIPJACK review. Interim Report: The Skipjack Algorithm.

43. Guimaraes, G., Souto, E., Sadok, D., & Kelner, J. (2005, August). Evaluation of security mechanisms in wireless sensor networks. In *2005 Systems Communications (ICW'05, ICHSN'05, ICMCS'05, SENET'05)* (pp. 428-433). IEEE.

44. Standard, A. E. (2001). Federal information processing standards publication 197. FIPS PUB, 46-3.

45. Wheeler, D. J., & Needham, R. M. (1998). Correction to xtea. Unpublished manuscript, Computer Laboratory, Cambridge University, England.

46. Lee, J., Kapitanova, K., & Son, S. H. (2010). The price of security in wireless sensor networks. *Computer Networks*, 54(17), 2967-2978.

47. Beaulieu, R., Treatman-Clark, S., Shors, D., Weeks, B., Smith, J., & Wingers, L. (2015, June). The SIMON and SPECK lightweight block ciphers. In *2015 52nd ACM/EDAC/IEEE Design Automation Conference (DAC)* (pp. 1-6). IEEE.

48. Mourouzis, T., Song, G., Courtois, N., & Christofii, M. (2015). Advanced differential cryptanalysis of reduced-round SIMON64/128 using large-round statistical distinguishers.

49. Khan, S., Ibrahim, M. S., Khan, K. A., & Ebrahim, M. (2015). Security analysis of secure force algorithm for wireless sensor networks. arXiv preprint arXiv:1509.00981.

50. Talbi, M., Barbarnoussi, C., & Adnane, C. (2013). Speech compression based on psychoacoustic model and a general approach for filter bank design using optimization. In *International Arab Conference on Information Technology* (ACIT 2013).

PART III

MOBILE TECHNOLOGY

Mobile technologies facilitate new digital supply chain processes and product life cycle management and consumption behaviors. For instance:

1. Live product performance allows us to do analytics performance benchmarking and gives a product manager overview.

2. Requirements-driven development allows us to gather all requirements and the software management in real time.

3. Management and optimization of product cost allows us to do product life cycle costing in real time.

4. Detail engineering is facilitated via an engineering control center in the cloud for mechanical, electrical/electronic, and software integration.

5. The digital twin facilitates the thing engineer in managing the registration (on-boarding) and hand-over (of the Thing definition) of tracked things during their progress or journey along the AIIoT.

6. Customer sales order creation is improved and more accurate, real-time price quotes can be provided.

7. Consumer behaviors are aggregated and analyzed in real time and service is personalized, optimized and targeted to the individual.

Chapter 5 presents a use case about the impact of the adoption of social media on the entrepreneurship ecosystem.

New technologies, such as RFID sensors, allow machines to interact with other machines via mobile technologies and cloud computing protected by cybersecurity, creating an internet of things that allows us to do big data analysis. Big data analysis systems use cognitive computing to enable on-demand 3D printing and advanced robotics to build and interact with the physical world around them. Connectivity is achieved via long-distance monitors that allow human users to control, operate and manufacture remotely, thus capable of local real-time awareness and influence, while continuously optimizing all processes through machine learning and predictive maintenance. Remote operators can view data *in situ* in 3D computer-generated worlds, with real-time data updates. They can view the remote real world from the viewpoint of the remote robot(s). Local operators can view additional layers of digital information, such as real-time data or instructions, and real-time assistance from remote operators, via augmented reality, 3D computer-generated shapes and animations projected on top of the real world, viewed through lenses or a screen.

To avoid costly and harmful errors, the interface to these new systems must clearly be as user-friendly as possible. It is the AIIoT developers and project stakeholders responsibility to take all precautions to develop systems with high usability, in order to help all users avoid mistakes, by testing the new systems thoroughly before deployment. The AIIoT engineer must learn and remember environmental and human safety and systems must be designed with the end-user and their goals and needs in clear focus during the entire development process. Chapter 6 presents the theory and a use case of User Experience (UX), User Interaction (UI) and Human-Computer Interaction design and evaluation procedures and principles.

- Chapter 5: The Impact of Social Media Adoption on Entrepreneurial Ecosystem

- Chapter 6: Human Factors for e-Health Training System: UX Testing for XR Anatomy Training App

CHAPTER 5

THE IMPACT OF SOCIAL MEDIA ADOPTION ON ENTREPRENEURIAL ECOSYSTEM

BODOR ALMOTAIRY,[1] MANAL ABDULLAH,[2] RABEEH ABBASI[2]

[1] Department of Information Systems, King Abdulaziz University, Jeddah, Saudi Arabia
[2] Department of Computer Science, Quaid-I-Azam University, Islamabad, Pakistan
Corresponding authors: balmetere0002@stu.kau.edu.sa; maaabdullah@kau.edu.sa; pakistan, rabbasi@qau.edu.pk

Abstract

Since entrepreneurs are an important driving force of economic growth, researchers should be helpful in developing greater strategic insight into innovation technology for this group. This chapter is a content analysis that seeks to systematize the studies carried out on the use of social media in the entrepreneurial ecosystem. Twenty-four studies were reviewed using a synthesis-and-interpretation-based approach. The results of the content analysis reveal the effectiveness of social media in connecting the key actors in the entrepreneurial ecosystem, such as partners, suppliers, universities, and resource providers, in many ways. The available literature suggests that social media – Twitter and Facebook in particular – have been the platforms most used by entrepreneurs. The presence of start-ups in social media is greater than established companies. Social media positively affects the performance of startups. The use of social media in the entrepreneurial ecosystem is affected by a number of variables such as the organization culture, region, gender, age, and business environment. Moreover, most of the studies follow a quantitative approach to measuring the frequency of the use of social media by small and medium enterprises (SMEs). The relevance of this study lies in the fact that it illuminates future research as it identifies the research gaps in the use of social media as a communication channel between SMEs and other stakeholders in the entrepreneurship ecosystem.

Keywords: Social media, entrepreneurship ecosystem, startups, entrepreneurs, Twitter, Facebook, LinkedIn, SMEs

Emerging Extended Reality Technologies for Industry 4.0.
Edited by Jolanda G. Tromp *et al.* Copyright © 2020 Scrivener Publishing

5.1 Introduction

In the last few decades, new information and communication technologies have taken the world of entrepreneurship by storm. The market dynamics and the competitiveness of businesses – be they established companies or startups – have been challenged by the increasing power of the internet and internet-based social media. These new technologies have a significant impact on how entrepreneurs operate and how they interact with each other [1]. They provide new ways of firm-to-firm communication and information sharing and thus link companies to the different players in the ecosystem [1-3].

Social media is a set of "virtual communities" that allow users to sign up for a public profile and establish a network of relationships with people of same interests [4]. Advances in information technologies, such as the advent of Web 2.0 and the rise of social media applications (Facebook, LinkedIn, Twitter, Slack, etc.) have revolutionized the communication landscape. People can now connect with their real-life friends or make new friends with whom they interact and exchange news. It is noteworthy, however, that social media platforms have more to them than mere chatting and networking. Their impact on news, politics, the economy and marketing should not be downplayed [5]. For instance, social media platforms have modernized business management and strategic thinking, and they have introduced a new form of firm-to-firm and firm-to-ecosystem communications [6]. It is for this reason that they are being hailed as a great asset for individual entrepreneurs who are wary of entering the market [7]. They help attenuate uncertainty and give new businesses a good start [8]. Moreover, social media allows the entrepreneur to diversify their communication tactics, claim new customers and manage crises [5]. In today's competitive and complex business world, entrepreneurs need to be constantly present on social media to interact with their customers and communicate with the different stakeholders [9]. By increasing their presence on social media, entrepreneurs increase their crisis management skills.

The number of social media applications and platforms is increasing every day. To ensure their survival, these applications and websites work hard to offer unique features that make them stand out from the rest. Each of these applications seem to provide their users with different functions and uses. For example, Facebook is now considered as the largest online-based social network with 2.2 billion active users per month. Its uniqueness lies in the way it allows friends and family to connect and communicate easily. Other platforms, such as LinkedIn, choose to focus on professional matters to enrich the job market with growing individual experience [10]. However, Twitter seems to be the best platform for entrepreneurs due to its follow and share feature [7].

The motivation behind this chapter was the scarcity of literature on the role of social media in the entrepreneurial ecosystem. This chapter is a content analysis that seeks to systematize the studies carried out on the use of social media in the entrepreneurship ecosystem. It defines the entrepreneurial ecosystem in detail to establish the link between social media and the ecosystem. Then, it reviews and analyzes twenty-four studies carried out on the issue. Finally, it reports the latest findings and finds the gap in the literature, which will enlighten future researches.

To ensure relevance and replicability, this chapter adopts a systemic approach. A systemic review reflects a satisfactory trustworthiness of the existing body of literature [11]. The purpose of this approach is to discover, summarize and analyze any relevant literature in the light of transparency and replicability [11].

The remaining parts of this chapter are organized as follows: Section 3.2 discusses the theoretical background. Then, Section 3.3 explains the methodology followed in this chapter. Section 3.4 defines the entrepreneurial ecosystems based on previous studies. Finally, Section 3.5 reviews and analyzes the studies carried out on the issue of using social media by entrepreneurial ecosystem stakeholders.

5.2 Background

This section discusses the theoretical background that defines SMEs and their role in economic growth, the importance of social media in the business world, and the relation between the entrepreneurs' success and their social relationship.

5.2.1 Small and Medium-Sized Enterprises (SMEs)

There is a significant variance in the way SMEs are defined. It seems that the notion of SMEs defies formal definitions [12]. Different criteria are used to define this type of business, such as the amount of economic activity, status within the country [13], capital assets, labor skills, level of turnover, legal status, method of production and type of activity [12]. Whatever the definition may be, it is evident in the literature that SMEs play an important role in the economy of any nation. These types of businesses have a high potential to generate jobs, increase exports and bring innovations to young entrepreneurs. SMEs are a fertile ground to experiment with new forms of innovation in order to empower young entrepreneurs. This cannot be achieved unless a strong supply chain is created to improve competitiveness [13].

5.2.2 Social Media

Social media has become essential for business [13]. Facebook and Twitter are considered the most used social media [10]. However, Twitter seems to be the best platform for entrepreneurs due to its follow and share feature [7].

Twitter is a microblogging platform that offers an effective way for people to interact through the creation and sharing of tweets. Its effectiveness is enhanced by its 280-character limit that suits people who are looking for quick, precise and to the point information [7]. The character limit increases the speed and the frequency of tweets on a daily basis [14]. Moreover, Twitter allows its users to choose whom and what to follow and once they are done following, the follower will automatically receive all updates of the followed user, including tweets, news and information. This feature makes the microblogging application an effective tool to disseminate information [15] and to enjoy transparency with little or no filtering of the content [16]. This accounts for the popularity of Twitter in the business world as a communication platform between companies and their customers and between companies and the different stakeholders. In fact, a review of the biographical profiles of Twitter's most active members reveals that the majority of them introduce themselves as entrepreneurs [7].

Social media is, then, an asset in the hands of young entrepreneurs who seek to connect with their ecosystems. This chapter hypothesizes that social media platforms have radically changed the entrepreneurial ecosystem, which is in line with the findings of many studies [7, 8]. Traditional forms of communication within the ecosystem were inefficient, which impedes economic growth and sustainability. The ineffectiveness of the ecosystem in the pre-social media era made it difficult for entrepreneurs to access and share information [1]. The idea of this chapter was born out of the intersection between social media and the business world. Given the effectiveness of social media (Twitter in particular) as a communication platform, startups should employ it to build and extend a large network of business relationships. The assumption behind this chapter is that Twitter can be effectively used to enhance firm-to-firm and firm-to-ecosystem interaction for SMEs.

5.2.3 Social Networks and Entrepreneurial Activities

The use of social networks in entrepreneurial activities is growing in importance. There have been numerous studies on how social networks benefit entrepreneurial activities [17, 18]. It has been found that social networks help entrepreneurs to have access not only tangible resources, such as labor and capital [19, 20], but also to intangible resources, including social support, information, reputation and risk-taking habits [20-22]. Moreover, social networks make it possible for entrepreneurs to create new business ideas [23], and enhance business performance [22]. Another way these networks can benefit business is by alleviating uncertainty and enlightening decision-making [24]. Access to venture capitalists is another key benefit provided by social networks, as investors are more likely to be interested in business proposals by people in their networks [25]. Intangible resources, such as knowledge and experience through social networks, are also key factors of the success of startups [26]. It can be argued, therefore, that having strong network connections is a prerequisite to success.

However, the status quo of research in this field points to a few pitfalls. First, these studies were keen to establish a connection between social networks and entrepreneurship. However, the outcome of these studies was highly judgmental, with a tendency to crudely categorize them as strong, weak, mutual, or highly influential [27-29]. Another bunch of studies relied on informal networks. These include business acquaintances, personal contacts, friends and families, spouses, mentors and many other types of informal networks [30-34]. Focusing on informal networks is likely to undermine the findings regarding the network dynamics [35]. The problem with informal and personal networks is that they don't capture the dynamics of the large entrepreneurial ecosystem. Accordingly, a more rigorous approach that takes into consideration the different stakeholders of the ecosystem is needed to establish the relationship between social networks and entrepreneurial activities. Most of the research done so far has focused on the micro (individual level) of social network. What still needs to be studied is the relationship between the individual and organization, inter-organization and inside the whole ecosystem.

5.3 Analysis Methodology

This chapter is a content analysis that seeks to systematize the studies carried out on the use of social media in the entrepreneurship ecosystem. It consists of three sections. The first section defines the entrepreneurial ecosystems based on previous studies. This definition seeks to establish the link between social media and the ecosystem. The second section reviews and analyzes twenty-four studies carried out on the issue. This section aims at reporting the latest findings and finding the gap in the literature, which will enlighten future researches.

5.4   Understanding the Entrepreneurial Ecosystem

Entrepreneurship plays a vital role in the economic growth and stability of any nation. It is through entrepreneurship that the gaps and the shortcomings of the national economic systems are addressed. The launching of new businesses should aim at filling these gaps. However, entrepreneurship is not a unilateral process, as it is contingent on the environment in which the entrepreneur operates. For instance, the success of Silicon Valley is largely due to the systematic cooperation between venture investors, entrepreneurs, researchers, anchor companies and business supporters [36]. These key players make up what is referred to in the literature as the "entrepreneurial ecosystem" [37]. It is a socio-economic framework, with different actors who collaborate together to promote initiatives and entrepreneurship at the local level. However, what these actors really are has been a matter of variance among scholars.

There have been several attempts at defining and understanding the entrepreneurial ecosystem. The diversity of studies on the topic reflects two verities about the ecosystem. First, the entrepreneurial ecosystem is not a constant entity. It is a multifarious concept that adjusts to the socio-economic changes, which accounts for the addition of new factors in every new study. Second, the ecosystem is culture specific. The actors that affect entrepreneurship vary from one geographical region to another.

One of the first theories of the ecosystem as a systemic entity recognizes it as a complexity of actors (basically environmental) that determine the regional performance of the ecosystem [38]. This conceptualization stresses the locality or the regionalism of the different factors and assigns a symmetrical role to each of the factors. Later attempts departed from the notion of a systemic entity to investigate what these actors really are. For example, a study carried out in Washington D.C. in 2001 identified social capital, venture capital, support services of entrepreneurship, entrepreneurs and universities as active players in the entrepreneurial environment of the region [39]. The results of this study differ from another study done in Boulder, Colorado. The latter recognizes six factors in the ecosystem: spin-off firms, networks (both formal and informal), incubators, culture and physical infrastructure [40]. This concept of the ecosystem highlights the importance of the interaction between these six elements to create the entrepreneurial environment.

Over the last decade, interest in the entrepreneurial ecosystem has taken a turn from identifying the different elements to highlighting their roles as anchors for entrepreneurial innovations and activities. For instance, the World Economic Forum (2013) identifies eight factors "accessible markets, human capital/workforce, funding and finance, support systems, government and regulatory system, education and training, universities, and cultural support." All of these elements intersect with a previous study carried out by Isenberg [41]. Theories of the ecosystem continue to develop in recent years. What is remarkable in recent years is the tendency in the literature to use categorical labeling to group those factors that are similar in nature. In 2014, the ecosystem was defined as the systemic collaboration of three major factors:

1. Entrepreneurial actors (both existing and potential)

2. Entrepreneurial corporations (firms, banks, venture investors) and

3. Institutions (universities, public agencies and financial institutions) [42].

The relevance of this categorization lies in the way it categorizes the factors into three types: entrepreneurship, and the type of support it can access either financially or in the form of research and planning. Another attempt at categorizing these actors appeared in the same year from the Center for Rural Entrepreneurship [43]. Within this study, the ecosystem is the sum of the five Cs: "Capital (financial resource), Capability (entrepreneur and owner skill set), Connection (resource and relationship network), Culture (the local communities' perception and support of entrepreneurship) and Climate (regulatory, economic development and policy environment)."

In 2017, another attempt at presenting the actors in the form of categories was published. In this study, the ecosystem is introduced as a community made up of two levels: the system level and the socioeconomic contextual level [44]. This view focuses on the socioeconomic environment as a matrix for entrepreneurship. This implies that entrepreneurial activities are set by their socio-economic environment and that these activities vary across cultures. Similarly, the factors of the ecosystem can be grouped into three classes: cultural attributes (attitudes towards entrepreneurship in a specific culture as told by the success stories), social attributes (support from investment capital, mentors and talent) and material attributes (tangible support from universities and policymakers) [45]. These three categories are equally important and mutually contingent on their support of entrepreneurship. It is noteworthy, however, that no definition of the ecosystem can be exhaustive unless it recognizes culture-specific parameters [46]. The dynamics of the entrepreneurial ecosystem vary from one country to another and largely depend on the organizational context and the level of economic development. What these studies have tried to do is identify the different actors involved in the entrepreneurial ecosystem. However, the nature of the relationship between these elements still needs to be investigated.

Focusing on the constituent elements of the ecosystem does not account for the internal relationships between them. Studying the different ways these elements interact with each other is a necessary step if we are to understand the dynamics of the ecosystem. Otherwise, how can such disparate elements as social capital and networks be reconciled? The past five years have been characterized by two tendencies in the research on the ecosystem. The first tendency has been – as discussed above – to classify these elements into big generic categories. The second tendency is a remarkable shift from an "*element-based approach*" to a "*connection-based approach*" [47]. A system-based approach has significant implications not only for pioneering entrepreneurs, but also for policymakers. It provides them with an exhaustive view of how the performance of a business is mediated by a bunch of economic activity [48]. One way of studying the dynamics of the ecosystem is by looking at spin-off from the prism of a local anchor company, like "entrepreneurial recycling" [49].

In 2018, there was an attempt to account for the social connectivity among entrepreneurs. The connections that this study established were long-term and region-based [50]. Another attempt [51] analyzed the entrepreneurial ecosystem in respect to the interaction between six stakeholders, they are government programs and agencies support, academic and research institutions, entrepreneurial finance, the infrastructure (human, legal, and physical), market-supporting institutions, and the entrepreneurship mindset shaped by local culture. Figure 5.1 shows these stakeholders.

The shortcoming of these connections is that they do not explain the day-to-day activities of entrepreneurs. Measuring daily activities is a prerequisite to understanding how the different stakeholders interact with each other. What entrepreneurs are keen to obtain is state-of-the-art information to help them cope with the volatile nature of the market and technological innovations.

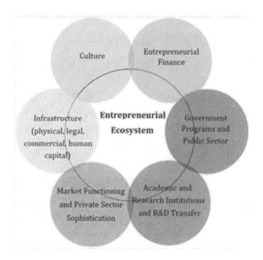

Figure 5.1   The entrepreneurship ecosystem actors.

5.5   Social Media and Entrepreneurial Ecosystem

Applying the systemic review, Table 5.1 summarizes the findings of twenty-four studies on the use of social media as a communication tool between the entrepreneurs, startups, and SMEs and the different stakeholders in the ecosystem. Special focus has been put on startups and SMEs. A synthetical discussion is presented in the subsections following the review. The attributes shown in the table are: the purpose of the study, the stakeholders and social media sites that were targeted by the study, the sample size, the method used to analyze the samples, and finally the relevant findings.

Table 5.1   Comparison of studies of entrepreneurship activities in social media.

Study	Study Purpose	Target	Social media	Sample Size	Method	Relevant Findings
[1]	Content analysis of interaction between startups and organizations of support in developing countries.	Support Organizations & startups	Twitter	3200 tweets	SNA techniques	• There is interaction between startups and support organizations as per their technology profile, business model and region. • The profile of the startup determines the interaction behavior.
[2]	The impact of social media on emerging existing entrepreneurial firms, B2B relationship through resource mobilization.	Firms	Facebook and Twitter	8000 Facebook /Twitter posts, and 8 Interviews	Hand labeled	• Facebook and Twitter increase the firms' network engagement, information sharing, collaboration, reconfiguration processes, operations and coordination.
[3]	Understanding the active factors and stakeholders in the innovation startup ecosystem	The Entrepreneuri al l Ecosystem	Twitter	An ongoing project in 33 European Countries. 200,000 tweets and 1,792 stakeholders	SNA techniques	• Social media allows us to see the regional differences in startup and innovation ecosystem. Twitter has attracted the same stakeholders with an average of 88%. The remaining 12% were drawn otherwise.
[9]	Studying the effect of social media on business leadership	Entrepreneur s	General	An interview with 7 entrepreneurs.	Grounded theory coding	• Social media has a positive impact on entrepreneurial leadership. • Social media helps the company to manage its internal tasks and communication. • Social media is a database of human capital that helps build a network with other entrepreneurial leaders in the ecosystem.
[13]	Understanding why SMEs use social media	SMEs	Twitter	questionnaires in 144 SMEs	Partial least squares	• The decision to adopt social media by SMEs is determined more by the organization and the environment constructs than by technology.

Study	Study Purpose	Target	Social media	Sample Size	Method	Relevant Findings
[39]	Analyzing the presence of CEOs on SNS, and their use of Twitter as a communication tool.	CEOs	General	14,153 tweets	Statistics	• The Presence of startups in social media has a positive effect on their funding outcome. • Social media facilitates the entrepreneurial financing strategy by luring investors.
[53]	Who do entrepreneurs get inspiration from in terms of information?	Entrepreneurs	Twitter	74 active Entrepreneurs'	SNA-based metric to interrupt the network	• Entrepreneurs rely more on local sources for information. • In their early stages, entrepreneurs follow Twitter accounts from various sources. • At an advanced stage, entrepreneurs rely on sources that focus on entrepreneurship. • Entrepreneurship-focused sources are more popular among entrepreneurs.
[54]	Identifying the motivations, benefits and intentions for entrepreneurs to use online social media.	Entrepreneurs	Twitter	368 Turkish firms	Statistics	• Turkish young male entrepreneurs are aware of the benefits they can get from online social media.
[55]	Identifying the factors affecting online knowledge sharing on the performance of SMEs	Manufacturing SMEs	General	1291 questionnaire	Partial least squares	• Social online knowledge sharing is mainly driven by technological and organizational factors. This sharing mediated between HR and innovation practice.
[56]	Analyzing the speeches of Entrepreneurs on social media	Entrepreneurs	Twitter	219 M posts, authored by 135K entrepreneurs of 65 countries	Natural language processing	• African entrepreneurs display more negative emotions than the rest of the population. • Entrepreneurs from developed economies display more positive emotions than their counterparts in the developed world.
[59]	Identifying the factors that drive crowdfunding.	Startups	AngelList, Twitter, Facebook, and CrunchBase	744,036 AngelList, 10,156 CrunchBase, 37,761 Facebook and 70,563 Twitter companies' profiles	SNA techniques	• There is a positive correlation between social media engagement and the company's success to raise funds. When companies have no social media accounts, its likelihood to raise fund is only 0.04%. If it uses Facebook, it is 12.2 % and Twitter 10.2%.
[60]	Investigating the use of Twitter by Startups in EU	Startups' Founders	Twitter	15,192 Twitter's Accounts	Statistics	• There is a positive correlation between the use of Twitter in EU startups and the amount invested in the country per capita.
[61]	Studying the relationship between social media use and venture capital financing	Startups	Twitter	2,880 startups twitter account	Ordinary Least Squares (OLS)	• Only 25% are present, LinkedIn is by far the most elected SNS by CEOs. • Only 25% of those present on SNS are using their Twitter accounts.
[62]	Establishing a correlation between social networks in startups and their financial performance	Startups' Founders	Linked In	227 founders' accounts	Statistics	• LinkedIn Founder Profiles are positively correlated with success. The number of LinkedIn followers indicates the rate of fundraising by the company.
[63]	Studying the impact of social media on knowledge creation process in SMEs.	SMEs	General	A questionnaire in 96 SMEs	Ordinary Least Squares (OLS)	• Social media favors the innovation process by influencing three of the four knowledge creation processes.
[64]	Studying the relationship between social networks, innovation & performance, and absorptive capacity.	SMEs	Twitter	Questionnaire in 215 SMEs	Partial least squares	• There is positive correlation between social networks, innovation & performance, and absorptive capacity.
[65]	Studying how social media is used by opportunity-based entrepreneurs to meet their resource challenge.	Entrepreneurs	General	Interviews in 19 entrepreneurs	Grounded theory coding	• Entrepreneurs use social media to create new types of capabilities and to maximize efficiency by using social networks to solve their resource limits.
[66]	Identifying the factors of two stages of the business-creation process: opportunity discovery and creation	Entrepreneurs and CEOs	General	177 questionnaires	Partial least squares	• The use of social media decreases the negative effects of prior knowledge • Information got from social media may intervene with the finding of business opportunity as per previous knowledge and experience. Social media can disrupt business planning and model built upon the entrepreneur's previous knowledge and experience.
[67]	How do entrepreneurs use CoPs to express	Entrepreneurs	Young Entrepreneur .com	Observations	Case Studies	• Entrepreneurs use CoPs in a story-telling way, while the domain expert has little command on the discussion.
[72]	Measuring the effectiveness of online social media among entrepreneurs in the Arab Gulf	Entrepreneurs	Facebook	50 questionnaires	Statistics	• 87 % of the participants think that their Facebook profiles were helpful. • 98 % of the participants believe that social websites help entrepreneurs.
[74]	Studying the way social media technologies (SMT) improve the proficiency of firms and redefine business resources.	Firms	General	Questionnaires on 201 firms	Structural Equation Modeling	• The more a company uses the potential of connectivity and innovation of social media in its innovation process, the better its performance in the long-run.
[77]	Studying the use of social media by SMEs in North America.	SMEs	General	An Interviews in 12 SMEs	Case Studies	• Facebook is the most widely used platform. • The social media are used to claim new customers
[78]	Investigating the dialogic communication between stakeholders.	All stakeholders	Twitter	930 tweets posted by 93 accounts	Hand labeled	• 61 % of organizations use Twitter dialogically to conserve their visitors compared to 39 % who have no dialogic orientation.

5.5.1   Social Media Platforms and Entrepreneurship

Twitter and Facebook are the most popular social networks used by entrepreneurs. Their popularity in the entrepreneurial ecosystem can be easily ascribed to their popularity as social networks [52]. Accordingly, using these two social networks helps young entrepreneurs maximize their presence in the ecosystem and reach new potential customers and business partners. SMEs seem to be more active and present on social network than big companies [35]. The presence of the CEOs of big established companies on Twitter and Facebook is insignificant [35, 52]. Moreover, entrepreneurs have employed different social media platforms for diverse reasons.

5.5.2   The Drivers of Social Media Adoption

There are a few differences in the way social media is used in SMEs. The choice of one social platform over the other is determined by the type of services the platform provides [53]. However, there are other factors that influence the choice of a platform, such as the geographical location, organizational and environmental constructs of SMEs [13], gender and age [54], and technology and organization [55].

The studies have revealed that the discourse of the entrepreneurs is also different across cultures [56]. For example, the discourse of African entrepreneurs seems to be loaded with negative emotions, while that of the entrepreneurs from the developing economies is more positively loaded.

5.5.3   The Motivations and Benefits for Entrepreneurs to Use Social Media

Entrepreneurs use social media for different reasons, such as mobilizing financial resources, [57, 58], connecting with potential investors in an attempt to get funding [59-62], and connecting with other startups [61]. Another use of social media is to consult with advisors for knowledge creation, [63], the process of innovation [35, 55, 64] and innovation capabilities [65], which allows them to find more opportunities [66]. Moreover, novice entrepreneurs and CEOs of established companies seem to be looking for different things via social media: the former would search for any type of support from any source, while the latter are more interested in knowledge and experience [35, 52, 67].

5.5.4   Entrepreneurship Activities Analysis Techniques in Social Media Networks

According to the literature available, there are six techniques to analyze activities on social media:

- Social network analysis (SNA) techniques

- Natural language processing techniques

- Grounded theory approaches

- Statistical techniques

- Case study approaches

- Hand-labeled classification

5.5.4.1 *Social Network Analysis (SNA) Techniques*

Social network analysis (SNA) is a sophisticated field that joins statistics, social psychology, sociology, and graph theory. It is beneficial in extracting insights from networks and consequently solving problems [68]. As to entrepreneurship on Twitter, SNA was used to analyze the interaction between startups and organizations of support in developing countries. The authors used community detection algorithms and measures of density to understand the interconnectedness of the network, and betweenness centrality and degree centrality to recognize the role of a specific actor in the network [1]. SNA-based metrics are also used to analyze the data gathered around Twitter hashtags in order to understand the active factors and stakeholders in the innovation startup ecosystem [3].

To understand and identify the factors that drive crowdfunding, community detection algorithms were employed to cluster companies according to investors [59]. Another use of SNA was to reveal where entrepreneurs take information [35].

5.5.4.2 *Natural Language Processing Technique*

Natural language processing (NLP) is part of artificial intelligence (AI). NLP can understand and decode human language [69]. In the context of the study, NLP was used to analyze the speeches of entrepreneurs on social media [56].

5.5.4.3 *Grounded Theory Approaches*

Grounded theory is a research method that enables researchers to categorize and integrate the concerns of the population and produce it as theory. Simply put, the grounded theory provides researchers with guidelines to recognize categories and set relations between them. Thus, grounded theory gives framework to explain the phenomenon under study [70]. In the current literature, grounded theory was used to study the effect of social media on business leadership [9], and to study how social media is used by opportunity-based entrepreneurs to meet their resource challenges [65].

5.5.4.4 *Statistical Approaches*

Statistical methods are mathematical techniques, models, and formulas. Statistical methods are used to collect, organize, analyze, and interpret the raw research data [71]. Two statistical methods are employed in the previous literature to analysis the data; they are inferential statistics and descriptive statistics. Descriptive statistics provide information that represents the data in a particular manner. Inferential statistics, on the other hand, uses samples of data to make inferences and generalizations on the populations of these samples [71].

5.5.4.5 *Descriptive Statistics*

Descriptive statistics are used to describe a correlation between social networks in startups and their financial performance [62] to demonstrate that there are correlations between the UK startups' activity on Twitter and the amount of investments they get [60], in order to measure the effectiveness of online social media among entrepreneurs in the Arab Gulf [72] and analyze the presence of CEOs on SNS and their use of Twitter as a communication tool [52]. Identifying the motivations, benefits and intentions for entrepreneurs to use online social media [54].

Several studies used partial least squares method (PLS) to describe the entrepreneurship phenomena. PLS uses latent variables to estimate complex relationship of cause-effect models. PLS is becoming popular in management and entrepreneurship research [66].

As to entrepreneurship in social media, PLS was used to investigate the relation between environmental, organizational, and technological contexts and the adoption of social media by SMEs [13]. It was also used to discover whether employees' sharing knowledge through social media affects the relationship between innovation performance and human resource practice [55].

Another use of PLS is to study the relationship between social networks, innovation and performance, and absorptive capacity [64], and to identify the factors of the two types of business opportunity exploitations: opportunity discovery and creation [66].

Structural equation modeling (SEM) is another statistical description method used to analyze structured relationships between latent constructs and measured variables [73]. For example, SME was used by Garcia-Morales *et al.* [74] to study the relation between companies' usage of social media in their innovation process and their long-run performance.

5.5.4.6   *Inferential Statistics*

Ordinary least squares (OLS) is one of the linear regression methods, which uses samples of data to infer and generalize about the populations. OLS estimates the obscure parameters in a linear regression model by reducing the sum of squared errors between variable being predictor's values and the values predicted by the linear function [75]. Ordinary least squares were employed to study the relationship between social media use and venture capital financing [61], and to study the impact of social media on the knowledge creation process in SMEs [63].

5.5.4.7   *Case Studies Approaches*

Case studies are in-depth investigations on individuals, groups, events or communities. In case studies, the researchers gather the data from diverse sources and use various methods such as interviews and observations [76]. Some studies observed entrepreneurs' behaviors in social media [67]. They applied a case study in communities of practice (COPs) to identify how entrepreneurs express themselves and engage in conversations. Another case study of entrepreneurship activities in social media interviewed and studied in detail how SMEs in North America perceive social media [77] .

5.5.4.8   *Hand-Labeled Classification*

Some of the authors of previous literature labeled the data manually to investigate the impact of social media on emerging existing entrepreneurial firms B2B relationships through resource mobilization [2], and to investigate the dialogic communication between stakeholders [78].

5.6   Research Gap and Recommended Solution

5.6.1   Research Gap

There is increased interest in entrepreneurship research; however, focusing on the constituent elements of the ecosystem does not account for the internal relationships between them. Studying the different ways these elements interact with each other is a necessary step if we are to understand the dynamics of the ecosystem. Otherwise, how can such disparate elements as social capital and networks be reconciled?

Social media is a good way for entrepreneurs to interact with the other stakeholders in the ecosystem such as partners, suppliers, universities, and resource providers. Social media as a connection tool can also allow entrepreneurs to reach out to actual or potential customers for feedback and inquiries. It is also remarkable that startups are more active on

Twitter than established companies, which will have a positive affect on their performance in the long run. This is all the more so given the fact that social media positively affects the entrepreneurial leadership both intra-organizationally and inter-organizationally. What seems to be evident, however, is the effectiveness of social media in connecting the key actors in the entrepreneurial ecosystem in many aspects. This can range from crowdsourcing, to crowdfunding, to marketing. Accordingly, communication channels between SMEs and the whole ecosystem have to be in place. However, research on this topic is still in its infancy. While the studies reviewed in this chapter have managed to establish correlations between social media and the ecosystem, the work is largely quantitative.

What still needs to be studied is the potential of Twitter to create an interactive entrepreneurial ecosystem. There is a need to find a tool to facilitate the spreading of information between SMEs and other stakeholders; helping SMEs to expand their relations with other stakeholders in the ecosystem. Also, to help the different agents of the entrepreneurial ecosystem reach out to SMEs and provide them with the necessary support.

5.6.2   Recommended Solution

The concept of information diffusion process – alternatively called information propagation, information spread, or information dissemination – refers to the way information flows and moves between individuals and communities within the same social network [79, 80]. Researchers have developed several models to understand the diffusion processes. These models involve discovering the key players in information diffusion [81], what information is most diffused [82], in which directions the information flows [83], and how the information will diffuse in the future [84, 85].

Messages from key people in the network [86], such as leaders and managers, are more likely to be followed and shared by followers, and would thus reach the whole community via small world [87] and word-of-mouth [88] effects. Understanding the pattern of the information flow and finding some influential users with high levels of interaction and connection in social media, and using them to initiate the information spread, could increase the diffusion of information more quickly [89]. This is of the utmost importance since key people in the information network exercise their control over information spread and can choose to retain or spread it [90].

The level of information diffusion has inspired future research, which seeks to explore the use of Twitter as an information diffusion tool between entrepreneurial ecosystem stakeholders and SMEs. Researchers are studying the effectiveness of diffusing the information by detecting the influential users in the entrepreneurial ecosystem network on Twitter in order to discover their attributes and the attributes of their tweets.

5.7   Conclusion

This research is motivated by the scarcity of the literature on the role of social media in the entrepreneurial ecosystem. Through a systemic approach, the chapter has demonstrated that – so far – the work has focused on determining the different actors in the ecosystems and on demonstrating the effective use of social media in the ecosystem. Empirical evidence on the use of social media in the ecosystem is relatively scarce. What has been understood is the role of Twitter in creating an interactive entrepreneurial ecosystem. Further research is needed to explore the perspective of each stakeholder in the ecosystem to use the social network, especially in identifying the obstacles and barriers that hamper them.

Moreover, most of the studies reviewed in this chapter adopted a quantitative approach, focusing on the frequency of the use of Twitter by SMEs. The effects and the motivations behind using Twitter in the ecosystem are better grasped when approached qualitatively.

REFERENCES

1. Park, E., Hain, D. S., & Jurowetzki, R. (2017). Entrepreneurial Ecosystem for Technology Start-ups in Nairobi: Empirical analysis of Twitter networks of Start-ups and Support organizations. In Proceedings of the 17th DRUID Summer Conference, New York, NY.

2. Drummond, C., McGrath, H., & O'Toole, T. (2018). The impact of social media on resource mobilisation in entrepreneurial firms. *Industrial Marketing Management*, 70, 68-89.

3. Mohout, O., & Fiegenbaum, I. (2015). The power of Twitter: Building an innovation radar using social media. In *ISPIM Conference Proceedings* (p. 1). The International Society for Professional Innovation Management (ISPIM).

4. Kuss, D. J., & Griffiths, M. D. (2017). Social networking sites and addiction: Ten lessons learned. *International Journal of Environmental Research and Public Health*, 14(3), 311.

5. Gruber, D. A., Smerek, R. E., Thomas-Hunt, M. C., & James, E. H. (2015). The real-time power of Twitter: Crisis management and leadership in an age of social media. *Business Horizons*, 58(2), 163-172.

6. Kietzmann, J. H., Hermkens, K., McCarthy, I. P., & Silvestre, B. S. (2011). Social media? Get serious! Understanding the functional building blocks of social media. *Business Horizons*, 54(3), 241-251.

7. Fischer, E., & Reuber, A. R. (2014). Online entrepreneurial communication: Mitigating uncertainty and increasing differentiation via Twitter. *Journal of Business Venturing*, 29(4), 565-583.

8. Le, D. N., Bhatt, C., & Madhukar, M. (Eds.). (2019). *Security Designs for the Cloud, IoT, and Social Networking*. John Wiley & Sons.

9. Gratell, P., & Dahlin, C. J. (2018). How does social media affect entrepreneurial leadership: A qualitative study on entrepreneur's perceptions regarding social media as a tool for entrepreneurial leadership, Master's Thesis, Uppsala University.

10. Van Dijck, J. (2013). You have one identity: Performing the self on Facebook and LinkedIn. *Media, Culture & Society*, 35(2), 199-215.

11. Petticrew, M., & Roberts, H. (2008). Systematic reviews-do they work'in informing decision-making around health inequalities?. *Health Economics, Policy and Law*, 3(2), 197-211.

12. Cheng, W. H., Kadir, K. A., & Bohari, A. M. (2014). The strategic planning of SMEs in Malaysia: a view of external environmental scanning. *International Journal of Business and Society*, 15(3), 437.

13. AlSharji, A., Ahmad, S. Z., & Abu Bakar, A. R. (2018). Understanding social media adoption in SMEs: Empirical evidence from the United Arab Emirates. *Journal of Entrepreneurship in Emerging Economies*, 10(2), 302-328.

14. Java, A., Song, X., Finin, T., & Tseng, B. (2007, August). Why we twitter: understanding microblogging usage and communities. In *Proceedings of the 9th WebKDD and 1st SNAKDD 2007 Workshop on Web Mining and Social Network Analysis* (pp. 56-65). ACM.

15. Hidayanti, I., Herman, L. E., & Farida, N. (2018). Engaging customers through social media to improve industrial product development: the role of customer co-creation value. *Journal of Relationship Marketing*, 17(1), 17-28.

16. Lakshmi, K. R., & Sengottuvelu, C. (2017). Social media as a tool for brand building in the automobile industry. *TRANS Asian Journal of Marketing & Management Research (TAJMMR)*, 6(8), 19-29.

17. Aldrich, H. E., Rosen, B., & Woodward, B. (1987). The impact of social networks on business foundings and profit: a longitudinal study. *Frontiers of Entrepreneurship Research*, 154-168.

18. Lippmann, S., & Aldrich, H. E. (2016). A rolling stone gathers momentum: Generational units, collective memory, and entrepreneurship. *Academy of Management Review*, 41(4), 658-675.

19. Zimmer, C., & Aldrich, H. (1987). Resource mobilization through ethnic networks: Kinship and friendship ties of shopkeepers in England. *Sociological Perspectives*, 30(4), 422-445.

20. Bates, T. (1997). Financing small business creation: The case of Chinese and Korean immigrant entrepreneurs. *Journal of Business Venturing*, 12(2), 109-124.

21. Westhead, P., Wright, M., & Ucbasaran, D. (2004). Internationalization of private firms: environmental turbulence and organizational strategies and resources. *Entrepreneurship & Regional Development*, 16(6), 501-522.

22. Witt, P., Schroeter, A., & Merz, C. (2008). Entrepreneurial resource acquisition via personal networks: an empirical study of German start-ups. *The Service Industries Journal*, 28(7), 953-971.

23. Singh, R., Hills, G. E., Hybels, R. C., & Lumpkin, G. T. (1999). Opportunity recognition through social network characteristics of entrepreneurs. *Frontiers of Entrepreneurship Research*, 228241.

24. Autio, E., Dahlander, L., & Frederiksen, L. (2013). Information exposure, opportunity evaluation, and entrepreneurial action: An investigation of an online user community. *Academy of Management Journal*, 56(5), 1348-1371.

25. Fried, V. H., & Hisrich, R. D. (1994). Toward a model of venture capital investment decision making. *Financial Management*, 28-37.

26. Roure, J. B., & Maidique, M. A. (1986). Linking prefunding factors and high-technology venture success: An exploratory study. *Journal of Business Venturing*, 1(3), 295-306.

27. Bhagavatula, S., Elfring, T., Van Tilburg, A., & Van De Bunt, G. G. (2010). How social and human capital influence opportunity recognition and resource mobilization in India's handloom industry. *Journal of Business Venturing*, 25(3), 245-260.

28. Partanen, J., Mller, K., Westerlund, M., Rajala, R., & Rajala, A. (2008). Social capital in the growth of science-and-technology-based SMEs. *Industrial Marketing Management*, 37(5), 513-522.

29. Granovetter, M. (1983). The strength of weak ties: A network theory revisited. *Sociological Theory*, 1, 201-233.

30. Welsch, H. P., & Young, E. C. (1982). The information source selection decision: The role of entrepreneurial personality characteristics. *Journal of Small Business Management* (pre-1986), 20(000004), 49.

31. Renzulli, L. A., Aldrich, H., & Moody, J. (2000). Family matters: Gender, networks, and entrepreneurial outcomes. *Social Forces*, 79(2), 523-546.

32. Brderl, J., & Preisendorfer, P. (1998). Network support and the success of newly founded business. *Small Business Economics*, 10(3), 213-225.

33. Cooper, A. C., Folta, T. B., & Woo, C. (1995). Entrepreneurial information search. *Journal of Business Venturing*, 10(2), 107-120.

34. Ozgen, E., & Baron, R. A. (2007). Social sources of information in opportunity recognition: Effects of mentors, industry networks, and professional forums. *Journal of Business Venturing*, 22(2), 174-192.

35. Motoyama, Y., Goetz, S., & Han, Y. (2018). Where do entrepreneurs get information? An analysis of twitter-following patterns. *Journal of Small Business & Entrepreneurship*, 30(3), 253-274.

36. Saxenian, A. (1994). *Regional Advantage: Culture and Competition in Silicon Valley and Route 128*, Harvard University Press, Cambridge, MA.

37. Van de Ven, H. (1993). The development of an infrastructure for entrepreneurship. *Journal of Business Venturing*, 8(3), 211-230.

38. Spilling, O. R. (1996). The entrepreneurial system: On entrepreneurship in the context of a mega-event. *Journal of Business Research*, 36(1), 91-103.

39. Feldman, M. P. (2001). The entrepreneurial event revisited: firm formation in a regional context. *Industrial and Corporate Change*, 10(4), 861-891.

40. Neck, H. M., Meyer, G. D., Cohen, B., & Corbett, A. C. (2004). An entrepreneurial system view of new venture creation. *Journal of Small Business Management*, 42(2), 190-208.

41. Isenberg, D. J. (2010). How to start an entrepreneurial revolution. *Harvard Business Review*, 88(6), 40-50.

42. Mason, C., & Brown, R. (2014). Entrepreneurial ecosystems and growth oriented entrepreneurship. *Final Report to OECD, Paris*, 30(1), 77-102.

43. Wortman Jr, M. S. (1990). Rural entrepreneurship research: An integration into the entrepreneurship field. *Agribusiness*, 6(4), 329-344.

44. Audretsch, D. B., & Belitski, M. (2017). Entrepreneurial ecosystems in cities: establishing the framework conditions. *The Journal of Technology Transfer*, 42(5), 1030-1051.

45. Spigel, B. (2017). The relational organization of entrepreneurial ecosystems. *Entrepreneurship Theory and Practice*, 41(1), 49-72.

46. Acs, Z. J., Desai, S., & Hessels, J. (2008). Entrepreneurship, economic development and institutions. *Small Business Economics*, 31(3), 219-234.

47. Breznitz, D., & Taylor, M. (2014). The communal roots of entrepreneurial-technological growth-social fragmentation and stagnation: reflection on Atlanta's technology cluster. *Entrepreneurship & Regional Development*, 26(3-4), 375-396.

48. Feld, B. (2012). *Startup Communities: Building an Entrepreneurial Ecosystem in Your City*. John Wiley & Sons.

49. Mason, C. M., & Harrison, R. T. (2006). After the exit: Acquisitions, entrepreneurial recycling and regional economic development. *Regional Studies*, 40(1), 55-73.

50. Neumeyer, X., & Santos, S. C. (2018). Sustainable business models, venture typologies, and entrepreneurial ecosystems: A social network perspective. *Journal of Cleaner Production*, 172, 4565-4579.

51. Andonova, V., Nikolova, M. S., & Dimitrov, D. (2019). What Is an Entrepreneurial Ecosystem?. In *Entrepreneurial Ecosystems in Unexpected Places* (pp. 3-16). Palgrave Macmillan, Cham.

52. Capriotti, P., & Ruesja, L. (2018). How CEOs use Twitter: A comparative analysis of Global and Latin American companies. *International Journal of Information Management*, 39, 242-248.

53. Akula, S. C. (2015). The Influence of Social Media Platforms for Startups. *J Mass Communicate Journalism*, 5, 264.

54. Turan, M., & Kara, A. (2018). Online social media usage behavior of entrepreneurs in an emerging market: Reasons, expected benefits and intentions. *Journal of Research in Marketing and Entrepreneurship*, 20(2), 273-291.

55. Soto-Acosta, P., Popa, S., & Palacios-Marqus, D. (2017). Social web knowledge sharing and innovation performance in knowledge-intensive manufacturing SMEs. *The Journal of Technology Transfer*, 42(2), 425-440.

56. Kuff, L., Vaca, C., Izquierdo, E., & Bustamante, J. C. (2018, April). Mining Worldwide Entrepreneurs Psycholinguistic Dimensions from Twitter. In *2018 International Conference on eDemocracy & eGovernment (ICEDEG)* (pp. 179-186). IEEE.

57. Shane, S. (2012). The importance of angel investing in financing the growth of entrepreneurial ventures. *The Quarterly Journal of Finance*, 2(02), 1250009.

58. Eckhardt, J. T., Shane, S., & Delmar, F. (2006). Multistage selection and the financing of new ventures. *Management Science*, 52(2), 220-232.

59. Cheng, M., Sriramulu, A., Muralidhar, S., Loo, B. T., Huang, L., & Loh, P. L. (2016, June). Collection, exploration and analysis of crowdfunding social networks. In *Proceedings of the Third International Workshop on Exploratory Search in Databases and the Web* (pp. 25-30). ACM.

60. Lugovi, S., & Ahmed, W. (2015). An Analysis of Twitter Usage Among Startups in Europe.

61. Jin, F., Wu, A., & Hitt, L. (2017, January). Social Is the New Financial: How Startup Social Media Activity Influences Funding Outcomes. In *Academy of Management Proceedings* (Vol. 1, p. 13329). Briarcliff Manor, NY 10510: Academy of Management.

62. Banerji, D., & Reimer, T. (2019). Startup founders and their LinkedIn connections: Are well-connected entrepreneurs more successful?. *Computers in Human Behavior*, 90, 46-52.

63. Papa, A., Santoro, G., Tirabeni, L., & Monge, F. (2018). Social media as tool for facilitating knowledge creation and innovation in small and medium enterprises. *Baltic Journal of Management*, 13(3), 329-344.

64. Scuotto, V., Del Giudice, M., & Carayannis, E. G. (2017). The effect of social networking sites and absorptive capacity on SMES' innovation performance. *The Journal of Technology Transfer*, 42(2), 409-424.

65. Riverola, C., & Miralles, F. (2018, June). Entrepreneurs' Bricolage and Social Media. In *2018 IEEE International Conference on Engineering, Technology and Innovation (ICE/ITMC)* (pp. 1-5). IEEE.

66. Park, J., Sung, C., & Im, I. (2017). Does social media use influence entrepreneurial opportunity? A review of its moderating role. *Sustainability*, 9(9), 1593.

67. Hafeez, K., Foroudi, P., Nguyen, B., Gupta, S., & Alghatas, F. (2018). How do entrepreneurs learn and engage in an online community-of-practice? A case study approach. *Behaviour & Information Technology*, 37(7), 714-735.

68. De, S. S., Dehuri, S., & Wang, G. N. (2012). Machine Learning for Social Network Analysis: A Systematic Literature Review. *IUP Journal of Information Technology*, 8(4).

69. Cambria, E., & White, B. (2014). Jumping NLP curves: A review of natural language processing research. *IEEE Computational Intelligence Magazine*, 9(2), 48-57.

70. Strauss A, Corbin J. (1998) Grounded theory methodology learning objectives. In: *Strategies of Qualitative Inquiry*, Sage.

71. Bain, L. (2017). *Statistical Analysis of Reliability and Life-Testing Models: Theory and Methods*. Routledge.

72. Indrupati, J., & Henari, T. (2012). Entrepreneurial success, using online social networking: evaluation. *Education, Business and Society: Contemporary Middle Eastern Issues*, 5(1), 47-62.

73. Francis, D. J. (1988). An introduction to structural equation models. *Journal of Clinical and Experimental Neuropsychology*, 10(5), 623-639.

74. Garcia-Morales, V. J., Martin-Rojas, R., & Lardon-Lopez, M. E. (2018). Influence of social media technologies on organizational performance through knowledge and innovation. *Baltic Journal of Management*, 13(3), 345-367.

75. Cochrane, D., & Orcutt, G. H. (1949). Application of least squares regression to relationships containing auto-correlated error terms. *Journal of the American Statistical Association*, 44(245), 32-61.

76. Angelelli, C. V., & Baer, B. J. (Eds.). (2015). *Researching Translation and Interpreting*. Routledge.

77. Roy, A., Dionne, C., Carson, M., Maxwell, L., & Sosa, O. (2017, July). How Small and Medium-Sized Enterprises Perceived and Used Social Media. In *ECSM 2017 4th European Conference on Social Media* (p. 264). Academic Conferences and publishing limited.

78. Rybalko, S., & Seltzer, T. (2010). Dialogic communication in 140 characters or less: How Fortune 500 companies engage stakeholders using Twitter. *Public Relations Review*, 36(4), 336-341.

79. Christakis, N. A., & Fowler, J. H. (2007). The spread of obesity in a large social network over 32 years. *New England Journal of Medicine*, 357(4), 370-379.

80. Zhang, Y., & Wu, Y. (2012). How behaviors spread in dynamic social networks. *Computational and Mathematical Organization Theory*, 18(4), 419-444.

81. Wu, X. D., Li, Y., & Li, L. (2014). Influence analysis of online social networks. *Chinese Journal of Computers*, 37(4), 735-752.

82. Kleinberg, J. (2003). Bursty and hierarchical structure in streams. *Data Mining and Knowledge Discovery*, 7(4), 373-397.

83. Newman, M. E. (2003). The structure and function of complex networks. *SIAM Review*, 45(2), 167-256.

84. Liu, D., Wang, Y., Jia, Y., Li, J., & Yu, Z. (2014). From strangers to neighbors: Link prediction in microblogs using social distance game. *Diffusion Networks and Cascade Analytics*, WSDM.

85. Guille, A., Hacid, H., Favre, C., & Zighed, D. A. (2013). Information diffusion in online social networks: A survey. *ACM Sigmod Record*, 42(2), 17-28.

86. Aral, S., & Walker, D. (2012). Identifying influential and susceptible members of social networks. *Science*, 337(6092), 337-341.

87. Watts, D. J., & Strogatz, S. H. (1998). Collective dynamics of 'small-world' networks. *Nature*, 393(6684), 440.

88. Jansen, B. J., Zhang, M., Sobel, K., & Chowdury, A. (2009). Twitter power: Tweets as electronic word of mouth. *Journal of the American Society for Information Science and Technology*, 60(11), 2169-2188.

89. Subramani, M. R., & Rajagopalan, B. (2003). Knowledge-sharing and influence in online social networks via viral marketing. *Communications of the ACM*, 46(12), 300-307.

90. McFarlane, J. (2016). Exploring individual status and collaboration: three studies using social network analysis methods, Dissertation, Towson University.

CHAPTER 6

HUMAN FACTORS FOR E-HEALTH TRAINING SYSTEM: UX TESTING FOR XR ANATOMY TRAINING APP

ZHUSHUN TIMOTHY CAI,[1] OLIVER MEDONZA,[1] KRISTEN RAY,[1] CHUNG VAN LE,[2] DAMIAN SCHOFIELD,[1] JOLANDA TROMP[3]

[1] Human Computer Interaction Program, State University of New York, Oswego, USA

[2] Duy Tan University, Da Nang, Vietnam

[3] Center for Visualization and Simulation, Duy Tan University, Da Nang, Vietnam

Corresponding authors: jolanda.tromp@duytan.edu.vn; zcai@oswego.edu; omedonza@oswego.edu; kray@oswego.edu; levanchung@duytan.edu.vn; schofield@cs.oswego.edu

Abstract

This chapter describes the usability evaluation of the user interface to the e-Health training application AnatomyNow, a 3D computer-generated fully interactive model of the human body for medical students. The user interfaces with the tablet and smartphone application are reviewed here. We systematically assessed the UX/UI of AnatomyNow, using the classic HCI and UX/UI design and evaluation principles as a guideline. We established that UX plays a significant role when developing e-Health mobile-learning systems and the design principles can be applied effectively to improve the usability of this e-Health and mobile-learning application. This chapter first presents the design principles and fully describes how they are applied to the design and evaluation of the application. It is not an exhaustive research report on these design principles but rather an argument for the importance of high usability UX design and evaluation solutions, in order to deliver the best in e-Health and mobile-learning systems and user experiences, illustrated by applying these principles.

Keywords: Human anatomy training, extended realities, usability, 3D models, e-Health

6.1   Introduction

Human factors and ergonomics are important for the design of human-computer interaction (HCI) and involve usability tests. We applied the rigorous HCI usability tests on the tablet and phone apps of the e-Health extended reality (XR) learning system for anatomy training: AnatomyNow. AnatomyNow consists of a suite of 3D simulations (smartphone, tablet, AR and VR). It was developed by the Center of Visualization and Simulation (CVS) in Duy Tan University, Vietnam [1]. AnatomyNow consists of a 3D model of the human body, which students can view and interact with using their smartphone, tablet, virtual reality headset, and augmented reality headset and 3D big screen projection in the classroom. The full report of our assessment can be found in [2] and is reported here. The 3D human model consists of eight human systems, with more than 3000 interactive elements of human anatomy, with their respective names and definitions, based on more than 30,000 records in the database. In this study, we report on the results of testing the UI/UX for the AnatomyNow learning interface on the smartphone, tablet and 3D screen interface design. Our assessment is based on the principles of usability; design choices that identify which design works better for the user and leads to a higher overall usability score [4-18].

6.2   Mobile Learning Applications

Mobile learning, or M-learning, is increasingly being used in education due to the popularization of smartphones and tablets among students [13] and is a harbinger of learning in the future [12]. According to Crompton [4], M-learning is "learning that takes place on handheld devices." It is suggested that M-learning can be achieved by using personal electronic devices in different contexts through social and content interactions. In defining handheld devices, laptops are excluded; instead smaller devices such as smartphones, tablets, iPods, and mobile phones constitute handheld devices [5, 8, 11]. As stated by Trentin and Repetto [5], M-learning focuses on facilitating the mobility of the learner, while interacting with portable technologies, making new ways of consuming and rehearsing learning materials a reality.

Using mobile tools for creating learning aids and materials is also becoming an important part of informal learning [6]. Some of the benefits of M-learning are as follows: learning is more accessible [8], mobile learning is convenient because it can take place anywhere [8, 9]; it is often self-paced and promotes 21st century skills [6]. Furthermore, studies have indicated that M-learning can lead to a more effective learning experience [10]. In the study conducted by Evans [10], students felt that M-learning was a more effective revision tool than their textbooks and more efficient than their own notes in helping them to learn. Thus, taking into consideration all the above factors suggests that M-learning has the potential to enhance curriculum, instruction, and information retention.

6.3   Ease of Use and Usability

According to the definition of the International Organization for Standardization (ISO), usability means "the extent to which a system, product or service can be used by specified users to achieve specific goals with effectiveness, efficiency, and satisfaction in a specified context of use" [3].

6.3.1 Effectiveness

Effectiveness depends on whether users can complete tasks completely and accurately. According to ISO, it means "the accuracy, completeness, and lack of negative consequences with which users achieved specified goals." The negative consequences include economic and environmental harm and harm to health. It can be measured by two methods: the user's ability to complete the tasks or the number of errors made when doing tasks. The effectiveness of a system is 100% when users successfully finish the task; it is 0% when users fail to finish the task or give up. Effectiveness is the core factor of usability, since usability does not exist if users cannot finish tasks. In our research, we used task completion rate (TCR), as the measure for effectiveness.

6.3.2 Efficiency

Efficiency depends on how fast users can finish tasks when using the system. According to the ISO [3], it is "the resources expended in relation to the accuracy and completeness with which users achieve goals." It measures how many resources, such as time and energy, are used by users when completing tasks. Factors of efficiency include task completion time and learning time. Using efficiency, designers have a way to obtain the completion time of certain tasks and examine the factor that slows users down. In our study we use Time on Task (ToT) as the measure for efficiency.

6.3.3 Satisfaction

Satisfaction depends on whether the system meets the satisfaction needs of users. According to the ISO [3], satisfaction is the "positive attitudes, emotions and/or comfort resulting from the use of a system, product or services." The satisfaction is subjective and deeply connected with the other two usability metrics: effectiveness and efficiency. How and how fast a user can finish tasks using a system influences the user satisfaction toward the system. In our study, we use two questionnaires to measure user satisfaction of each task and the overall application: After-scenario Questionnaire (ASQ) and Post-Study System Usability Questionnaire (PSSUQ).

When designing a user interface for an M-learning system it is also important to take into consideration a series of UX design principles, which are based on scientific laws. By implementing UX principles one can significantly bolster the usability of a digital interface. According to research by Chopra [16], implementing Fitts' law, further described below, increased the efficiency rate on an eCommerce website by 34%. Below, we discuss these UX principles or laws – Hick's law, Miller's law, Fitts' law, and the von Restorff effect – on the usability of the M-learning system AnatomyNow.

6.3.3.1 Miller's Law

Miller's law suggests the average person can only keep seven (plus or minus two) items in their working memory at a given time. In 1956, George Miller stated that the span of instantaneous memory and complete judgment were restricted to about seven bits of data. A bit is the amount of information necessary to make a choice between two items. In other words, the quantity of bits which can be transmitted reliably through a channel is limited. If the amount of data exceeds the channel capacity within a certain amount of time it will lead to confusion, producing an incorrect judgment. Therefore, overloading a user interface with information can harm the user's processing speed.

Whenever we interact with a new system our brain goes through a process of learning. The mental effort required during this learning period is called cognitive load. Cognitive load can be affected in an M-learning user interface by too many choices, too much thought required, or lack of clarity. If an M-learning system violates any of the above factors the brain will require processing and takes up mental resources that don't help users understand the content, leading to incorrect decisions and to unsatisfactory and inefficient task completions overall, due to the number of errors made. Thus, to avoid this error it is necessary to design an interface by avoiding unnecessary elements, creating consistent design patterns, minimizing available choices, and displaying available choices as chunked groups.

In this M-learning system, we noticed that when it came to the body system page the number of options were linearly placed. Only three possibilities were visible at a single time. This design was not optimal for task completion because a user would have to scroll quite a lot to progress through all the available options. As Miller's law states, a user can process up to seven (plus or minus two) items in their working memory at a given time. Therefore, we conclude that the UI system design was not taking advantage of Miller's law, and that it was restricting the efficiency of the user progress through the menu options. Hence, we decided to redesign the system page where the user would be able to view nine items at a single time. Since eight pieces were at the highest range of the users working memory, we chunked the functions into groups of three, thereby helping the user process the load much more efficiently and reducing the time taken on a task. Thus, making the interaction a much more efficient and satisfying experience.

6.3.3.2 Hick's Law

Hick's law states the time it takes to decide increases with the number and complexity of choices. Hick's law (or the Hick-Hyman law) is named after British and American psychologists William Edmund Hick and Ray Hyman. In 1952, they examined the association between the number of items present and a user's reaction time. According to their findings, the more stimuli to select from, the longer it takes the user to decide to make a choice between available stimuli. Users with a multitude of choices take significantly more time to interpret the data and select a single specific choice, thereby giving them more work than required.

Thus, when designing an interface, it is important to take into consideration the available number of choices visible to the user. To create an efficient interface, it is necessary to limit the number of options available. This prompts the user to make quick decisions and leads them to the information quicker without any distractions. This law is supplementary to that of Miller's law, a designer must not overload the user with too much information and limit the available information to no more than seven (plus or minus two) items in a single screen. Thus, it is essential to remove all information that is not required and create a simplistic design.

When redesigning this M-learning system, we took into consideration the number of clickable functions on the 3D object screen. We noticed there was a multitude of tasks that were not directly related to the process of the M-learning system. Hence, we reduced the number of clickable items on the screen from twenty to eight. These eight items were those most required when it came to interacting with the system at that point. Therefore, we decided to only incorporate the essential functions for the user to communicate with the system, thereby increasing the efficiency in task completion. With this design change, the user can complete a task faster and not waste time to decipher the options and select a single specific choice. This design implementation reduces the time taken on work by lowering the number and complexity of choices.

6.3.3.3 *Fitts' Law*

Fitts' law, coined by psychologist Paul Fitts in 1954, describes the relationship between the amplitude, size, precision, and speed of rapid movements [19]. In essence, the precision and speed for a human to move a pointer (mouse cursor or finger) to a target depends on the target size and target distance from the pointer. The bigger the target or shorter the distance, the faster and more precise the movement will be.

Fitts' law is widely used by user experience and user interface designers. Conventions such as creating large buttons for core functions on user interfaces are influenced by Fitts' law. Bigger buttons support faster and easier user interaction with the system, which increases the efficiency and user satisfaction of the system. A study showed that increasing the left navigation menu size resulted in a 34% increase in the conversions of an eCommerce website [16]. By utilizing Fitts' law in user interface design, designers created derivative terms such as infinite edges and corners. Infinite edges and corners are the four edges and corners of a computer monitor. Since a mouse cursor cannot move past these edges and corners, users can move the cursor as fast as they can to these locations, creating an effect similar to locations having infinite size. Different companies, such as Microsoft [20] and Apple, have been utilizing the infinite edges and corners for their most used functions. For example, the taskbars of both companies' operating systems are located at the bottom infinite edges, and the "Close" functions are located at the top left or top right infinite corner.

Based on Fitts' law, we resized and relocated the buttons on the 3D model page for users to interact with them easily. The buttons we redesigned are related to the 3D model, which is the core function of the application. The newly designed buttons have a size of 1.5cm × 1.5cm, which is 87.5 percent bigger than the original buttons (0.8cm × 0.8cm). The location of the original buttons is hard to reach because they are located at the top left area of the screen, which creates a long distance between the buttons and user's thumb. We relocated the buttons to the bottom of the screen for easy access. In essence, the newly designed buttons are bigger in size and have a shorter distance to users' thumbs to assist users in completing tasks faster and easier compared to the original design.

6.3.3.4 *von Restorff Effect*

Humans tend to remember uncommon things better than ordinary objects. If an item is unique in a list of other common elements, the memory of item will be stronger compared to other objects. This phenomenon is called the von Restorff effect (also known as isolation effect) and was first coined by Hedwig von Restorff, a German psychiatrist, in 1933. Later research also suggests people's attention is easily drawn to salient and distinctive stimuli, which explains why people remember them better [18]. Professionals in different fields use the von Restorff effect to helps users memorize critical information. For instance, advertisers and marketers who built advertisements using the von Restoff effect created unique and creative ads that significantly changed consumers' behavior [17]. The von Restorff effect is also pervasive in the field of UX, where information is highlighted for easy memorability and to suggest its importance or current states. For instance, nearly all eCommerce websites have a check out button which is unique in size and color compared to other information to assist users in noticing and remembering the location of the button quickly.

In the original design, all the buttons are similar and they stay unchanged after users press them. We utilized the von Restorff effect by increasing the size of the important buttons and adding a highlight effect on the selected buttons. This change should help users memorize the location and status of these buttons better.

6.4   Methods and Materials

We assessed the UX of AnatomyNow, the human anatomy training application, developed by the Center of Visualization and Simulation (CVS), Duy Tan University in Vietnam, to supplement educational materials for students learning human anatomy. The product contains a 3D human model which students can view and interact with using their smartphone, and rehearse the names of the parts. Ten systems of the human body are modeled and there are more than 3000 movable parts. We assessed the smartphone version of this M-learning application.

We conducted a comparison between the original design of the user interface and our new design of the user interface. In UX/UI terms this is often referred to as an A/B test, where A is the original UI and B the new UI design. See Figures 6.1 to 6.4 for examples of the original UI and the redesign.

As shown on the left of Figure 6.1, the original navigation page has only three cards on one screen. On the right, the redesigned navigation page shows eight cards on one screen.

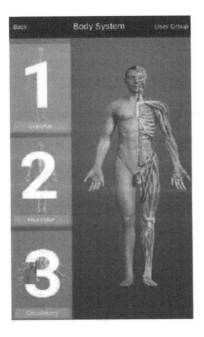

Figure 6.1   (left) Original navigation page with three cards on one screen; (right) redesigned navigation page with eight cards on one screen.

As shown on the left of Figure 11.2, the original 3D model page has twenty buttons. On the right, the new 3D model page has eigth buttons.

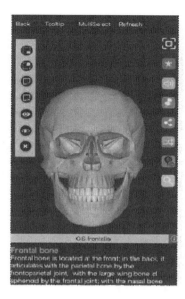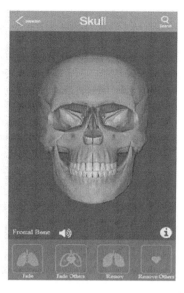

Figure 6.2   (left) The original 3D model page with 20 buttons; (right) new 3D model page with 8 buttons.

As shown on the left of Figure 6.3, the original buttons are too small and far away from a user's thumb. On the right, the redesigned buttons are bigger in size, and located at the bottom of the screen.

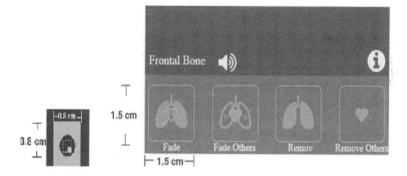

Figure 6.3   (left) The original buttons were small and located far from the thumb; (right) redesigned buttons are bigger and located at the bottom of the screen.

Figure 6.4 shows the redesigned buttons with a highlight effect.

- *Hardware*: iPhone 6s to run both applications. The smartphone has a display size of 4.7 inches, and a resolution of 750×1334 pixels.

- *Software Prototype*: We built the mockup of the new design for the AnatomyNow UI as a prototype, using Axure prototype building software. The prototype was built to such an extent that participants could finish the twelve essential tasks of the application.

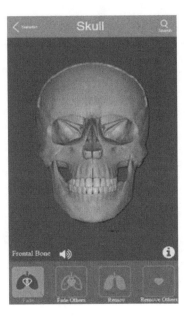

Figure 6.4   The redesigned buttons have a highlight effect.

- *Participants*: The potential subjects were recruited at random across the world. A total of 17 young adults took part in this procedure. All participants had prior knowledge in operating a phone. All participants were fluent in English.

- *Tasks*: To compare the usability of the applications, we created twelve tasks with scenarios for participants to complete during the experiment, see Table 6.1. These tasks are related to participants' navigation process and 3D model interaction process using both systems.

Table 6.1   Scenarios and tasks, as used in the experiment.

1. You are studying anatomy and hope to learn more about the nervous system. **Locate the Nervous system.**
2. You want to know the name of the bone on your forehead. **Locate the bone on the forehead of the skull (frontal bone)**
3. You want to see what through the Frontal Bone. **Fade frontal bone**
4. You are done studying what is behind the Frontal Bone. **Undo the last task.**
5. You want to isolate the frontal bone, so you can study it carefully. **Remove everything BUT the Frontal bone.**
6. You are done studying frontal bone. **Undo the last task.**
7. You want to view the whole skull without the frontal bone highlighted. **Deselect the frontal bone.**
8. You want to know a body part named Zygoma. **Find Zygoma.**
9. You want to refresh the 3D model so it returns to the original state. **Refresh the 3D model.**
10. You want to put three body parts together and make a group. **Create a body system group with first three body parts.**
11. You want to delete the group you created. **Delete the group you created.**
12. You want to read the description of the frontal bone. **Find the description of the frontal bone.**

- *After-Scenario Questionnaire (ASQ)*: We used the ASQ to measure the user satisfaction of the twelve individual tasks. The ASQ is a three-item questionnaire measuring ease of task, satisfaction with task duration, and satisfaction with support information.

- *Post-Study System Usability Questionnaire (PSSUQ)*: We used the PSSUQ to measure the overall user satisfaction of the two systems. The PSSUQ is a questionnaire developed by IBM to measure user satisfaction with computer software and application, probing ease of systems, ease of tasks, user satisfaction with error recovery, user satisfaction with support information, and overall user satisfaction.

- *Procedure*: Participants were separated into two groups to perform the task using one of the two versions. They were asked to read and sign the consent form. Then we informed them that the experiment is about testing the software, not their ability to complete tasks. After that, participants were asked to read the task description and say "Start" to start doing the task and say "Forfeit" to end the task at any time. When participants were performing the tasks, experimenters recorded whether tasks were completed or not. Experimenters also recorded the time for participants to finish the task. Then, participants filled out the ASQs after each task. After participants completed all the tasks, they filled out the PSSUQ.

6.5 Results

6.5.1 Task Completion Rate (TCR)

Tables 6.2 and 6.3 present the results of descriptive statistics and independent t-test conducted to test the average TCR of participants using the two applications. The difference between the original version ($M = 72.6\%$, $SD = 0.15$) and the new version ($M = 86.1\%$, $SD = 0.11$), is approaching significance $t(14) = 2.083$, $p = 0.056$.

Table 6.2 Descriptive statistics for the average TCR.

	Group	N	Mean	SD	SE
TCR	Original	7	72.6%	0.15	0.057
	New	9	86.1%	0.11	0.037

Table 6.3 Results of independent t-test for TCR.

	t	df	p
TCR	-2.083	14.00	0.056

Table 6.4 presents the average TCR for each task. The results suggest that the new version has a higher TCR for all the tasks expect Task 5 and Task 9.

Table 6.4 Descriptive statistics for the average TCR of individual tasks.

Task 1	Original	7	71.4%	0.488	0.184
	New	9	100.0%	0	0
Task 2	Original	7	100.0%	0	0
	New	9	100.0%	0	0
Task 3	Original	7	85.7%	0.378	0.143
	New	9	100.0%	0	0
Task 4	Original	7	57.1%	0.535	0.202
	New	9	77.8%	0.441	0.147
Task 5	Original	7	100.0%	0	0
	New	9	100.0%	0	0
Task 6	Original	7	71.4%	0.488	0.184
	New	9	88.9%	0.333	0.111
Task 7	Original	7	85.7%	0.378	0.143
	New	9	77.8%	0.441	0.147
Task 8	Original	7	14.3%	0.378	0.143
	New	9	88.9%	0.333	0.111
Task 9	Original	7	71.4%	0.488	0.184
	New	9	11.1%	0.333	0.111
Task 10	Original	7	100.0%	0	0
	New	9	100.0%	0	0
Task 11	Original	7	71.4%	0.488	0.184
	New	9	100.0%	0	0
Task 12	Original	7	42.9%	0.535	0.202
	New	9	88.9%	0.333	0.111

6.5.2 Time-on-Task (TOT)

Table 6.5 and Table 6.6 present the results of the descriptive statistics and independent t-test conducted to test the average TOT for users to finish the twelve tasks using the two applications. The result revealed a significant difference between the original version ($M = 22.57$, $SD = 7.41$) and the new version ($M = 8.78$, $SD = 3.06$), $t(14) = 5.089$, $p < .001$.

Table 6.5 Descriptive statistics for the average TOT.

Group	N	Mean	SD	SE
Original	7	22.57	7.41	2.80
New	9	8.78	3.06	1.02

Table 6.6 Results of independent t-test for TOT.

	t	df	p
TOT	5.089	14.00	< .001

Tables 6.7 and 6.8 show the descriptive statistics and independent t-test results of the average TOT of each individual task. Among the twelve results, seven of them (Task 1, 3, 4, 5, 8, 11 and 12) are significant. There was no t-test result for Task 9 due to low

task completion rate. Also, it is worth mentioning that Task 9 is the only task that the participants spend more time on the new version than the original version.

Table 6.7   Descriptive statistics for the average TOT of individual tasks.

	Group	N	Mean	SD	SE
Task 1	Original	5	28.47	19.85	8.88
	New	9	2.95	1.82	0.61
Task 2	Original	7	16.49	11.27	4.26
	New	9	15.24	9.31	3.10
Task 3	Original	6	36.06	24.02	9.80
	New	9	9.85	8.75	2.92
Task 4	Original	4	37.13	36.52	18.26
	New	7	3.67	3.76	1.42
Task 5	Original	7	19.19	9.28	3.51
	New	9	8.67	10.02	3.34
Task 6	Original	6	5.28	4.72	1.93
	New	8	2.85	3.21	1.14
Task 7	Original	6	10.19	7.57	3.09
	New	7	6.31	10.00	3.78
Task 8	Original	3	74.15	46.66	26.94
	New	8	17.74	7.66	2.71
Task 9	Original	5	5.60	5.73	2.56
	New	1	18.00	NaN	NaN
Task 10	Original	7	25.29	16.17	6.11
	New	9	17.16	8.99	3.00
Task 11	Original	5	15.60	11.37	5.09
	New	9	1.81	1.11	0.37
Task 12	Original	3	17.16	13.13	7.58
	New	8	4.64	2.96	1.05

Table 6.8   Independent t-test results of TOT of each task.

	t	df	p
Task 1*	3.959	12	0.002
Task 2	0.244	14	0.811
Task 3*	3.032	13	0.01
Task 4*	2.506	9	0.034
Task 5*	2.149	14	0.05
Task 6	1.153	12	0.271
Task 7	0.777	11	0.454
Task 8*	3.621	9	0.006
Task 9[a]	NaN		
Task 10	1.284	14	0.22
Task 11*	3.732	12	0.003
Task 12*	2.753	9	0.022

6.5.3   After-Scenario Questionnaire (ASQ)

Tables 6.9 and 6.10 present the results of descriptive statistics and independent t-test conducted to test the average TOT for users to finish the twelve tasks using the two applications. The results revealed a significant difference between the original version ($M = 4.77$, $SD = 1.01$) and the new version ($M = 6.31$, $SD = 0.53$), $t(15) = -4.026$, $p = 0.001$.

Table 6.9   Descriptive statistics for the average ASQ score.

	Group	N	Mean	SD	SE
ASQ	Original	8	4.77	1.01	0.36
	New	9	6.31	0.53	0.18

Table 6.10   Results of independent t-test for average ASQ score.

	t	df	p
ASQ	-4.026	15.00	0.001

Twelve independent sample t-tests were conducted to measure the ASQ scores for each task of different versions of the applications (see Table 6.12). Seven out of twelve (Tasks 3, 4, 5, 7, 8, 11 and 12) results were significant.

Table 6.11   Descriptive statistics for the average ASQ score of individual tasks.

		Group	N	Mean	SD	SE
ASQ	Task 1	Original	8	5.667	1.208	0.427
		New	9	5.926	0.925	0.308
	Task 2	Original	8	6.25	0.661	0.234
		New	9	6.333	0.624	0.208
	Task 3	Original	8	3.875	1.221	0.432
		New	9	5.815	1.119	0.373
	Task 4	Original	8	4.167	2.168	0.766
		New	9	6.704	0.512	0.171
	Task 5	Original	8	4.75	1.571	0.555
		New	9	6.519	0.58	0.193
	Task 6	Original	8	5.083	1.9	0.672
		New	9	6.556	0.687	0.229
	Task 7	Original	8	4.917	2.158	0.763
		New	9	6.37	0.857	0.286
	Task 8	Original	8	2.625	2.504	0.885
		New	9	6.111	1.537	0.512
	Task 9	Original	8	4.625	2.56	0.905
		New	9	5.333	1.59	0.530
	Task 10	Original	8	6.375	0.825	0.292
		New	9	6.704	0.564	0.188
	Task 11	Original	8	4.5	2.337	0.826
		New	9	6.889	0.333	0.111
	Task 12	Original	8	4.375	2.2	0.778
		New	9	6.481	1.226	0.409

Table 6.12   Independent t-test results of the ASQ score of each task.

	t	df	p
ASQ	-0.5	15	0.624
Task 1	-0.267	15	0.793
Task 2	-3.419	15	0.004
Task 3*	-3.419	15	0.004
Task 4*	-3.154	15	0.007
Task 5*	-2.177	15	0.046
Task 6* Task 7	-1.868	15	0.081
Task 8* Task 9	-3.507	15	0.003
Task 10	-0.694	15	0.498
Task 11*	-0.969	15	0.348
Task 12*	-3.045	15	0.008
	-2.478	15	0.026

*$p < 0.05$

6.5.4   Post-Study System Usability Questionnaire (PSSUQ)

An independent sample t-test was conducted to examine the PSSUQ score of the two applications (see Table 6.14). The results revealed a significant difference between the original version ($M = 4.44$, $SD = 1.23$), and the new version ($M = 5.87$, $SD = 0.81$), $t(15) = 2.87$, $p = 0.01$.

Table 6.13   Descriptive plot for the average PSSUQ score.

	Group	N	Mean	SD	SE
PSSUQ	Original	8	4.44	1.23	0.43
	New	9	5.87	0.81	0.27

Table 6.14   Results of independent t-test for PSSUQ score.

	t	df	p
PSSUQ	-2.868	15.00	0.01

6.6   Conclusion

Our research addressed how we can use UX/UI design principles and laws to enhance the usability of the M-learning system AnatomyNow by applying these principles to create a more efficient, effective and satisfying interface for the learner. We demonstrated that UX assessments can play a significant role when developing the M-learning system. However, these findings are preliminary since ideally the sample size for representative and reliable statistical analysis is recommended to be larger. The purpose of this study was to work out and demonstrate how to redesign and test a new user interface design for evidence of increased usability (task completion rate, time-on-task, and user satisfaction) of the application. The results supported our hypothesis; the redesigned application has higher for TCR, and user satisfaction rate and lower for TOT. In essence, we found that the entire user experience when interacting with the system was significantly increased.

The results obtained from this experiment suggest that the redesign of the UI has had a significant impact on the usability of the user experience and interaction with the system. Overall time-on-task was significantly reduced in the redesigned system compared to the original system; furthermore, a significant increase in overall satisfaction of all tasks was observed through the scores obtained by the ASQ and PSSUQ. The redesigned interface was successful in creating a more effective, efficient and user-friendly XR-learning system. However, further studies are needed to investigate the successfulness of the application as a whole, teaching anatomy and the retention of the learned subject material.

REFERENCES

1. Le, C., Tromp, J. G., & Puri, V. (2018). Using 3D simulation in medical education: A comparative test of teaching anatomy using virtual reality, in: *Virtual Reality and Augmented Reality Healthcare and Medicine Applications: Design, Evaluation and LongTerm Use Implications.* Eds: Dac-Nhuong Le, Chung Le Van, Jolanda G. Tromp, Gia Nhu Nguyen, Scrivener Publishing Wiley.

2. Cai, Z., & Medonza, O. (2019). Applying UX Principles to an M-Learning System Increase in Usability: a Case Study, 2019 Research Report in partial completion of HumanComputer Interaction Master's, State University of New York in Oswego, USA.

3. ISO CD 9241-11: Ergonomics of human-system interaction - Part 11: Usability: Definitions and concepts (2015)

4. Crompton, H. (2013). A historical overview of mobile learning: Toward learner-centered education. In ZL Berge & LY Muilenburg (Eds.), *Handbook of Mobile Learning*, Routledge.

5. Trentin, G., & Repetto, M. (Eds.). (2013). *Using Network and Mobile Technology to Bridge Formal and Informal Learning.* Elsevier.

6. Koole, M. L. (2009). A model for framing mobile learning. In *Mobile Learning: Transforming the Delivery of Education and Training*, 1(2), 25-47.

7. Sharples, M., Taylor, J., & Vavoula, G. (2005, October). Towards a theory of mobile learning. In *Proceedings of MLearn 2005 conference 25-28 October, Cape Town, South Africa.* pp.1-9.

8. Crescente, M. L., & Lee, D. (2011). Critical issues of m-learning: design models, adoption processes, and future trends. *Journal of the Chinese Institute of Industrial Engineers*, 28(2), 111-123.

9. Sarrab, M., Elgamel, L., & Aldabbas, H. (2012). Mobile learning (mlearning) and educational environments. *International Journal of Distributed and Parallel Systems*, 3(4), 31.

10. Evans, C. (2008). The effectiveness of m-learning in the form of podcast revision lectures in higher education. *Computers & Education*, 50(2), 491-498.

11. Miraz, M. H., Ali, M., & Excell, P. S. (2018). Cross-cultural Usability Issues in E/M-Learning. arXiv preprint arXiv:1804.02329.

12. Beutner, M., & Ruscher, F. A. (2017). Acceptance of Mobile Learning at SMEs of the Service Sector. 13th International Conference Mobile Learning 2017, International Association for Development of the Information Society.

13. Kuhnel, M., Seiler, L., Honal, A., & Ifenthaler, D. (2018). Mobile learning analytics in higher education: Usability testing and evaluation of an app prototype. *Interactive Technology and Smart Education*, 15(4), 332-347.

14. Speicher, M. (2015). What is usability? a characterization based on ISO 9241-11 and ISO/IEC 25010. *arXiv preprint arXiv:1502.06792*. http://arxiv.org/abs/1502.06792.

15. Frkjr, E., Hertzum, M., & Hornbk, K. (2000, April). Measuring usability: are effectiveness, efficiency, and satisfaction really correlated?. In *Proceedings of the SIGCHI conference on Human Factors in Computing Systems* (pp. 345-352). ACM. [Retrieved from https://doi.org/10.1145/332040.332455.]

16. Chopra, Paras. "Usability Is Not Dead: How Left Navigation Menu Increased Conversions by 34% for an ECommerce Website." Blog, November 30, 2010. [Retrieved from https://vwo.com/blog/usabilityleft-navigation-menu-bar-conversions-ecommerce-website/.]

17. Mufti, O., Parvaiz, G. S., & Ullah, U. (2018). Creating Distinctiveness & Vividness in Ads Using Isolation Effect: A Case of Cellular Network Providers. *Journal of Managerial Sciences*, 12(1).

18. Taylor, S. E., & Fiske, S. T. (1978). Salience, attention, and attribution: Top of the head phenomena. In *Advances in Experimental Social Psychology* (Vol. 11, pp. 249-288). Academic Press.

19. Thumser, Z. C., Slifkin, A. B., Beckler, D. T., & Marasco, P. D. (2018). Fitts' law in the control of isometric grip force with naturalistic targets. *Frontiers in psychology*, 9.

20. Berkun, S. (2000). *Fitts's UI Law Applied to the Web*. Microsoft Developer Network.

PART IV

TOWARDS DIGITAL TWINS AND ROBOTICS

The move towards digital twins and robotics will transform industrial operations because it will equip machines with superior perception, integrability, adaptability, and mobility. Setting up industrial operations will be faster, including calibration, optimization, multiplication, commissioning and reconfigurations. This will facilitate more efficient and stable operations. Meanwhile, the cost of displays (AR, VR, 3D groupware (CAVE, IMAX, VOID)), sensors and computing power decreases and software increasingly replaces hardware as the primary driver of functionality. This allows us to do many tasks more economically than via the previous generation of the automated systems. Broadly speaking, it enables the self-controlled factory of the future. The exact form of the industrial operations and automated systems depends on the industry, the region, the people and company specific needs.

The predicted benefits are:

1. *Productivity*: Self-adjustment to changing parameters eliminates micro-stops of conventional robotics processes. It is significantly easier to set up and reconfigure than conventional robots, using suitable simulation software. It is also quicker at learning how to perform tasks, and has a rapid ramp-up of processes in AIIoT for production systems that need frequent adjustments in response to changeovers or customization requests.

2. *Quality*: It can perform more tasks that are hazardous or physically demanding for humans (for instance RSI); the machine-vision technology that improves robots' perception can also enhance safety (and has no limit spatially).

3. *Agility*: Advanced robotics can be used to automatically configure new production systems, meeting the AIIoT demands for more product variations, customized products and product redesigns, based on the "flexible cell manufacturing" structure.

The predicted social impacts are: 1) There will be a major impact on the workforce. To achieve ROI (positive economics for investment) robots must replace humans rather than support them. 2) Routine manual activities will become fully automated. Routine and non-routine activities will change, and the share of non-routine activities will increase for the human operator. Manual work will shift towards non-routine tasks, which means that workers must acquire more advanced skills. 3) New job categories will arise with tasks that require technical capabilities and soft skills (to manage the errors and problem solving that machines cannot handle). Companies must plan to accelerate the creation of industrial engineering jobs dedicated to robotics (developing and customizing robotics solutions).

The current perception of the maturity of the new technologies is low and our understanding of the possibilities is still developing. AR, VR, and AIIoT-enabled robotic systems use digital twins to integrate real-time and historical information about the product, service, and production system, protected by cybersecurity where necessary, and connected to the cloud for sharing when desirable. Chapter 7 presents an analysis of augmented reality interfaces for interactive historical information displays. Companies in the transportation, logistics technologies and automotive industries have the lead in implementing advanced simulation, visualization, and robotics; however, a lot of this work currently takes place in commercial companies and in research labs behind "closed-doors," and protected with patents.

In logistics, autonomous self-repairing, ML-enabled mobile robots for in-plant logistics and warehousing, will replace both fixed conveyor belts and automated guided vehicles (AGVs). They can autonomously supply work stations via ground transport, drone transport, perform picking, packaging and palletizing operations, and kitting tasks (but currently there is no fully realized technology for kitting). Sensors and machine learning are essential for the robot to identify, pick, and handle unsorted or flexible parts in bins. At the time of this writing, it is only recently that the first demonstrators for this have been showcased. They can control in-line quality by automatically adjusting equipment parameters in response to perceived quality. They can recognize damage and perform automated inspections of remote or large or very small parts, autonomously move testing equipment to the place where it is needed, and perform maintenance, including in conditions that are hazardous for humans.

Implications for industrial operations and companies are the need for a number of action steps to establish three enablers:

1. Define the target picture of the future factory,

2. Build organizational competencies,

3. Design the system architecture.

The vision of the future factory should encompass the implementation of multiple automation technologies, and must define key transition steps, test solutions rapidly, collaborate on pilot programs with other manufacturers of robotics and other producers, to rapidly scale up solutions that perform well at the pilot stage in the relevant area of operations.

Teaching, monitoring and managing advanced robotic systems requires employees to exercise both functional and soft skills, and smart learning management systems (LMS) can offer excellerated learning solutions. Robots can be trained in VR. Employees can be guided and trained in real time via AR and VR solutions. Chapter 8 presents a use case of an ML algorithm in an LMS.

- Chapter 7: Augmented Reality at Heritage Sites: Technological Advances and Embodied Spatially Minded Interactions

- Chapter 8: TELECI Architecture for Machine Learning Algorithms Integration in an Existing LMS

CHAPTER 7

AUGMENTED REALITY AT HERITAGE SITES: TECHNOLOGICAL ADVANCES AND EMBODIED SPATIALLY MINDED INTERACTIONS

Lesley Johnston,[1] Romy Galloway,[1] Jordan John Trench,[1] Matthieu Poyade,[1,*] Jolanda Tromp,[2,3] Hoang Thi My[4]

[1] School of Simulation and Visualisation, The Glasgow School of Art, Glasgow, UK

[2] Center for Visualization and Simulation, Duy Tan University, Da Nang, Vietnam

[3] Department of Computer Science, State University of New York, Oswego, New York, USA

[4] Department of Tourism, Hai Phong University, Hai Phong, Vietnam

*Corresponding author: m.poyade@gsa.ac.uk

Abstract

This chapter seeks to consider how issues of environment, realism and ideas of physical and virtual space are influencing developments in augmented reality (AR) within the context of heritage sites. It considers the technical challenges that AR applications face at these sites such as high computational demands, remote locations, scene detection and tracking, and the difficulty of virtually duplicating real-world environmental conditions convincingly. These technical innovations create a framework for all other aspects of the application, particularly in how we develop engaging user experiences, and facilitate new forms of interaction that look towards more performative and experiential forms of interpretation. This chapter looks at how the nature of AR offers opportunities to negotiate contemporary ideas of space in these sites and ways to explore them. Drawing upon examples of the technical challenges AR faces, the chapter aims to demonstrate the crucial impact this can have on user experience and the design of interactions. The academic definitions of presence sought within mediated interactions no longer fit these developing uses of AR. As such, further exploration of the term is called for, one that fits the nuanced forms of engagement and embodied experiences of cultural material being fostered.

Keywords: Augmented reality, cultural heritage, spatial interaction, museum exhibits, design

7.1   Introduction

Augmented reality (AR) takes multifaceted forms and has a great deal to offer the cultural heritage sector. In seeking to understand these forms before progressing to how they are evolving and being utilized within this sector, it will be useful to return to early definitions for the ideas that drive AR. In its basic classifications, it is real-time and interactive, registered in 3D space, and allows the overlaying of virtual elements onto a capture of a physical environment [1-3]. Often defined by its differences from virtual reality (VR) [1, 30], the capabilities of AR are in "enhancing real world objects and environments instead of replacing them" [30]. With rapid technological advancements and affordability of consumer-level mobile devices, and the resulting ubiquity of smartphones and tablets in recent years, AR has become widely available to the public [5, 11, 31, 44, 48, 51]. In addition, the emergence of user-friendly development platforms, such as Unity (2005) [52] and Vuforia (2015) [39], through which the public can create their own applications, have also contributed to the diversification to wider audiences.

Whilst Han, Jung and Gibson [19] remarked several years ago that AR was still a fairly new concept in its application to the tourist industry, it has experienced exponential growth in multiple sectors with the launching of AR platforms by multiple global brands [6], and has since become a valued commodity in the cultural heritage sector. Interactive AR affords museums and cultural heritage sites the capacity to enhance the visitor experience by effectively engaging the public and disseminating predominantly visual information in memorable ways [23]. This has not been a simply altruistic undertaking. tom Dieck and Jung [48] have demonstrated that the adoption of innovative technologies tends to both improve the user experience, and deliver economic value by increasing footfall and encouraging visitors to remain at the site for a longer period. In recent years, many cultural heritage institutions have implemented both museum-based and location-based AR services in attempts to increase visitor numbers to both urban and remote heritage destinations [22].

Both indoor and outdoor AR applications require the same functionality in smartphone device functionality: a camera, GPS, gyroscope, and acceleration sensors. Whilst both also deliver similar features and experiences – 2D and 3D visualization, navigation, and user interaction – outdoor mobile AR applications face additional difficulties [32, 40]. The number of calls for more user testing *in situ* within the study of such AR applications [10, 44], demonstrate an awareness in the field of just how much the environment shapes the interaction, even without being explicitly designed into the experience.

This chapter seeks to consider how issues of environment, realism and ideas of physical and virtual space are influencing developments in AR within the context of heritage sites. It considers the technical challenges that AR applications in these sites face, such as; high computational demands, remote locations, scene detection and tracking, and the difficulty of virtually duplicating real-world environmental conditions convincingly. These technical contexts subsequently create a structure for all other aspects of the application, particularly in how we may develop engaging user experiences, and facilitate new forms of interaction that look towards more performative and experiential forms of interpretation. This chapter looks at how the nature of AR offers opportunities to negotiate contemporary ideas of space in these sites and ways to explore them. Drawing upon examples of the technical challenges AR faces, the crucial impact this can have on user experience and the design of interactions will be discussed. The academic definitions of the presence sought within mediated interactions no longer fit these developing uses of AR that are inherently imbedded in both virtual and real space. As such, more exploration of the term is called for, one that fits the nuanced forms of engagement and embodied experiences of cultural material being fostered.

7.2 Augmented Reality Devices

Studies undertaken by Olsson *et al.* [35] and tom Dieck and Jung [47] demonstrate that since AR came into the public realm the user expectations of the AR experience have changed little; relevant, up-to-date information in an attractive style which provides a quality user experience and usable interface are aspects that are key to an application's success [57]. However, even more fundamental than these features is the requirement for an AR device to:

A) Permit effective AR interactions,

B) Be accepted by the public for the purpose of AR interactions, and

C) Be accessible and affordable to the public.

Early AR devices would not have met the criteria outlined above. As shown in Figure 7.1 below, the earliest devices typically utilized a bulky head-mounted-display (HMD) with cumbersome backpack containing a processing unit and a battery, such as that used by Vlahakis *et al.* for The Olympia Project to implement mobile AR [53].

Figure 7.1   An example of an early cumbersome HMD.

To provide a suitable degree of mobility, mobile devices must be capable of providing sufficient processing power, software framework, high graphical rendering capability, data management, wireless communication and tracking support [8]. Despite the advances of mobile technologies, these features are not yet built into many modern mobile devices.

Modern HMDs or AR glasses such as the HoloLens, Google Glass and Magic Leap One, as shown in Figure 7.2 [17, 42], are considered by many to be the preferred AR see-through interfaces, particularly as nowadays these are more user-friendly and lighter [8, 9, 38]. AR glasses, or see-through display technology, permit the user to still perceive the world around them whilst virtual images are integrated into the users field of view utilizing light field display technology, thus providing the user a sense of 3D immersion [20, 28].

Figure 7.2 Examples of see-through AR interfaces, both of which are lightweight and hands-free augmented reality glasses that permit the user to view the world around them; Google Glass (left) and Magic Leap One (right).

AR glasses allow hands-free selections of digital objects through the focus of gaze on a particular object or using voice command, permitting the user a greater aspect of freedom in their use. However, Chatzopoulos *et al.* [8] raised an interesting issue of definition, noting some controversy over whether these glasses ought to be classed as AR or mobile AR technology, as many provided functions are not relevant to a real-world content and so do not require tracking and alignment. Many of the Google Glass basic functions center on smartphone style interactions, i.e., sending messages, information searching and navigation [8]. In these functions the glasses operate more as a hands-free device than an AR device. Admittedly, these are base level interactions and numerous applications have been developed which allow a much greater and undeniably augmented experience. The HoloMuse application with the HoloLens for example, as shown in Figure 7.3, allows a hands-free augmented experience of artefacts through gesture control [8]. The user can interact.

Figure 7.3 Example of gesture-based interaction through the HoloLens and HoloMuse application.

The user can interact with digital objects through a set of gesture-based movements to create an active and intuitive interaction in a predefined environment [8, 38].

Jung [22] observed that there is limited research which has been undertaken on the adoption and acceptance factors involved in the selection and success of AR devices, although it is still apparent that smartphones and tablets have the favor of the wider audience to display AR despite the possibilities afforded by AR glasses [8, 41]. A non-exhaustive list of contributory factors for this is the initial cost layout for AR glasses, a general lack of social acceptance, convenience and the wish to avoid appearing too "touristy" [18, 26, 41]. Not only do many people already own smartphones powerful enough for this purpose, but the fact that they are less conspicuous seems to be a clear advantage in device selection. The trade-off between robustness, portability, graphical rendering capacity, network capability, computational power and battery life required for AR and interactions, means that smartphones and tablets are still the only realistic practical choice in heritage sites [26]. As such we will consider the smartphone or tablet as the default AR device discussed throughout this chapter unless expressly noted otherwise. Having briefly covered two of the three fundamental device requirements – fit for and accepted for the purpose by the public – we will move on to consider the requirement for AR devices to be able to effectively permit AR experiences by locating them in the correct location and orientation.

7.3   Detection and Tracking

As many AR applications seek to "bridge the gap" between the digital and real worlds [36], it is paramount that the digital content should be scaled and situated in the correct location and orientation within the real world. Enabling this many applications requires utilizing QR codes, or markers, which act as anchors fixing the virtual content into physical space. However, unlike in museums or urban heritage contexts, there is often a physical or ethical impediment prohibiting the application of markers to points of interest in many heritage sites [6]. This presents one of the primary barriers to functionality in AR, particularly when one of the most appealing features of mobile AR is its capacity to allow the user to interact virtually with augmented artefacts from a suitable distance without the potential risk of damage to the site [51]. If the scene registration is inaccurate due to poor detection and tracking, users will be dissatisfied with the experience and unlikely to endorse the application or return to the site to try again. Thus, Marques *et al.* [32] argued that AR must have high accuracy whilst avoiding latency for an improved level of user experience. Accurate registration is even more challenging within mobile AR applications for outdoor heritage sites due to the range of angles from which the site may be approached [6]. Furthermore, there are a range of environmental factors which can also affect marker detection and registration.

Typically, there exist several technologies to support location tracking in AR: Vision-based markers and/or natural features tracking; and Sensor-based: inertial, magnetic, electromagnetic, and ultrasonic tracking [8]. As marker-based methods are often not an option at heritage sites, natural feature tracking is a more suitable approach. This is a non-intrusive approach which tracks known extant points and regional features to determine the position of the camera in real time; Figure 7.4 shows a spread of such natural features identified in a rock-art example [36].

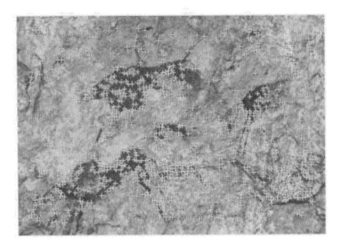

Figure 7.4 An example of natural feature-based point detection for using AR on rock art. Recognition of multiple known points is required to permit accurate registration of the augmented image [40].

Blanco-Pons *et al.* [6] suggest natural feature tracking is non-optimal for heritage sites which specifically have low contrast or high surface texture, i.e., rock art, as feature-based detection requires a suitable level of detail and contrast to allow a match to be made between digital models and the reference image on the application's database. Furthermore, Chatzopoulo *et al.* [8] and Blanco-Pons *et al.* [6] concur that this method can be hindered by light variation and self-occlusion, whilst the registration against the reference image can have a detrimentally high computational overhead. In addition, there is a consensus in the field that sensor-based tracking alone can lead to high registration errors, more particularly in outdoor settings [6, 40, 46]. Thus, a hybrid of both methods can be utilized to reduce inconsistencies, such as allowing natural feature-based tracking to reduce the drift of inertial sensors [40]. Shi *et al.* [46] have has demonstrated that utilizing such hybrid tracking method can increase registration accuracy by 20% over simply using GPS location-based tracking alone. Effective point detection and tracking through either one or a combination of these methods allows applications to establish the relevant scene without any inaccuracies or latency which may detract the user from the interactive experience they are instantiating. Once the virtual content is placed in the correct location, the next fundamental requirement to allow a user to begin an engaging and convincing experience is the degree of realism with which the augmented and physical scenes are blended [9, 10].

7.4 Environmental Variation

In addition to the difficulties faced in anchoring AR viewpoints to the physical world, the juxtaposition between fluctuating natural light and static digital light represents another barrier to realizing a convincing scene [45]. To convincingly blend the digital and real worlds, environmental factors must be taken into consideration when designing the augmented experience. For instance, libraries and software development toolkits, such as Google's platform ARCore, are now going to considerable lengths to develop real-time light variation functionality to help 3D objects blend as realistically as possible into their physical environment [54].

As one of the most common uses of AR in the heritage field is visually overlaying a digital reconstruction of the virtual past over the present scene, it is important that the two blend together effectively to create a convincing amalgamation. For applications seeking to only give an indicative representation of a 3D model to facilitate information transfer or promote the gamification of a site, this is a lesser issue. However a convincing degree of realism would still be considered an optimal outcome. The above reflection notices the difficulty and importance of placing and orientating the digital data; efforts which can be undermined when environmental conditions depicted within the digital data are incongruous with the real world, thus preventing a high degree of immersion and optimal user experience [45].

Within the confines of a museum's stable and controlled environment, AR can be designed to reflect the lighting conditions of the known space. This is considerably less challenging than developing AR applications which exhibit matching lighting conditions to an outdoor environment [32]. AR applications for outdoor environments must accommodate for the fact that both the light and environmental conditions are in constant flux. Therefore, implementing AR applications able to detect and dynamically replicate realistic environmental factors, particularly light and shadow, is an important progression for real-time rendering of augmented digital models [4]. This is known as photometric registration [4], and there have been several methods developed to effectively mimic real-time environmental conditions. For instance, Rohmer *et al.* [59] used a smartphone's depth sensor to implement real-time color correction through altering the white balance of the image, i.e., the relative warmth or coolness perceived from the light source, dependent upon the white balance detected by the sensor to render increasingly photorealistic images.

Seo *et al.* [45] further built upon this concept and included color temperature compensation to synchronize the image with the approximate color temperature of the sun depending on the time of day. This meant that low intensity color temperature could be applied near dusk and dawn, whilst higher intensity would be more appropriate around noon. This change in color tone throughout the day is demonstrated in Figure 7.5.

Figure 7.5   A range of white balance settings which match color temperature at set times, increasing consistency of color tone with the real scene.

This blends the color of the virtual object with the predicted color tone of the real scene, causing visual consistency between the two for the user [45].

The potential realism of the scene can then be further increased by synchronizing the displayed environmental conditions with weather forecast conditions using network connections, allowing real-time weather events, currently limited to rain, snow and wind, to be duplicated on the augmented image. However, such an approach has not been trialled yet in the context of mobile AR [45]. For instance, the absolute illuminance values would be calculated as a function of the degree of cloud and any changes of environmental illumination would be dynamically reported on augmented models in real time, as shown in Figure 7.6. However, depending upon how the device is held, if the angle of the device is superior to −75 degrees, then the estimation of absolute illuminance is problematically prone to errors [4].

Figure 7.6   An example of real-world shadow creation under varied environmental conditions; virtual teapot (left) and real teapot (right).

The degree of ambient scene illuminance is detected by the smartphone's ambient light sensor and this data is used to detect sunlight intensity. The phone's geospatial sensors then relay location, orientation and time to the app, which can then calculate and render a plausible real-time depiction of scene luminance onto the augmented image [4]. In concurrence with Seo *et al.* [45], Barreira *et al.* [4] suggest synchronizing to a weather forecast server to establish the current degree of cloud coverage – cloudy, partly cloudy, or clear skies – and from this generate a dynamic shadow of the augmented models to mimic real-time conditions. For instance, the absolute illuminance values would be calculated as a function of the degree of cloud, and any changes of environmental illumination would be dynamically reported on augmented models in real-time. However, depending upon how the device is held, if the angle of the device is superior to −75 degrees, then the estimation of absolute illuminance is problematically prone to errors [4].

In addition, the dynamic shadows of Barreira *et al.* [4] reportedly only operated under an on-or-off scenario and could not correctly depict the shadow of an object which is half in shade and half not. Also, a method has not yet been found to smoothly transition the presence of shadow on and off with lighting change. Despite these issues and possible errors, this method could greatly contribute to increase the level of realism with which augmented reconstructions can be viewed, thereby removing the disparity between digital models and the real scenery, making the experience more immersive and convincing for the user.

Once these technical restrictions of tracking, registration and environmental incoherency are overcome, AR applications will be able to overlay the required data onto the scene at the correct location and orientation in a visually convincing way. With such advancements, it is becoming increasingly feasible for realistic and engaging AR experiences to occur in increasingly complex physical environments, thereby opening up a host of opportunities for new forms of interaction. These developments within AR technology that render devices more lightweight, socially acceptable and mobile, run in tandem with developments in the type of experiences now sought in the heritage sector. Namely, more effective experiences based on performative interactions.

7.5 Experiential and Embodied Interactions

Within museum methods of interpretation, Messham-Muir [34] noted two significant shifts: digital media for information display, and the employment of "affective modes of communication" in interpretation material. While his discussion was specifically applied to museums we may apply it to heritage interpretation more generally, and look to how the latter shift in interpretative methods might feed into the use of the multimedia displays.

Messham-Muir denoted a move towards sensory engagement of audiences, in part through emphasis on embodied interactions with spaces and artefacts [34]. He outlined this by citing the writing of Chakrabarty [58] and a transition within the museum model from a pedagogical approach to a more performative one, where the viewer is implicit within the construction of meaning. He suggests that the former structure of interpretation suppressed the physical bodily experience to promote abstract reasoning, and the contemporary performative gives rise to the embodied and sensory experience.

However, amongst these developments Messham-Muir [34] noted a gulf; between the adoption of multimedia within these spaces and their use in the rise in embodied performative interpretation. By way of explanation, he noted the physicality understood to be inherent in the latter, and an opposing consideration of intangibility in the former. A stance echoed by Witcomb [55], whose critique of unfulfilling digital interactions within heritage sites, considered it in part due to the treatment of digital media as immaterial.

Towards overcoming this divide, there are some approaches that attempt to rematerialize the technology within the interactions. One particular methodology emphasizes the physical material parts at work within all methods of digital interaction: the button, touchscreen or phone, even the floor you position yourself on [21]. Rather than focusing on separation by categorization between AR/VR and tangible user interfaces, Hornecker and Buur [21] compared media while emphasizing that there is a tangible element to all of them. In their study, they use a framework that identifies digital interactions as an act that happens in physical space with material forms. Building upon Dourish's ideas of embodied interaction within HCI, they suggest activation of this tangible element can lead to rich bodily movement [13].

It has been noted that a primary disadvantage of smartphone use in AR is users having to hold the device up for prolonged periods of time, leading to fatigue; subsequently, developers must consider this in the design of their applications [18]. Even through this incidental effect of prolonged interaction with a mobile device, the importance of physical elements within the AR user experience is noticeable. In their study on embodied interactions for promoting cognitive processes, Li and Duh [30] cite the potential of mobile AR to influence how users position and move themselves. Adhering to theories of powerful routes to understanding as "grounded in bodily interaction in real space and time," they note potential in designing with and for physiological qualities and space within AR.

Spatial Interaction and Embodied Facilitation are identified as two major themes at play within digitally mediated interactions. To design an application with spatial interaction in mind, Tromp [50] suggests considering the function of the real, virtual and augmented space and the objects in it, as the user infers meaning from the objects in the spatial configuration and the enabled interactions. Tromp distinguishes three layers of spatial interaction that need to be considered in the interaction design: architectural, semantic and social (Figure 7.7 [50]), which change form, location and meaning over time, based on the embodied interactions of the users in the real and augmented space.

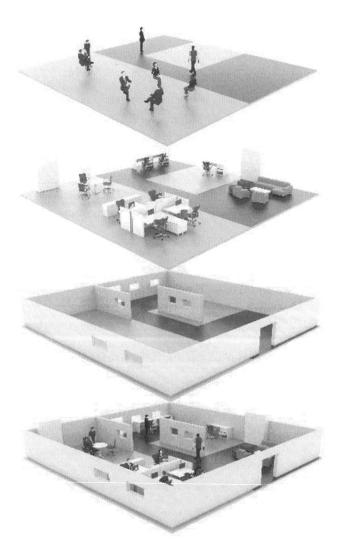

Figure 7.7 Virtual and augmented design space consists of layers of meaning: architectural, semantic, social, and temporal.

Additionally, Tromp [49] shows the human-computer interaction feedback loop; namely, the scripts that get triggered once the user interacts with the virtual or augmented representations, and the importance of these preprogrammed responses from the computer resulting from user actions. This continuous feedback loop is essential for the temporary embodiment process, where the user becomes one with the augmented reality tool and the real-world objects that are being augmented, and exhibits the resulting successful task flow in an augmented reality user interaction (Figure 7.8).

Certainly, the definitions of "presence" proposed by Floridi [15] and Benyon [5] fit more comfortably within AR's current uses. The sense of presence develops via interaction, during consistent, timely and believable feedback from the interactions in VR or AR and illustrates the manner in which VR interaction differs from VR interaction (see Figure 7.8. While the user in VR interacts directly with the objects in the Virtual World, the AR user has to locate the trigger object in the Augmented World to perceive the overlay, the augmented display that shows the triggered augmentation on top of the real object(s) or spaces.

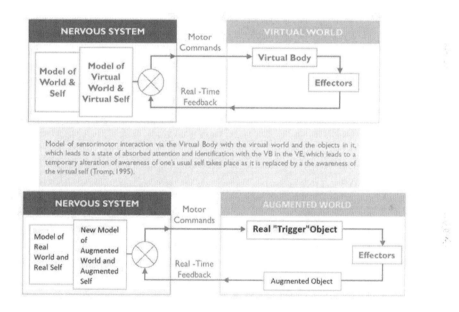

Figure 7.8   A user constructs a sense of presence from successful interaction with the virtual or augmented world (adapted from Tromp [49]).

The complexity of the AR design challenges is further illustrated when we consider the mapping between the real world and the augmented or virtual (twin) world. In an augmented reality use case and a virtual (twin) reality use case, the user decides the order of their actions until they engage with an interactive sequence relating to a virtual or augmented object, person or space. The user interactions with VR and AR systems are not as linear and therefore not as predictable and harder to design for as the user interactions with a 2D application. In VR and AR, users can roam the space freely and execute tasks in their own sequence and may not find all interactive elements if they are not obvious. It can be helpful to consider the design space for VR and AR interaction. When designing user interactions and applications, the design space can be deconstructed to identify the generic task flow within the free-flowing user task interactions of VR and AR interactions. Embodied interactions take place in relation to the objects, spaces and in multi-user applications, and in relation to the other participants, as shown in Figure 7.9. User interactions take place on a:

- Social level: design challenges to facilitate multi-user collaborations,

- Semantic level: design challenges to facilitate object interactions,

- Architectural level: design challenges to facilitate navigation through space,

- Temporal aspect: design challenges to facilitate interaction with people, objects and spaces which move or change over time.

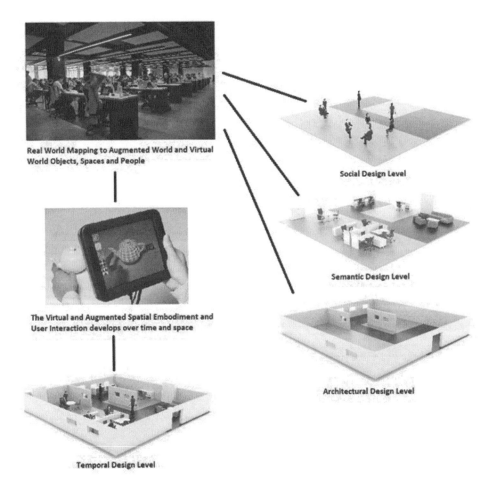

Figure 7.9 Virtual and augmented design space consists of layers of possible interactive functionality and optimization of the user interactions in terms of task-flow and interaction-feedback loop mappings between real world, virtual world and augmented world/object at the architectural, semantic, social, and temporal level [50].

Descriptions of layering digital and real, can be seen in various forms from Layar [27] or Yelp's Monicle [56].

Hornecker and Buur suggest considering both the user's ability to move objects and themselves as input. To design for Embodied Facilitation, we must use the construction of both the digital and physical space to influence, promote or obstruct certain actions. These "embodied constraints" or facilitators within the design are so central to the experience, that for any interaction to feel effective for the user, it is recommended they be considered within the design process [21]. With such uses of AR, Liao and Humphreys [31] identify potential for new forms of embodiment, where media space and bodies coexist.

Using AR to accommodate bodily movements in order to facilitate cognitive processes was an explicit aim of the TombSeer project [37]. An application at the Royal Ontario Museum, it utilized a Meta holographic headset within an empty replica of an Egyptian tomb, and focused on engaging two senses – sight and gesture – to recreate artefacts that were physically unavailable (Figure 7.10 [37]).

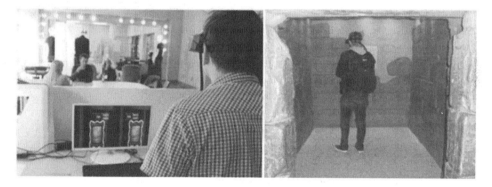

Figure 7.10   AR within the TombSeer project: testing functionality of gaze selection with the Meta headset (left), and *in-situ* testing within the replica of an Egyptian tomb (right).

As outlined within its design, this development sought to avoid the stand and read paradigms typically presented in museums [37] and, as such, movement was facilitated largely through gestural activity similar to that of the HoloMuse application discussed above. Users were able to pick up and move digital artefacts, interrogating them, placing them in assigned areas in order to trigger events, and point at paintings on the walls to trigger animated visualizations, or make hieroglyphs appear larger within the field of view.

In AR, two of the most common bodily interactions are navigation and manipulation of digital objects [30]. Whereas the link between navigation and spatial awareness may seem more direct, the manipulation of digital objects seems less so. However, Li and Duh [30] note within gestural input an ability to handle spatial information, and, in this, an intuitiveness of interaction that strengthens the ties between physically occupied space and the digital one.

Presented as a critique of mobile guides that lead to isolate and disconnect the visitor from the physical space and the objects, Koterwas, *et al.* [25] present different ways of providing additional content to exhibition displays. The Pocket Curator and re-sOUnd applications are examples of projects built to foster interactions relating to being physically present in a space, and work to create embodied experiences towards the enhanced understanding of digital objects on display [25]. The Pocket Curator presents seven objects within a museum, each augmented with at least two audio clips and one animation or interactive experience. One of these interactive experiences concerns a Victorian box filled with "inscrutable antique electronics" [25]. The user lines up an outline of the box through the camera view, the outline of the physical box itself acting as a feature marker to instantiate the application. This reveals a button that once pressed makes a bell resonate at the other end of the gallery display, seeking to recreate the object's use in an early demonstration of wireless technology. Another interaction takes the user step by step through using a virtual sextant to configure coordinates: lining up the handheld device with the horizon, finding the sun relative to its position within the location that day, and converting to latitude data. These experiences "cause the environment itself to react" [25], and have the effect of influencing the user to consider themselves in the space, contributing to a feeling of presence in the experience and at the site.

The re-sOUnd application presents digital versions of historic musical instruments, and allows users to interact with them through their smartphone. Using gestures like blowing into the device microphone or drawing a finger across the displayed bows, the user elicits recordings of the instruments [25]. The popularity of these interactions in comparison to the audio clips and animations that were also offered within the museum display, speaks to the ability of these experiential and embodied forms to successfully engage audiences.

7.6   User Experience and Presence in AR

Presence is often closely related to ideas of physical immersion and psychological engagement in a mediated digital environment [29, 33]. There have been several attempts to measure presence, although most have focused on media experiences surrounding virtual reality [29]. The ITC-Sense of Presence Inventory (ITC-SOPI) is an attempt to build a baseline to quantify presence using a questionnaire across various media forms. This broad scope of media experiences uses an inclusive framework that we see echoed in further studies in the field [21], and works more effectively to illuminate the variety of uses advancing these technologies.

However, despite the questionnaire's broad scope, it is brief in its inclusion of interactive forms and sadly does not include AR. Yet, in fostering a sense of aura and presence in an interaction, Brown [7] sees great capabilities within the specific technology. Interestingly the traits Brown sees as giving AR the qualities to imbue presence within an interaction are the loss of keyboard and mouse, which allow it into "the spatial world," acting more readily within our physical realm of experience [7]. This tie between notions of space and the experiential power of a medium is something that has been reflected in the work of Lessiter *et al.* [29].

Before looking at how AR may imbue presence through an interaction, a closer look at how we define this term is necessary. In the ITC-SOPI definitions are based on early discussions of presence that surround the transparency of the medium within the user experience, an inability to detect the mediation that feeds the illusion of being elsewhere [29]. Here the relevance of how presence plays into a user's experience is in understanding "that an illusion is generated whereby a user senses that she/he is located somewhere other than her/his physical environment" [29]. How do these measurements of presence, concerned with achieving a sense of being physically located in another place [14] and notions of "being there" [3], fit in the context of AR? Particularly as previously identified with adding to the physical environment rather than eclipsing it?

Floridi [15] contests early definitions of presence tied up in the failure to notice mediation. He argues instead for extended ideas of space and interactions beyond it. Benyon [5] also acknowledges the complicated nature of applying these definitions to contemporary spaces in which the virtual inhabits the real. Indeed, Benyon [5] refers to the spaces created by AR as hybrid, "blended" spaces, and identifies potential for developing experiences that make people feel present in such augmented environments.

Certainly, the definitions of presence proposed by Floridi [15] and Benyon [5] fit more comfortably within AR's current uses. Descriptions of layering digital and real, can be seen in various forms; from Layar [27] or Yelp's Monocle [56], with users augmenting public places with their digital content, to many conventional museum applications, providing additional curatorial content to physical artefacts. One particular study concentrating solely on the way a virtual avatar moves in relation to the physical layout of the room AR is deployed in, finds how it can drastically alter user experience [24]. In these uses we see complicated notions of space evolving from embedding the digital within the physical.

Taking this further, some cite AR explicitly as a tool for consuming place and negotiating encounters of space [30], stating that it offers new ways of moving through and enacting place [16]. The significance of these uses is a sense of presence with an emphasis tied not to being elsewhere, but to feeling physically present here [5]. This tension between physical space and the virtual, creates interesting issues from a design perspective [30].

Within the re-sOUnd application previously mentioned, it was found that users felt that the provided interactions contributed to an enhanced engagement within the exhibition space, promoting a real sense of the displayed objects [25]. This echoes findings about presence within mediated interactions, that suggest it is often tied to a user's ability to interact with the virtual, creating a strong perception-action link between the user and the display [29]. In contrast to the way TombSeer's gestures created a sense of physical interaction with the digital augmented environment [37], those of the Pocket Curator create a sense of feedback from the digital space within the physical space. This suggests that spatially minded interactions foster a sense of presence in an embodied space in AR, whether virtual or real.

While we may discuss what it means theoretically for AR to facilitate these contemporary modes of experience between virtual and digital spaces, the technical innovations necessary to enable such interaction, as we have seen earlier, require overcoming difficult problems. Only once these are developed enough to perform effectively and efficiently, can we create a rewarding and engaging user experience.

7.7 Conclusion

This chapter has sought to provide a high-level overview of the technical and interactive aspects of AR which relate to heritage sites, both indoor and outdoor, through the recent literature of the sector. There is an interdependent relationship between the development of hardware and software in AR and the resultant capacity for complex and rewarding user experiences. As the technology develops to make the practical interactions increasingly streamlined, accurate and dynamic, particularly in more challenging locales, the richness of interactions asked of the medium increases. This is particularly so in terms of expanding the scope of AR beyond the visual, towards more experiential and embodied encounters with cultural heritage. As the use of digital technologies increasingly occurs within cultural heritage sites, so does the virtual space of such media. Yet there is still an apparent absence of design guidance on how to craft these new "multiple reality environments" [5]. We must evolve discussions of presence within digital interactions solely from ideas of being in another place; acknowledging that it is also now possible to achieve engaging AR experiences through fostering the presence of the user within the interaction and the site itself.

This overview has highlighted that AR holds rich possibilities for enhancing exhibition spaces, offering opportunities for embodied experiences and intuitive interaction with exhibited artefacts and their digitally associated models. However, as the demand for experiential and performative modes of interpretation coupled with the proliferation and availability of AR grows, there still appears to be a gap between the two. Applications for heritage sites predominantly continue to be an extension of the labeling system that contextualizes artefacts and paintings. This may be due in part to a serious lack of research into user experience and feedback [11, 12, 44]. With more focus on user experience, testing *in situ* and iterative development with user feedback, the quality of AR applications would be expected to improve faster. Several of the examples discussed in this chapter have attempted this throughout the design process, and the quality of the experiences they foster consequently seem to be improved. The examples given are evidence of what can be achieved: performative interactions that lead to understanding through experience. There is still a great deal of research required to ensure that the de facto standard of AR experiences in this sector deliver personalized and meaningful interactions, and that it does not simply become a flash-in-the-pan novelty [18, 35].

REFERENCES

1. Azuma, R. (1997). A survey of augmented reality. *Presence: Teleoperators and Virtual Environments*, 6(4), 355-385. Doi:10.1162/pres.1997.6.4.355

2. Bach, B., Sicat, R., Beyer, J., Cordeil, M., Pfister, H., (2018). The hologram in my hand: How effective is interactive exploration of 3D visualizations in immersive tangible augmented reality? *IEEE Transactions on Visualization and Computer Graphics*, 24(1). doi: 10.1109/TVCG.2017.2745941

3. Barfield, W., Zeltzer, D., Sheridan, T. B., & Slater, M. (1995). Presence and performance within virtual environments. In W. Barfield & Furness, T. A. (Eds.). *Virtual Environments and Advanced Interface Design* (pp. 473-541) Oxford:Oxford University Press.

4. Barreira, J. Bessa, M., Barbosa, L. and Magalhaes, L. (2018). A context-aware method for authentically simulating outdoors shadows for mobile augmented reality, *IEEE Transactions on Visualization and Computer Graphics*, 24(3), pp. 1223-1231. doi: 10.1109/TVCG.2017.2676777.

5. Benyon, D. (2012). Presence in blended spaces. *Interacting with Computers*, 24(4), pp. 219-226. https://doi.org/10.1016/j.intcom.2012.04.005

6. Blanco-Pons, S., Carrin-Ruiz, B. and Lerma, J. L. (2018). Augmented reality application assessment for disseminating rock art, *Multimedia Tools and Applications*. doi: 10.1007/s11042-018-6609-x.

7. Brown, D. (2007). Te Ahua Hiko: Digital Cultural Heritage and indigenous Objects, People and Environments. In Cameron, F., and Kenderline, S. (Eds.), *Theorizing Digital Cultural Heritage*. MIT Press Scholarship Online. https://doi.org/10.7551/mitpress/9780262033534.001.0001

8. Chatzopoulos, D., Bermejo, C., Huang, Z., & Hui, P. (2017). Mobile augmented reality survey: From where we are to where we go, *IEEE Access*, 5, pp.6917-6950. doi: 10.1109/ACCESS.2017.2698164.

9. Chen, H. Lee, A.S, Swift, M, Tang, J.C. (2015). 3D collaboration method over HoloLensTM and SkypeTM end points, In *Proceedings of the 3rd International Workshop on Immersive Media Experiences*. pp. 27-30. doi: 10.1145/2814347.2814350.

10. Damala, A., Cubaud, P., Bationo, A., Houlier, P., & Marchal, I. (2008). Bridging the gap between the digital and the physical: Design and evaluation of a mobile augmented reality guide for the museum visit. *Proceedings of the 3rd International Conference on Digital Interactive Media in Entertainment and Arts - DIMEA'08*, 120. https://doi.org/10.1145/1413634.1413660

11. Dey, A., Billinghurst, M., Lindeman, R. W., & Swan, J. E. (2018). A systematic review of 10 years of augmented reality usability studies: 2005 to 2014. *Frontiers in Robotics and AI*, 5(April). https://doi.org/10.3389/frobt.2018.00037

12. Ding, M. (2017). Augmented reality in museums. *Arts Management and Technology Laboratory, Carnegie Mellon University*. online Available at https://amtlab.org/blog/2017/5/augmented- reality-in-museums. Accessed on [15th March 2019]

13. Dourish, P. (2001). *Where the Action Is: Foundations of Embodied Interaction*, Massachusetts: MIT Press.

14. Draper, J. V., Kaber, D. B., & Usher, J. M. (1998). Telepresence. *Human Factors*, 40, pp.354-375. https://doi.org/10.1518/001872098779591386.

15. Floridi, L. (2005). The philosophy of presence: From epistemic failure to successful observation. *Presence: Teleoperators and Virtual Environments*, 14(6), pp. 656-667. https://doi.org/10.1162/105474605775196553

16. Graham, M., Zook, M. and Boulton, A. (2012). Augmented reality in urban places: Contested content and the duplicity of code, *Transactions of the Institute of British Geographers*, 38(3), pp. 464-479. doi: 10.1111/j.1475-5661.2012.00539.x.

17. Haesner, M., Wolf, S., Steiner, A., Steinhagen-Thiessen, E. (2018). Touch interaction with Google Glass -Is it suitable for older adults?, *International Journal of Human Computer Studies*. Elsevier Ltd, 110(October 2016), pp. 12-20. doi: 10.1016/j.ijhcs.2017.09.00

18. Han, D. I., tom Dieck, M. C. and Jung, T. (2018). User experience model for augmented reality applications in urban heritage tourism. *Journal of Heritage Tourism*. Taylor & Francis, 13(1), pp. 46-61. doi: 10.1080/1743873X.2016.1251931.

19. Han, D., Jung, T. and Gibson, A. (2014). Dublin AR: Implementing augmented reality (AR) in tourism, in *Information and Communication Technologies in Tourism*. New York: Springer International Publishing, pp. 275-277. doi: 10.1016/s0160-7383(01)00025-1

20. He, Z., Sui, X., Jin, G., Cao, L. (2018). Progress in virtual reality and augmented reality based on holographic display, *Applied Optics*, 58(5), p. A74. doi: 10.1364/ao.58.000a74

21. Hornecker, E. and Buur, J. (2006). Getting a grip on tangible interaction: a framework on physical space and social interaction. In *Proceedings of the SIGCHI Conference on Human Factors in Computing Systems (CHI '06)*, Cutrell, R. J., and Olson, G (Eds.). New York, USA: ACM pp. 437-446. DOI: http://dx.doi.org/10.1145/1124772.1124838

22. Jung, T. H., Lee, H., Ching N., & tom Dieck, M. C. (2018). Cross-cultural differences in adopting mobile augmented reality, *Cultural Heritage Tourism Sites*, 30(3), pp. 1621-1645.

23. Kim, H., Matuszka, T., Kim, J.I., Kim, J., & Woo, W. (2017a). Ontology-based mobile augmented reality in cultural heritage sites: information modeling and user study. *Multimedia Tools and Applications*, 76(24), pp. 26001-26029. doi: 10.1007/s11042-017-4868-6

24. Kim, K., Maloney, D., Bruder, G., Bailenson, J. N. and Welch, G. F. (2017b). The effects of virtual human's spatial and behavioral coherence with physical objects on social presence in AR. *Computer Animation and Virtual Worlds*, 28(3-4), pp. 1-9. https://doi.org/10.1002/cav.1771

25. Koterwas, T., Suess, J., Billings, S., Haith, A., and Lamb, A. (2018). *Augmenting reality in museums with interactive virtual models*. In Jung, T. and Tom Dieck, M. C. (Eds.), 2018. *Augmented and Virtual Reality*. Springer. pp. 365-370. 10.1007/978-3-319-64027-3_25.

26. Kounavis, C. D., Kasimati, A. E. and Zamani, E. D. (2012). Enhancing the tourism experience through mobile augmented reality: Challenges and prospects, *International Journal of Engineering Business Management*, 4(1), pp. 1-6. doi: 10.5772/51644.

27. Layar, (2009). *Layar, version 8.5.3, mobile app*. Available at https://www.layar.com/mobile-download/. Accessed on: 15th March 2019.

28. Lavalle, S. M. (2017) *Virtual Reality*. Cambridge University Press. Available at: http://vr.cs.uiuc.edu/.

29. Lessiter, J, Freeman, J., Keogh, E, and Davidoff, J. (2001). A cross-media presence questionnaire: The ITC-sense of presence inventory, In *Presence: Teleoperators and Virtual Environments*, 10(3), pp. 282-297.

30. Li, N., and Duh, H. B. (2013). Cognitive issues in mobile augmented reality: An embodied perspective. In: Huang, W., Alem, L. and Livingston, M. (Eds.), *Human Factors in Augmented Reality Environments*. Springer. pp.109-135.

31. Liao, T. and Humphreys, L. (2015). Layar-ed places : Using mobile augmented reality to tactically reengage , reproduce , and reappropriate public space. *New Media and Society*, 17(9), 1418-1435. https://doi.org/10.1177/1461444814527734.

32. Marques, L. F., Tenedorio, J. A., Burns, M., Romao, T., Marques, J., & Pires, A. (2017). Cultural heritage 3D modelling and visualisation within an augmented reality environment, based on geographic information technologies and mobile platforms. *Architecture, City and Environment*, 11(33), pp. 117-136. doi: 10.5821/ace.11.33.4686.

33. McMahan, A. (2003). Immersion, engagement, and presence: A method for analyzing 3-D video games. In: Wolf, M. and Perron, B., (Eds.), 2003. *The Video Game Theory Reader*. New York, US: Routledge, Taylor & Francis Group. pp. 67-86.

34. Messham-Muir, K. (2005). Affect, interpretation and technology. *Open Museums Journal*, 7(November 2005), 1-13.

35. Olsson, T., Krkkinen, T., Lagerstam, E., Vent-Olkkonen, L. (2012). User evaluation of mobile augmented reality scenarios. *Journal of Ambient Intelligence and Smart Environments*, 4(1), pp. 29-47. doi: 10.3233/AIS-2011-0127.

36. Panou, C., Ragia, L., Dimelli, D., Mania, K. (2018). An architecture for mobile outdoors augmented reality for cultural heritage. *ISPRS International Journal of Geo-Information*, 7(12), p. 463. doi: 10.3390/ijgi7120463.

37. Pedersen, I. and Mirza-Babaei, P. (2017). More than meets the eye: The benefits of augmented reality and holographic displays for digital cultural heritage. *Journal on Computing and Cultural Heritage*, 14(3), pp. 145-148. doi: 10.1002/j.1467- 8438.1993.tb00956.x.

38. Pollalis, C., Fahnbulleh, W., Tynes, J., & Shaer, O. (2017). HoloMuse: Enhancing engagement with archaeological artifacts through gesture-based interaction with holograms., *Proceedings of the Tenth International Conference on Tangible, Embedded, and Embodied Interaction (TEI'17)*, pp. 565-570. DOI: 10.1145/3024969.3025094.

39. PTC Inc., (2015). *Vuforia, version 8.0.10*. Available at https://www.vuforia.com/ Accessed on 17th March 2019.

40. Rao, J., Qiao, Y., Ren, F., Wang, J., & Du, Q. (2017). A mobile outdoor augmented reality method combining deep learning object detection and spatial relationships for geovisualization. *Sensors*, 17(9), 1951. DOI: 10.3390/s17091951.

41. Rauschnabel, P. A A. (2018). Virtually enhancing the real world with holograms: An exploration of expected gratifications of using augmented reality smart glasses. *Psychology & Marketing*, 35(8), 557-572. DOI: 10.1002/mar.21106.

42. Regaldo, A. (2018). *Magic Leap One*, MIT Technology Review, 121(2).

43. Rekimoto, J. and Ayatsuka, Y. (2000) CyberCode: Designing augmented reality environments with visual tags. *Proceedings of DARE 2000 on Designing Augmented Reality Environments*, 303(9), 1-10. https://doi.org/10.1145/354666.354667

44. De, S. M., & Churchill, E. F. (2013). Mobile augmented reality: A design perspective. In Huang, W., Alem, L. & Livingston, M. (Eds.). *Human Factors in Augmented Reality Environments*. Springer. pp. 139-164. DOI: 10.1007/978-1-4614-4205-9.

45. Seo, S., Kang, D., & Park, S. (2018). Real-time adaptable and coherent rendering for outdoor augmented reality. *EURASIP Journal on Image and Video Processing*, 2018(1), pp. 1-8. DOI: 10.1186/s13640-018-0357-8.

46. Shi, Z., Wang, H., Wei, W., Zheng, X., Zhao, M., Zhao, J., & Wang, Y. (2016). Novel individual location recommendation with mobile based on augmented reality. *International Journal of Distributed Sensor Networks*, 12(7). DOI: 10.1177/1550147716657266.

47. tom Dieck, M. C., & Jung, T. (2018). A theoretical model of mobile augmented reality acceptance in urban heritage tourism. *Current Issues in Tourism*, 21(2), 154-174. DOI: 10.1080/13683500.2015.1070801.

48. tom Dieck, M. C., & Jung, T. H. (2017). Value of augmented reality at cultural heritage sites: A stakeholder approach. *Journal of Destination Marketing & Management*, 6(2), 110-117. DOI: 10.1016/j.jdmm.2017.03.002.

49. Tromp, J.G., (1995). Presence, telepresence and immersion: The cognitive factors of embodiment and interaction in virtual environments, In *Proceedings of the FIVE'95 (Framework for Immersive Virtual Environments) Conference*, Queen Mary and Westfield College, pp.39-51

50. Tromp, J.G., (2001) *Systematic Usability Design and Evaluation for Collaborative Virtual Environments*. Thesis, Doctor in Philosophy. University of Nottingham.

51. Tscheu, F., & Buhalis, D. (2016). Augmented reality at cultural heritage sites. In Inversini, A. & Schegg, R. (Eds.), *Information and Communication Technologies in Tourism 2016*, (pp. 607-619). Springer, Cham. DOI: 10.1016/s0160-7383(01)00025-1.

52. Unity Technologies (2005). *Unity, version 2018.3.5*. Available at https://unity3d.com/unity/whats-new/2018.3.5 Accessed on: 17th March 2019.

53. Vlahakis, V., Karigiannis, J., Tsotros, M., Gounaris, M., Almeida, L., Stricker, D., ... & Ioannidis, N. (2001). Archeoguide: first results of an augmented reality, mobile computing system in cultural heritage sites. In *Proceedings of the 2001 Conference on Virtual Reality, Archeology, and Cultural Heritage*, pp. 131-140. DOI: 10.1145/584993.585015.

54. Wiggers, Kyle, (2018). ARCore 1.6 improves ambient lighting, polishes screen capture and recording, *VentureBeat*, URL; https://venturebeat.com/2018/12/07/arcore-1-6-improvesambient- lighting- polishes-screen-capture-and-recording/ accessed, June, 2019

55. Witcomb, A. (2007). The materiality of virtual technologies: A new approach to thinking about the impact of multimedia in museums. In Cameron, F. & Kenderline, S. (Eds.), *Theorizing Digital Cultural Heritage: A Critical Discourse*, pp. 35-48. MIT Press.

56. Yelp (2009). *Yelp Monocle, mobile app*. Available at https://play.google.com/store/apps/details?id=com.yelp.android&hl=en_GB. Accessed on: 15th March 2019.

57. Boboc, R. G., Duguleana, M., Voinea, G. D., Postelnicu, C. C., Popovici, D. M., & Carrozzino, M. (2019). Mobile augmented reality for cultural heritage: Following the footsteps of ovid among different locations in Europe. *Sustainability*, 11(4), 1167. DOI: 10.3390/su11041167.

58. Chakraborty, A., & Nanni, F. (2017). The changing digital faces of science museums: A diachronic analysis of museum websites. *Digital formations*, 112, 157-172.

59. Rohmer, K., Jendersie, J., & Grosch, T. (2017). Natural environment illumination: Coherent interactive augmented reality for mobile and non-mobile devices. *IEEE Transactions on Visualization and Computer Graphics*, 23(11), 2474-2484.

CHAPTER 8

TELECI ARCHITECTURE FOR MACHINE LEARNING ALGORITHMS INTEGRATION IN AN EXISTING LMS

V. Zagorskis, A. Gorbunovs, A. Kapenieks

Distance Education Study Center, Riga Technical University, Latvia
Corresponding authors: viktors.zagorskis@rtu.lv; aleksandrs.gorbunovs_1@rtu.lv; atis.kapenieks@rtu.lv

Abstract

Nowadays, e-learning service systems generate huge amounts of data, including both information directly about student behavioral and activity data within the information system during the learning process. System users' activity and behavioral patterns during the learning process have a crucial role in determining learners' needs and offer them the most suitable, appropriate learning content and personalized learning path, thus contributing to learning efficiency. Moreover, adaptive learning management systems ought to ensure an availability to identify possible gaps in the knowledge space of learners. In this chapter authors propose a new adaptive e-learning service system architecture, implementing machine learning technique and utilizing algorithms for predictive modeling, simulation, and forecasting, which allows the learning management system to learn from user activity data and offer them the unique personalized learning.

Keywords: Artificial intelligence, boredom, learning experience, learning management system, machine learning, predictive modeling

8.1   Introduction

The motivation for new IT projects in the domain of Learning Management Systems (LMS) often is, of course, to increase learning process efficiency under the pressure of instant updates of content and technology [5]. But this segment also includes IT-based monitoring and evaluation of a series of actions based on learning process quality indicators, for example, in the context of receiving assignments or processing learners complaints.

Obviously, technology-based formats dominate in education [6]. For instance, print texts are dominant in many educational institutions starting from early learning [12, 13], and students use keyboards entering texts. At the same time, we understand that the need to enter formulas or draw figures on surfaces of mobile devices manually is a more accurate and authentic way to reflect learners' thoughts.

In the education market, the reason for improving LMS with clear documentation is, for example, due to the emergence of new multimedia standards with new hardware devices and software interfaces. Clear documentation of processes in LMS usually occurs for two reasons. Firstly, so that the employees involved in the education process can orientate themselves in their daily work. Here, we consider employees learning process proposers, content proposers, content developers, designers, and trainers. Secondly, because the documentation is used in the context of legal requirements or for obtaining specific standards-based certification.

We imply that ISO 9001 is the standard in education and training [14], whereas, ISO 29990 defines how non-formal education should be organized. To be more specific, quality of education management is expressed in concepts, frameworks and standards addressing the following target groups:

1. Teachers / trainers / tutors

2. Directors / headmasters

3. Quality managers / inspectors / evaluators

4. Administrative staff

In general, standards define requirements for skills and competencies necessary to manage the staff of educational and training organizations in order to develop and maintain their own quality management system. Also, standards are crucial to identify organizational pitfalls in existing, newly created or updated LMS. Learning process administration is not only crucial for following guidelines correctly, but also for approaching students in the right and effective way in order to preserve their personality.

Our aim was to invent yet another approach to adapt LMS based on the virtual student (VS) concept. Here, Virtual Student is an algorithmic software or Intelligent Agent helping to evaluate quantitative and qualitative performance:

1. of existing LMS after adaptation to VS requirements,

2. in new LMS designs, starting with revealing of concepts and architecture.

Overall, there exists more than one intelligent agents classification scheme proposed by Russel and Norvig [16] and Weiss [20]. We followed the Russel and Norvig classification involving five agent groups: simple reflex agents, model-based reflex agents, goal-based agents, utility-based agents, and learning agents. In our use case, the most appropriate agent to start with is a learning agent. Also, the learning agent can act either as a single instance or in groups known as: multi-agent systems. In the current work, we imply a single instance model.

In this document, we introduce the TELECI architecture elements implementing primary real student (RS) interaction with updated LMS. Also, we have expectations that Virtual Student activity has to be similar to RS behavior. Therefore, VS agent specifications should be based on the real student and LMS interactions model.

We propose guidelines for TELECI system implementation, two well-known approaches used to create software-based IT project architecture: a) a top-down approach, and b) a bottom-up approach. Architecture, in praxis, is a complex and multifaceted notion; therefore, we create multiple views, presenting architecture from different perspectives and with varying accuracy [7].

Also, we distinguish the information such as a) standards and b) explanation of taken decisions that is hard to present in a picture. In that case, we use other artifacts, e.g., text, math or code snippets describing the substance of the system or its parts. We follow the Business Process Management and Notation standard BPMN 2.0 [15].

The following sections introduce TELECI architecture elements based on real student initial steps in thier learning path, reveal a use case implementing machine learning technique, and discuss possible data acquisition and measurement issues identifying learner activity.

8.2   TELECI Architecture

In this section, we propose the architecture of LMS system capable of implementing a virtual student's model beside a real student's learning path to clarify TELECI upgrades for existing LMS. Firstly, we introduce TELECI interface to a real LMS. Next, we describe a real student (RS) learning experience in TELECI upgraded LMS. Finally, we clarify some specific processual interactions with an upgraded LMS-based TELECI approach.

8.2.1   TELECI Interface to a Real LMS

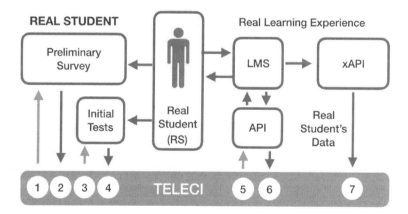

Figure 8.1   A real student learning experience operating in LMS after upgrades based on the TELECI approach.

In Figure 8.1 the TELECI constituent for an upgradable LMS is shown. In the proposed architecture, the TELECI component has seven interfaces to communicate with LMS; each interface has a unique sequence number, which in the current presentation is assumed to be uni-directional. In fact, every LMS has an application programming interface (API) which is more or less complete for extensions programming and access to LMS backend layer. TELECI architecture proposal has seven specified interfaces:

1. IF1 - TELECI output to Preliminary Survey Component (ToPSC)

2. IF2 - TELECI input from Preliminary Survey Component (TiPSC)

3. IF3 - TELECI output to Initial Test Component (ToITC)

4. IF4 - TELECI input from Initial Test Component (ToITC)

5. IF5 - TELECI output to Application Programming Interface (ToAPI)

6. IF6 - TELECI input from Application Programming Interface (TiAPI)

7. IF7 - TELECI input from Experience API (TixAPI)

Since TELECI requirements determine LMS upgrades, in the following text, we use TELECI notation considering LMS as a part of the TELECI system, if not otherwise specified.

8.2.2   First RS Steps in the TELECI System

In this section, we describe the first steps for a real student in the TELECI system (LMS after TELECI initiated upgrades). As the "first steps" we denote activities just before the start of the learning course.

To clarify a real student behavior, we refer to Figure 8.1. Architectural upgrades for existing LMS include two new essential system components: a) Preliminary Survey component and b) Initial Tests component.

The TELECI system can have its own front interface to interact with RS, implementing all necessary Preliminary Survey and Initial Tests functionalities. This subject relates to the TELECI system component design and implementation phase. For additional information on the subject, follow the proposed scheme in Figure 8.1.

Interaction among system components in Figure 8.1 is shown using arrows. Initially, TELECI system injects some settings utilizing interfaces IF1, IF3, and IF5. Settings include initial questions for the Preliminary Survey (interface IF1) along with LMS control information (interface IF5). Also, default settings for the Initial Knowledge Test (interface IF3) can be uploaded.

In the TELECI approach, before a student takes the course or its parts, learning content has to be adapted to the student's skills and learning style. Figure 8.2 depicts the diagram of Real Student interaction with LMS operating under control of the TELECI system.

Here, a preliminary survey is the essential process to identify most probabilistic learning style for a student taking this survey. In general, the learner's psychological characteristics can be identified using various techniques and methods [16].

Principally, even handwriting analysis can be used for detection of personality traits [3]. Therefore, various machine learning techniques (supervised and unsupervised) can be adapted to identify and classify learners in distinct groups. Moreover, cycle-wise operations help to build models predicting the learner's behavior. Some research aimed to find partner matching [9, 10].

In TELECI architecture, after identification of a learning style by analyzing Preliminary Survey results, specific algorithms build and deploy individually adapted Knowledge Tests.

As depicted in Figure 8.2, Knowledge Test results are reported to learners, to staff, and used to build ADAPTED course content.

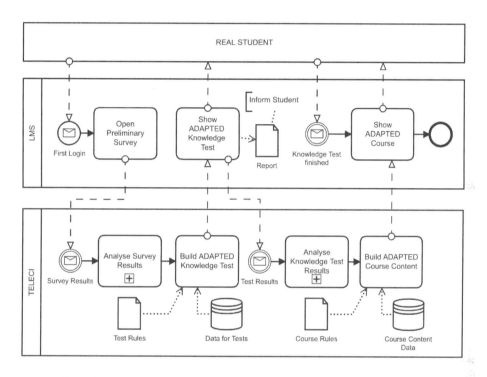

Figure 8.2   Knowledge tests and course content adaptation process diagram.

8.2.3   Real Student Data for VS Model

Data collected from the first real students' experience can be used to determine the computerized virtual student model. The probabilistic modeling approach is commonly practiced and widely used in various machine learning techniques [2, 3].

Figure 8.3 depicts the process of Preliminary Survey analysis in more detail. It is intuitively clear that data gathered from RS interaction with LMS include different reactions on modalities of data – textual information, images, audio, and video. Students' attention, perception, and response differ if LMS proposed content has multimodal properties. When building the VS model, it is essential that the model contains identifiable variables corresponding to the data observed from real students.

Since very distinct statistical properties characterize each modality, the patterns, combined in a joint representation, capture the real-world concept that corresponds to the data. In the TELECI system, each modality of data obtained from a Preliminary Survey is characterized by having distinct statistical properties that help to create a probabilistic model for identification of the personality traits of learners.

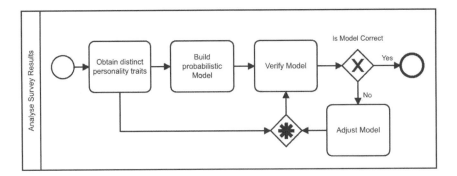

Figure 8.3   Detailed process of Preliminary Survey analysis.

8.2.4   TELECI Interface to VS Subsystem

In the previous Section 8.2.1, we discussed a plan for real student interaction with LMS after upgrades proposed by TELECI architecture. The interfaces (IF1 to IF8) were defined. Here, we present another set of seven specific interfaces necessary for virtual student functionality:

1. IF8 - TELECI output to Cognitive Energy-Based VS Model Component (ToCEM-VS),

2. IF9 - TELECI input from Cognitive Energy-Based VS Model Component (TiCEM-VS),

3. IF10 - TELECI output to Default VS Properties Component (ToDP-VS),

4. IF11 - TELECI input from Default VS Properties Component (TiDP-VS),

5. IF12 - TELECI output to LMS Plugin (ToLMSP-VS),

6. IF13 - TELECI input from LMS Plugin (TiLMSP-VS),

7. IF14 - TELECI input from Virtual Student Experience API (TixAPI-VS)

All the interfaces (IF9 to IF14) organized as internal connections among TELECI components and presented only for demonstration of consistency and similarity of learning paths for RS and VS.

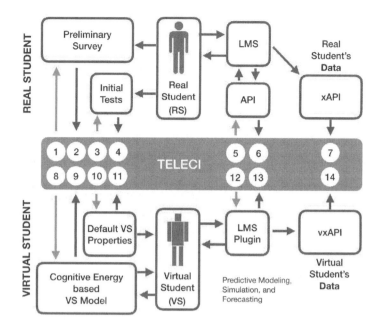

Figure 8.4   TELECI Interface to VS subsystem.

Virtual student operates on the same foundation of a previously proposed concept based on the model of cognitive energy flow [4]. The model involves tokens representing discrete cognitive energy portions needed for focusing attention on the learning object (LO).

Figure 8.5 illustrates that the learning energy network model for VS operation is an isolated learning network. The network has boundaries and rules for virtual student operations for sensing, reasoning (perception, cognition) and acting. Also, the learning network binds energy consumption or production. In the model are specified three top-class energy-related objects for the ecosystem and their properties:

(1) System Energy Depot - E^D

(2) Virtual Student's Energy Buffer - E^{VS}, and

(3) Learning Object Energy Storage - E^{LO}.

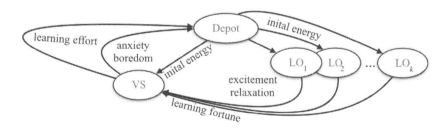

Figure 8.5   Energy flow model for virtual student's ecosystem: System Energy Depot (Depot), Virtual Student's Energy Buffer (VS), and k Energy Storages for Learning Objects (LO$_1$ ... LO$_k$).

8.2.5 TELECI Interface to AI Component

Artificial intelligence (AI) component is a part of the TELECI system. Although, for consistency sake, we include interfaces IF15 and IF16 specifying the architectural style of the system at large, in Figure 8.6 we define interfaces (IF15, IF16) on the system landscape.

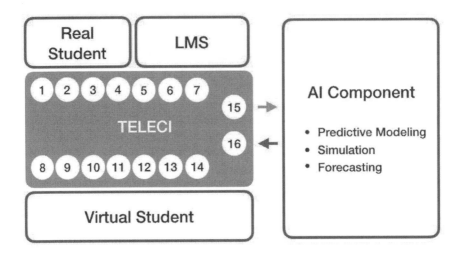

Figure 8.6   TELECI interface to AI component.

The AI component has two subcomponents: Machine Learning and Real Data Processing.

- First, the machine learning subcomponent utilizes algorithms for predictive modeling, simulation, and forecasting. In some sense, virtual student also applies and uses ML algorithms.

- Second, real data processing cares about data acquisition, mining, and RS or VS patterns recognition, preparing data ready for ML algorithms. Therefore, the border between VS, ML, and real data processing is fuzzy enough on the current architectural abstraction level.

8.3   Implementing ML Technique

In this section, we discuss further TELECI architecture adaptation based on preliminary experiments. Here, we refer to our previous works implementing ML classification utilizing handwriting on mobile surfaces.

During the learning process, learners receive small regular assignments with content that relates to learning objectives. Learners are asked to interact with learning content. After learners apply a response in a handwritten form, the captured handwriting style is partially processed, analyzed locally and sent to an application running machine learning algorithms to identify specific patterns.

8.3.1   Organizational Activities

From an instructional point of view, we propose the following activities:

1. Producing a micro-learning content including learning units for interaction with learners with the aim to initiate a response in the form of handwriting.

2. Micro-learning content delivery to learners using online network communication protocol HTTP/2 and utilizing the internet browser on a mobile device.

3. Sequential acquiring of personal handwriting data.

4. Partial data processing employing the computational power of a mobile device.

5. Data delivery for further analysis, particularly for application of machine learning algorithms utilizing Google API.

6. Building of the unsupervised machine learning models.

7. Identifying indicators of learner's boredom variability over time.

8. Recognizing boredom related clusters.

8.3.2 Data Processing

Data Recognizing involves Web application, partially sharing the responsibility for the experiment with a set of algorithms and a set of resources (see Figure 8.7).

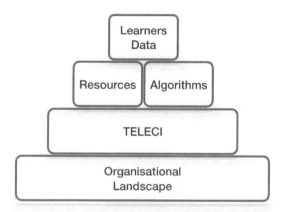

Figure 8.7   The organizational landscape environment holds TELECI system controlling learners' data gathering, distribution, and flow among computational and storage resources.

Mainly, a JavaScript-based algorithm collects user interaction with mobile device surface, identifying touching style (one finger or more) coordinates on HTML Canvas component. At first, HTML Canvas API collected DATA along with time stamp is processed for eventual locally controlled feedback. Next, collected DATA prepared for delivery to cloud computing resources with the aim of utilizing Google API by applying machine learning methods. Finally, processed data was used for the preparation of insights, visualization, and control of the learning process.

8.3.3   Computing and Networking Resources

For experiment organization, we involve both computational and communications resources. A mobile device with a surface for interaction is suitable for the experiment. Today, computational power and networking capability of the average mobile device are sufficient for the operations research, and therefore more detailed specification is out of the scope of this study. The role of mobile resource in the experiment is the CLIENT.

Another computational power for the experiment provided by cloud computing resource organized on Apache CloudStack deployed on institutional hardware maintained by Riga Technical University and hosted in Riga, Latvia. Cloud-based support allows us to scale resources easily on demand for the amount of memory or the number of processors needed. The role of cloud-based resource in the experiment is the SERVER. Also, the SERVER side provides DATA storage according to the DATA Model.

As the computational power which is more complicated for production, however, quite easy to use for prototyping and experimentation, we decided to employ the side part Google computational resources achievable through Google API. Here, we accept Google help to engage its artificial intelligence using machine learning libraries (e.g., TensorFlow 2.0, an open-source Python library developed by the Google Brain labs). The role of Google resource in the experiment is the AI-ML.

All the resources involved in the experimental setting communicate over the network. Mobile devices use a 4G network (depends on the provider). Further quantitative description of connections among SERVER, CLIENT, and AI-ML is out of the scope of this study.

In conclusion, this subsection described a mobile device (CLIENT) that is used to 1) communicate with the server side of the experimental setting, 2) deliver micro-learning content to the learner, 3) gather handwriting data from the device surface, 4) add a time stamp to data, and 5) deliver data to the SERVER side. The SERVER communicates with AI-ML to delegate resource-consuming tasks to GOOGLE. Also, SERVER side provides delivery of data queries, insights, visualization, and control of the learning process.

8.3.4   Introduction to Algorithm

In this section, we omit a detailed description of a software stack used to implement the algorithm. However, the data model will be sketched out later on in the text, helping to interpret results.

8.3.4.1   Recent Findings

To build the algorithm, we followed the best findings and practice using adaptive mobile learning [4, 8]. Also, we took into consideration some relevant findings starting from initial ideas [17], and following through the pitfalls, issues and challenges [1] to recent achievements [11, 19] that researchers have figured out in handwriting recognition.

We also took into consideration reported results of researchers to try to find out about learners' mathematical reaction time by analyzing not only the starting and ending time of the quiz, but also each subevent within the test or examination. Some researchers focused on such learning process properties as question reading time, mathematical (or logic) reaction time, answer input time, and navigation usage time [18].

8.3.4.2   Algorithm Components

Based on recent research findings and available technology, we propose an algorithm adaptable to the variations of learners' perception and specific cognitive abilities.

We named the algorithm the *Simple Boredom Identification Algorithm*, otherwise known as the Simple Algorithm for Boredom Identification (SABI).

The SABI algorithm uses the following variables and data models:

- **Response Time Window (RTW)**: A time window that allows the acceptance of all handwritten symbols entered on the mobile device surface;

- **Threshold Time (ThT)**: An average task completion time, individually recorded for each user, including initial delay;

- **Drawing as a Matrix (DaaM)**: A two-dimensional array holding handwriting sketched drawing captured from the mobile device surface after forming process completion;

- **Drawing Start Time (DST)**;

- **Drawing End Time (DET)**;

- **Active Drawing Time (ADT)**;

- **Calibration Timeouts (CalTo)**: An array holding timeout settings for each calibration round;

- **Drawing Animation (DAnim)**: An array holding drawing process animation over the forming time;

- **Reference Drawing (RefD)**: A reference to file on the SERVER side that holds the screen displayed on the CLIENT device. The data model for RefD includes screen (a browser window) settings gathered from CLIENT device;

- **Google Transactions Model (GTM)**: A data model helping to reconstruct system dynamics;

- **Server Data Model (SDM)**: Used by Data Analytics Module.

Figure 8.8 depicts SABI algorithm key variables. Usually, after starting the LO content demonstration, an initial delay occurs before reacting on visual information: to perceive, to think, and begin to act. Due to natural reasons, each experiment produces random data characterized by some essential statistical moments, e.g., mean value and variance.

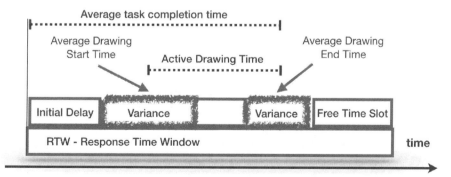

Figure 8.8   SABI algorithm key variables in action.

The essential novelty of the SABI algorithm is that the response time window (RTW) is adjustable to learners properties. In short, the SABI algorithm operates as follows: IF the learner's response time grows AND becomes longer than expected from calibration results, THEN the learner is classified as bored.

Calibration of the SABI algorithm starts using a game-like approach. Let's describe the Calibration Game.

8.3.5 Calibration Experiment

For the first experiment with system calibration, we create a dynamic WEB content consisting of 10 slides displayed in a sequence on the viewable area on the mobile device surface. Each slide remains visible for some time. After that, a slide is changed to another. For example, if each slide shown lasts for one second, during a 10-second time interval learners got ten different messages.

Initially, a user opens the web browser on the mobile personal learning environment, named CLIENT. After connection to the TELECI site, follows the formal registration procedure by entering the familiar nickname. For simplicity's sake, we accept only 4-digit "nicknumbers," similar to the PIN code for a phone or bank card.

In the first round, we give one symbol representing a single digit number per slide. Since all experiment participants are familiar with elementary numbers, the sequence is displayed with the rate equal to 2 digits per second. The first round is quite easy because the numbers are dynamically presented in a natural progression: from 0 to 9.

Therefore, after the first round participants were introduced to this simple information to remember, we assume that all learners remembered the numbers presented and their sequence. That is a crucial assumption for calibration.

In the second round, we propose to draw over the given numbers a finger or by stick depending on the device and learners' habits. Complementing the algorithm, we use the following logic: after the moment when the user touches the surface for the first stroke in a number, the algorithm starts a countdown timer to identify the time window for input acceptance. By default, the time window size is one second. In the case of writing lasting longer than one second, the algorithm just branched to waiting until any pressure to the surface is released. Now, the handwritten drawn number is prepared for the transfer to the SERVER. Along with 1) a final drawing of the number, 2) start event timestamp, 3) stop event timestamp, 4) a drawing process animation over time, and 5) reference to displayed learning problem (a number shown in the screen) are sent to SERVER. After data is received, the SERVER applies some normalization to the drawing and utilizes Google API to identify the number. A supervised machine learning algorithm responds with a probability distribution among possible outcomes from 0 to 9, and Not a Number (NAN). According to the algorithm, the SERVER should decide regarding the next instructional steps. Since the SERVER already knows the number displayed to the CLIENT, it is quite easy to determine how to respond. After entering all of the ten digits, the second round is finished.

In the third round we repeated the first round reversely, displaying numbers from 9 to 0.

In the fourth round, we again proposed drawing over the numbers appearing on the screen reversely. The algorithm applying time window for handwriting numbers is equal to that described in round two.

In the fifth round, a calibration is performed which includes the task of redrawing numbers in an up-going sequence – number by number – without time limitation; although a hard timeout limitation value is stored in the (CalTo) array. The algorithm should respond to each handwritten symbol with a typed one number guessed by ML-AI.

In the sixth round, the calibration includes the task of redrawing numbers in a downgoing sequence – number by number – without time limitation. However, there exists a hard timeout limitation value stored in the (CalTo) array. The algorithm should respond to each handwritten symbol with a typed one number guessed by ML-AI.

For the method used in experiments, we use no more calibrations due to concerns about users becoming bored or anxious.

As follows from the calibration experiment, the system is calibrated to recognize learner's handwritten numbers. The method used for boredom detection involves threshold time (ThT) monitoring in combination with factors from drawing animation (DAnim) array learned on the calibration stage.

Finally, at this stage the learning system is ready to switch to a micro-learning mode and deliver some learning content.

As recent findings [11] show, further directions to extend the algorithm to experiment with online handwriting recognition are possible.

Usually, in the micro-learning approach, after content presentation follows the assignment. We argue that to identify the learner's possible state of boredom in advance, we have to motivate learners to respond to tasks using the handwriting method.

We suggest organizing the learning process by formulating a preliminary survey, initial tests, and most of the following assignments to prepare for handwriting. Such an approach gives more data to process. Therefore, more data provides more information. On one hand, more data to operate with offers better accuracy for application of ML methods. On the other hand, in large-scale applications, additional unexpected delays can occur due to data processing. In either case, algorithms leverage with data produced by active users.

8.4 Learners' Activity Issues

Learners' outcomes and learning efficiency in educational e-service information systems could be improved by introducing adaptive solutions in information systems (IS) design [9]. System users' activity and their behavioral patterns during the learning process have a crucial role in determining learners' needs and offer the most suitable, appropriate learning content and personalized learning path. Learners' activities on their learning path produce data from interaction to learning object. Here, we consider the learning object (LO) to be a self-contained piece of instructional material. Produced interaction data is also fundamental to giving useful recommendations to course tutors and instructional designers regarding necessary improvements in learning objects: both course content and LO types (video, text, etc.). Moreover, knowing the characteristics of user actions, it is possible to reveal other behavioral properties of users like boredom or engagement level of the learning content acquisition.

Learning speed, ability to learn without interaction, background knowledge level, levels of an ability to apply prior knowledge and skills, mouse clicks and time spent indicating LO type preference, dropout forecasting user's location tracking which might give dropout forecast, system user's participation in discussions indicating his/her self-confidence level, and the number of asked questions and feedback, are all events and curious questions in a time-frequency domain that ought to be analyzed and considered within LMS.

Mainly, a sequence of events at a time $e_i(t)$ represented as a process with eventual users' activities taking place during the technology-enhanced learning process in IS (see Figure 8.4).

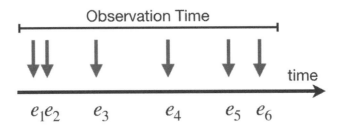

Figure 8.9　Learning related events { an arrival process.

It might be said that the total experiment events space (E) includes the series of events, i.e.:

$$E := \{e_1, e_2, \ldots, e_n\} \tag{8.1}$$

Each event invokes a response from LMS as new content delivery to a learner or as sending of learner's data to LMS. Because of natural origins, the frequency of events is not a constant value. The user can start the retrieval of different learning objects at arbitrary time moments. Technically, there are no problems identifying learner's and LO interaction start event; in LMS users interact with system interface and such events can be easily logged. Usually, a while after the first event, events can be easily counted and arrival process statistics can be inferred.

Inter-arrival time variation among events requests is common in service systems. Analysis of user activity data will allow us to conclude the user's learning style. Besides, by conducting user self-assessment surveys, we will get one more data for analysis. By comparing both data files, we can reach a conclusion about user behavior patterns and learning styles. As a result, IS can learn from user activity data and offer a personalized learning path to him/her.

A similar but not same approach was introduced at the 5th Annual GIFT Users Symposium. In order to ensure system adaptivity, the individual concepts across all lectures (e.g., videos, quizzes, etc.) were identified [20, 21].

Also, time spent for acquisition of different LOs may vary. If x_i is the time interval spent by a learner interacting with an LO in the system, it is self-evident that the learner's total learning time consists of the sum of the time spent working with each LO:

$$X(learning) = x_1 + x_2 + \ldots + x_n \tag{8.2}$$

Equation (8.2) is a simple model characterizing a learner experience and effort with some specific LO; each event could be distinguished by the LO type chosen and time spent by the particular learner.

Here, we use additional notation– various types of LOs can be interpreted as different information translation channels. We can determine the time spent on interacting with different kinds of LO delivery channels by individual learner and express counter numbers $x_1 \ldots x_n$ as the sum of several time sets which correspond to the specific delivery channel (i.e., x_{video} – video LO, x_{text} – textual LO, x_{ex} – exercises LO, x_{quiz} – quiz LO):

$$X(learning) = \sum_i x_{video} + \sum_j x_{text} + \sum_k x_{ex} + \sum_l x_{quiz} \qquad (8.3)$$

Again, equation (8.3) gives the total time spent in interaction with LOs under the assumption that LMS can identify how long the learner interacts with different LOs. Such a simple model is efficient enough under the assumption that interaction with each LO type is identified with some acceptable error.

More often, learners use the PC screen with several simultaneous channels proposed for learning. Usually, LMS is designed to build mixed content, such as videos, text blocks, illustration, etc., in one screen. In this case, in one learning unit, instructors were allowed to put more than one channel for simultaneous interaction.

Nowadays, instructional designers follow state-of-the-art practices to engage learners with new LMS design and content. Even the same content, but enveloped in different frames can have a disparate impact on the attention time of learners [18].

In Figure 8.10, we present a schematic diagram of a use case; simultaneously available channels encoded by the Real Learner. Modality detection from learner's data involves decoding of attention time and interaction sequence with LOs. Since the learner's behavior data is encoded with errors determined by undetectable "behavior noise" $N(t)$, the decoding process, in general, leads to detection errors.

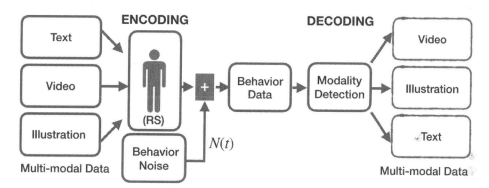

Figure 8.10   The model of behavior noise impact on data produced by Real Learner. Modality decoding can lead to detection errors.

Usually, if the problem is to separate LO channels, the reason is that LMS cannot separate interaction objects because of specific architecture and design; one online-content page has many objects. In some cases, teaching organizations provide learning content along with misleading advertisements.

Only some specific techniques such as ECG and eye-gaze tracking on LO along with mouse pointer or mouse scrolling detection can reduce encoded "behavior noise." In that case, extra effort and equipment are needed to detect the learner's behavior with acceptable precision.

Obviously, if an organizational problem is getting to know a learner's interaction time with LOs separated by channels, legacy LMS design is not optimized for channel separation. In general, serious upgrades are needed.

The problem becomes more real in the case of PC usage in online-learning process because of ineffectual screen space usage.

In general, LMS design for desktop computers is not optimized for channel separation.

At the moment, there is still a technically unsolved problem – to identify the learner's interaction time with LO. A small learning object requires less time to interact. It is common for distractions to divert the student's attention and happens regardless of his/her conscious energy or diligence.

Here, we address an intuitively clear idea regarding possible focused attention time detection error. The smaller the LO and time expected to be spent on it, the less likely is a possible prediction error in the interaction time (see Figure 8.11).

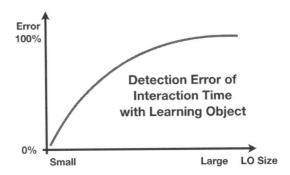

Figure 8.11 Interaction time detection error. A small learning object requires less time to interact. Distractions produce "behavior noise."

In the case of presentation of LOs as significant monumental texts, videos, etc., learners definitely will be distracted. In this case, the cumulative error of interaction time measurements will grow due to technical limitations in identifying distraction moments. Therefore, the "behavior noise" used in our model (see Figure 8.10) will also grow.

In conclusion: 1) the smaller the LO, the more precise is the learner's attention to detect the LO, and 2) the content design ought to follow minimalistic guidelines.

8.5 Conclusion

Modern e-learning service systems produce extensive data, including direct information on both the learner's behavioral and activity data within the information system during the learning process. As a result, the learning management system (LMS) may give the student the most relevant recommendations and appropriate content for further learning.

Learning management systems can perform an analysis of the student's interests by supplying relevant learning objects based on the learner's behavioral patterns. Artificial intelligence, in general, and machine learning play a more and more significant role, explicitly improving accuracy and efficiency in such adaptive solutions continuously.

Most LMS cannot identify separate interaction objects because of legacy architecture and design. Such systems are harder to be adapted for new TELECI architecture proposals. However, a more dominant role is played by the adaptation of LMS for instructional design.

From an instructional point of view, to get more reliable interaction time measurements, we find mobile devices to be more effective in the learning process: one LO type per screen, simple clear content, shorter texts and videos, adaptable sequential content, and small tests.

Prospective adaptive learning management systems ought to ensure an availability to identify possible gaps in learners' knowledge space. Also, adaptive e-learning systems offer them personalized learning paths based on their learning preferences, activities and behavior patterns within the system. Learners ought to have the opportunity to choose any available learning plan from the list offered by e-learning system, as well as build a personalized learning path.

Acknowledgment

This research was supported by a grant from the European Regional Development Fund (ERDF/ERAF) project "Technology Enhanced Learning E-ecosystem with Stochastic Interdependences - TELECI," Project No.1.1.1.1/16/A/154.

REFERENCES

1. Abuzaraida, M. A., Zeki, A. M., & Zeki, A. M. (2013, March). Problems of writing on digital surfaces in online handwriting recognition systems. In *2013 5th International Conference on Information and Communication Technology for the Muslim World (ICT4M)* (pp. 1-5). IEEE.

2. Bishop, C. M. (2006). *Pattern recognition and machine learning.* Springer Science + Business Media. ISBN 978-0387-31073-2. URL http://research.microsoft.com/en-us/um/people/cmbishop/prml/.

3. Bixler, R., & D'Mello, S. (2013, March). Detecting boredom and engagement during writing with keystroke analysis, task appraisals, and stable traits. In *Proceedings of the 2013 International Conference on Intelligent User Interfaces* (pp. 225-234). ACM.

4. Cinquin, P. A., Guitton, P., & Sauzeon, H. (2019). Online e-learning and cognitive disabilities: A systematic review. *Computers & Education*, 130, 152-167.

5. Dabbagh, N., Benson, A. D., Denham, A., Joseph, R., Al-Freih, M., Zgheib, G., ... & Guo, Z. (2015). *Learning Technologies and Globalization: Pedagogical Frameworks and Applications.* Springer. ISBN 978-3-319-22962-1. DOI: 10.1007/978-3-319-22963-8.

6. Dunn, J., & Sweeney, T. (2018). Writing and iPads in the early years: Perspectives from within the classroom. *British Journal of Educational Technology*, 49(5), 859-869. DOI: 10.1111/b-jet.12621

7. Ford, N., Parsons, R., & Kua, P. (2017). *Building Evolutionary Architectures: Support Constant Change.* O'Reilly Media, Inc. ISBN 978-1-491-98636-3

8. Fox, A. (2016). Microlearning for effective performance management. *TD Magazine*, 70(4), 116-117.

9. Gorbunovs, A., Timsans, Z., Zuga, B., & Zagorskis, V. (2017). Conceptual design of the new generation adaptive learning management system. *International Journal of Engineering & Technology*, 7(2.28), 129-133.

10. Gromann, I., Hottung, A., & Krohn-Grimberghe, A. (2019). Machine learning meets partner matching: Predicting the future relationship quality based on personality traits. *PloS One*, 14(3), e0213569. DOI: 10.1371/journal.pone.0213569

11. Keysers, D., Deselaers, T., Rowley, H. A., Wang, L. L., & Carbune, V. (2016). Multi-language online handwriting recognition. *IEEE Transactions on Pattern Analysis and Machine Intelligence*, 39(6), 1180-1194. DOI: 10.1109/TPAMI.2016.2572693

12. MacKinnon, D. P., & Fairchild, A. J. (2009). Current directions in mediation analysis. *Current Directions in Psychological Science*, 18(1), 16-20. DOI: 10.1177/0963721410370295

13. Loerts, T., & Heydon, R. (2017). Multimodal literacy learning opportunities within a grade six classroom literacy curriculum: constraints and enablers. *Education* 3-13, 45(4), 490-503. DOI: 10.1080/03004279.2016.1139608

14. Natarajan, D. (2017). *ISO 9001 Quality Management Systems*. Springer International Publishing. ISBN 3319543822, 9783319543826.

15. von Rosing, M., White, S., Cummins, F., & de Man, H. (2015). *Business Process Model and Notation-BPMN*. URL http://www.omg.org/spec/BPMN/2.0.

16. Russell, S. J., & Norvig, P. (2016). *Artificial Intelligence: A Modern Approach*. Malaysia; Pearson Education Limited. ISBN 0137903952.

17. Tappert, C. C., Suen, C. Y., & Wakahara, T. (1990). The state of the art in online handwriting recognition. *IEEE Transactions on Pattern Analysis and Machine Intelligence*, 12(8), 787-808. DOI: 10.1109/34.57669.

18. Vagale, V., & Niedrte, L. (2011). E-learning system individualization for intellectual ability measurement. In *Perspectives in Business Informatics Research. In Local Proceedings of the 10th International Conference*, BIR 2011 (pp. 200-207).

19. Wang, G., Zhang, X., Tang, S., Zheng, H., & Zhao, B. Y. (2016, May). Unsupervised clickstream clustering for user behavior analysis. In *Proceedings of the 2016 CHI Conference on Human Factors in Computing Systems* (pp. 225-236). ACM. DOI: 10.1145/2858036.2858107.

20. Weiss, G. (Ed.). (1999). *Multiagent Systems: A Modern Approach to Distributed Artificial Intelligence*. MIT press.

21. Zagorskis, V., & Kapenieks, A. (2018). Impact of LMS selection on students activity. In *Proceedings of the 10th International Conference on Computer Supported Education - Volume 1: CSEDU*, pages 505-512. INSTICC, SciTePress, 2018. ISBN 978-989-758-291-2. DOI: 10.5220/0006810205050512.

PART V

BIG DATA ANALYTICS

Before Big Data can be used for Big Data Analytics it needs to be prepared for incorporation into the business analytics software. Data needs to be homogenized and aggregated, and privacy and security need to be protected and applied using masking and anonymization. Data is collected, cleaned and sold by intermediaries, brokers and multi-vendors, creating new cataloging services and new business models.

The early AIIoT adopters of big data analytics for business intelligence will have the market advantage due to their business intelligence, giving them superior profit and loss (P&L) management skills. They will be the "digital natives," familiar and adept at using the digital domain for their professional and personal lives. They are the ones who are able to convert data into information, information into knowledge, and knowledge into wisdom, and thus they will rapidly gain the competitive advantage, because they have greater access to greater wisdom, and therefore greater opportunity and prosperity, than others. McKinsey's 2019 report predicts an estimated reduction of total machine downtime of 30-50%; a 45-55% increase of productivity in technical professions through automation of knowledge work; costs for inventory holding reduced by 20-50%; costs to maintain quality are reduced by 10-20%; forecasting accuracy increases more than 85%; reduction of time to market of 20-50%; and a 10-40% reduction of maintenance cost. Chapter 9 presents a use case in modeling enterprise innovation management.

With this knowledge and power, also comes responsibility. There is a global need for interoperability between AIIoT devices and a worldwide digital industrial transaction and transportation track. This means that it is of great importance to develop proprietary and collective data formats and valuation, and a collective responsibility to use open architectures, creating a collective wisdom that shares best practices by adopting common smart regulatory solutions for cross-border transactions and other international and global challenges that require international cross-cultural collaboration and innovation. Chapter 10 presents a use case that addresses the goal of global sustainability and aspects of the "peak oil" situation by exploring the use of simulation to optimize diesel engine processes.

- Chapter 9: Enterprise Innovation Management in Industry 4.0: Modeling Aspects

- Chapter 10: Using Simulation for Development of Automobile Gas Diesel Engine Systems and Their Operational Control

CHAPTER 9

ENTERPRISE INNOVATION MANAGEMENT IN INDUSTRY 4.0: MODELING ASPECTS

V. Babenko

Department of International E-Commerce and Hotel and Restaurant Business, V. N. Karazin Kharkiv National University, Ukraine
Corresponding author: vitalinababenko@karazin.ua

Abstract

In the current Industry 4.0 environment, any enterprise is forced to make urgent management decisions of choosing effective innovation control. The purpose of this research is dynamic optimization of management of innovative processes of the enterprise. The main method for solving the problem is the method of detecting the reachable areas. Using this method, we work out the scenario of optimal innovation management in the presence of risks. A meaningful and formal statement of the model of management of innovative processes of the enterprise is developed. A general solution algorithm is proposed and a model of multicriteria optimization of enterprise innovation management is offered. The proposed algorithm allows the creation of numerous effective methods for implementing a computer simulation of a solution to the problem of management of innovative processes of the enterprise. It opens the perspective of developing computer information systems that support making effective management decisions in conditions of uncertainty and lack of information.

Keywords: Innovation management, dynamic optimization, minimax, guaranteed result, program control, adaptive control

9.1   Introduction

Changes that occur in the industry under the influence of information technology significantly help to increase the quality of products and services. This increases loyalty and customer satisfaction. Manufacturers also do not want to remain a loser, and new approaches and business models born in Industry 4.0 allow them to earn more, and therefore invest in improving products.

The term "Industry 4.0" first appeared in Europe in 2011 at one of the industrial exhibitions in Hanover. The German government spoke of the need for a wider use of information technologies in production. A specially created group of officials and professionals developed a strategy for turning the country's industrial enterprises into "smart" ones. Other countries followed this example by actively exploring new technologies. In addition, the term "Industry 4.0" is a synonym for the Fourth Industrial Revolution. A consequence of the movement is that today the material world connects with the virtual. As a result, there are new cyber-physical complexes united in one digital ecosystem. Robotic manufacturing and smart plants are one of the components of the transformed industry. The Fourth Industrial Revolution means that there is increasing automation of all processes and stages of production. At the same time, economic principles are preserved, since robotic production is more energy efficient, accompanied by less waste and scrap.

In modern economic conditions, any enterprise forced by management to adapt its resource capabilities to external and internal conditions, must take into account the risks associated with the instability and complication of socioeconomic conditions of the domestic and foreign markets.

These factors require companies to react promptly through the adoption of urgent managerial decisions on the choice of effective innovation process management, which involve the replacement of raw materials, the production of innovative products, adjustment of energy prices and other factors of production, which ultimately leads to the need to use innovative technologies and related equipment at the production stage. Thus, these and other factors related to the peculiarities of innovative production make it necessary to solve the problem of choice from a possible alternative to optimal enterprise management control during the production process in conditions of uncertainty and the resulting risk.

Effective implementation of tasks associated with these processes requires the use of appropriate tools: economic and mathematical models, methods and algorithms for solving problems of optimizing process management in conditions of uncertainty and the resulting risk using modern information technology that allows reproduction, and therefore explore, predict and manage the behavior of an object using a model.

Thus, the developed economic-mathematical model of innovation management processes and methods for their solution should be based on the system of such conceptual conditions:

1. Innovative process management of an enterprise is complicated by the presence of a subjective component, which is reflected by uncertainty and the resulting risk.

2. Management of innovative processes is based on the choice of optimal control of the set of alternatives. This production system is a set of interconnected elements, each of which carries out a certain processing of some raw material or semi-finished product into a finished product. During the production process, taking into account the specifics of production under the influence of the external and internal environment, it may be necessary to choose innovation management processes based on a production plan that takes into account the peculiarities of the application of relevant

innovative technologies, new types of raw materials, equipment, etc., which forms a set of alternatives to possible innovation process management.

3. Modeling in takes place in uncertain conditions and, due to this risk, characterizes the complexity of interrelated tasks (financial, economic, industrial, etc.) and various parameters, and consists of a system of models. The enterprise is a complex social and economic system which is constantly developing and interacting with the external environment, the parameters of which change over time.

4. To improve the practical value of the results, the task of modeling in the innovation process management investigates the development of the process in time. It is dynamic and creates conditions for a more complete, adequate reflection of the process in the time aspect and creates opportunities for the choice of management not only at the final moment of time, but throughout the studied period.

5. Taking into account the possibility of obtaining financial and economic indicators of the company's activity and innovation process management at selected time intervals, the modeling task of enterprise innovation processes management (EIPM) is discrete. In such models, in the role of time parameters there is a finite number of discrete numeric values with a given starting point of time, a fixed period between any two adjacent moments of time and a finite term.

6. To optimize innovation processes management we use a multicriteria model. As criteria for optimization in the EIPM model, we can select different economic indicators such as total profit, cost, raw material consumption, energy intensity, return on assets, etc. Also, taking into account the specifics of innovative processes management, we should consider innovation process quality management criteria such as the indicators of the economic effectiveness of innovative processes implementation, the net present value of innovation processes, the profitability of the innovative processes, the life cycle of the innovation product, the environmental safety of innovative products, etc.

7. The decision-making process in conditions of uncertainty and the resulting risk leads to the need to solve the task of the best choice in conditions with incomplete information about the system under consideration. At the same time, there are existing approaches to solving such problems such as, static models and use of a stochastic modeling apparatus, for which knowledge is required of the probabilistic characteristics of the main parameters of the model and special conditions for the implementation of the considered process. However, for the stochastic modeling machine, special conditions are needed (for example, a large set and homogeneity of a sample of values), which in practice is usually difficult to execute. Taking into account the specifics of agricultural production, where, in particular, the risks are not dependent on us and there are uncontrolled parameters, to solve the task of innovation processes management we propose the use of a minimax approach or finding a guaranteed result. This means that the minimum guaranteed optimal management of the worst (maximal) vector of heterogeneous risks is least comparable with similar values for others.

8. In innovation process management tasks it is necessary to develop a mathematical model of programmatic and adaptive management. Implementation of program management of innovative processes predicts the entire study period. However, with the actual process in each period, a situation may arise in which there is a change in model parameters (raw material suppliers, financial indicators, the impact of risks with less

significant values, etc.). In this case, it is necessary to provide a procedure for adapting the model to the current state of the process. In such cases, the process of adaptive innovative processes management should be organized to refine the results of innovative processes program management, taking into account changes in the economic environment and the current state of the process.

Taking into account the conceptual conditions, the model for enterprise innovation management processes represents a dynamic multicriteria task of optimizing several target functions on a given set of optimal goals with a complex Y criterion:

$$Y = F(f_k(, u(t), v(t))) \to opt, k = \overline{1..m} \tag{9.1}$$

where

- m is the number of target functions to be optimized;

- f_k is the partial optimization functions ($k = \overline{1..m}$);

- $x \in X$ is the input parameters;

- $u(t) \in U$ is the vector of management of the set of possible alternatives;

- $v(t) \in V$ is the risk vector; and

- t is the time.

The solution of the EIPM optimization task is to find such a management $u(t) \in U$, in which, from the point of view of a set of partial criteria put forward at the suggestion of management of the enterprise, the implementation of an integrated risk optimization criterion is ensured.

Such an approach to modeling in the innovation management process of enterprise provides management flexibility, allows taking into account the uncertainty factor in the form of various risks and simulation errors that arise in the process of modeling when selecting criteria for optimizing the task of management in order to investigate the effectiveness and priority of innovation processes from a variety of possible alternatives.

9.2 Conceptual Model of Enterprise Innovation Process Management

Taking into account the information presented above and based on the foundations and principles of mathematical modeling and optimal control theory, we proceed to the modeling of EIPM. This process takes place in stages to design system models. First, develop a conceptual economic and mathematical model of the EIPM. This is an important stage of modeling, since at this stage the main content of the model is determined, which is developed on the basis of adopted conceptual provisions [5]. This takes into account the following features:

a) Formulation of the modeling problem;

b) The structure of the model; and

c) Possible methods and means of solving the modeling problem.

Formulate the model in a meaningful setting. For example, a plant is planning to introduce the innovative processes, that is, switching to output based on the model. This process takes into account various types of production factors, raw materials, options for the use and storage of raw materials, intermediate and final products, the influence of various production and external factors, including other components of the process and may consist of certain technological methods of production organization involving the use of existing or replacement (partial or complete) technological equipment.

Innovation process management is implemented in some periods of the life cycle of innovative processes during its implementation in the enterprise. The innovation management process includes the values of the volume production of new products, the vector replenishment material and labor resources for its production and the vector of current investments for the innovation processes implementation, which form the management scenario of the corresponding innovative processes. It is possible to use different innovative management process scenarios depending on the variation of the values of the corresponding components of the innovation processes.

It is necessary to carry out such rational innovative process management with the corresponding scenario on the set time interval of its life cycle by choosing from a variety of alternatives of possible management actions, so that the general criterion efficiency of innovative processes is the maximum [12]. At the same time, if several options for the introduction of different innovation processes based on appropriate innovative technologies are considered, it is also necessary to make a choice between them and find rational management according to the selected criteria [3].

Having developed a meaningful economic and mathematical model of innovative process management, we proceed to its formal formulation and development in several stages [4].

Equation (9.2) shows the formation of the economic and mathematical model of EIPM [2]. Let's introduce designations:

$$\bar{x}(t) = (x_1(t), x_2(t), \ldots, x_n(t))' \in R^{\bar{n}} \tag{9.2}$$

The phase vector characterizing a condition management of innovation processes (availability of the production volume of the enterprise, financial, investment, technological, other production resources, etc.) in the period of time t [1].

To describe the process of innovation process management, it is necessary to know the initial values of the system parameters (at the beginning of the studied time interval). Consider its structure. It includes the volume of production, other initial production resources, etc., and also investments directed to innovative processes. Due to the initial investment of I_0, equipment, production resources and other necessities for the "start-up" are purchased by the individual entrepreneur. Because the amount of initial investment is a key factor for realization of the investment project, in the phase vector $\bar{x}(0)$ select them separately, that is

$$\bar{x}(0) = \{x_0, I_0\}$$

Process EIPM described by vector of discrete (recursive) equation:

$$\bar{x}(t+1) = A(t)\bar{x}(t) + B(t)\bar{u}(t) + C(t)\bar{v}(t), \quad \bar{x}(0) = \{x_0, I_0\} \tag{9.3}$$

where

- $t \in \overline{0, T-1} = \{0, 1, 2, \ldots, T-1\}$ is the discrete moments of time, divided by a period of a month, quarter, or year chosen by management;

- $\overline{0,T}$ is the given period of time ($T > 0$ and integer);

$\bar{x}(t+1) \in R^{\bar{n}}$ is the phase vector characterizing the state of management of innovative processes in the period of time $(t + 1)$ and consists of vectors of volumes of production, production stocks, expenses, financial resources and volumes of investments which were formed in the period of time $(t + 1)$ (stocks in the period $(t + 1)$).

Let's consider the formation (9.2) on the example of the vector production volumes of the enterprise, where $x_i(t + 1)$ is the number of i-th type of products $i \in \overline{1, n}$ formed in the warehouse prior to the beginning of the time period $(t + 1)$ (inventory of products in the period $(t + 1)$), which is formed from stocks $x_i(t)$ of the previous time period and the products produced at the enterprise for the time period t.

Equation (9.3) consists of three components, which we consider below (the remnants of unrealized products for the period, manufactured products in the period and the impact of risks for the studied period of time).

- The remnants of unsold goods in period $t + 1$. Note that if at the beginning of the time period t there were stocks in the amount of $x(t)$, then by the end of this period, that is, by the beginning of the time period $t + 1$, only a part equal to $A(t)\bar{x}(t)$;

    - $A(t) = \|a_{ii}(t)\|_{i \in \overline{1, n}}$ is the diagonal matrix characterizing the sales of products (matrix of "sales") over a period of time $\overline{t, t + 1}$;
    - $\bar{x}(t) = (x_1(t), x_2(t), \ldots, x_n(t))' \in R^n$ is the vector of stocks of production in the period t ($t \in \overline{0, T - 1}$) in which each i and coordinate $_i(t)$ designates volume of production of the i-th type $i \in \overline{1, n}$ (n is the total number of types of products), R^n is the n-dimensional vector space of vectors columns.

- Manufactured products in period $t + 1$ (vector $B(t)\bar{u}(t)$), where $\bar{u}(t) \in R^p$ is the vector of management of innovative processes (management action), the components of which are the intensities of the use of the j-th technological method of production of products (according to the corresponding innovative processes) in the time period t, $p \in N$ in which each j-th coordinate is the value of the volume production of material and labor resources and investments for innovative processes, ($j \in \overline{1, n}$), $\forall t \in \overline{0, T - 1}$, $\bar{u}(t) \in U_1$, and U_1 is a finite set of alternatives, which limits the resource management impact;

$B(t) = \|b_{ij}(t)\|_{i \in \overline{1, n}, j \in \overline{1, p}}$ is the "technological matrix" of production, the components of which can be represented by the j-th way, which corresponds to the organization of production ($j \in \overline{1, p} = \{1, 2, \ldots, p\}$) in the time period t ($t \in \overline{0, T - 1}$, $T > 0$), which is characterized by the vector $(b_{1j}(t), b_{2j}(t), \cdots, b_{nj}(t))$ norms of expenses of resources for the manufacture of a unit volume production of the i-th species ($i \in \overline{1, n}$). If $b_{ij}(t) < 0$, the value $b_{ij}(t)$ determines the cost of the i-th ingredient $i \in \overline{1, n}$ during the j-th mode of production in the time period.

A term that takes into account the impact of risks, modeling errors on products in the period $t+1$ (vector $C(t)\bar{v}(t)$, where $\bar{v}(t) \in R^q$ is the risk vector which affects the production and storage of products, that is, the process of vector formation $\bar{x}(t + 1)$, $q \in N$. For example, investment payments (or their shortfall), short supply of components, spoilage agricultural products during storage or transportation, noncompliance with the quality requirements of raw materials or finished products, insufficient investment, etc.; $\forall t \in \overline{0, T - 1}$, $\bar{v}(t) \in V_1$ is the convex, closed and limited polyhedron in R^q.

$C(t) = \|c_{il}(t)\|_{i \in \overline{1, n}, l \in \overline{1, q}}$ is the matrix consisting of coefficients listing the impact of the risk vector on the products of each type.

$A(t)$, $B(t)$, $C(t)$ are the matrices of dimensions $(n \times n)$, $(n \times p)$ and $(n \times q)$ respectively, formed on the basis of preliminary information from the enterprise reporting documents, available statistical data on the considered process, with the help of experts, economic forecasts and other sources through the use of data evaluation methods and solving a separate task of identification of the parameters of the system under study.

9.3 Formation of Restrictions for Enterprise Innovation Management Processes

As introduced in the previous section, the management vector of innovation processes and the risk vector

$$\bar{u}(t) = (u_1(t), u_2(t), \ldots, u_p(t))' \in R^p$$

in the system (9.1) each pair $(\bar{u}(t)\bar{v}(t))$ must satisfy such a given restriction:

$$(\bar{u}(t), \bar{v}(t)) \in UV(t) = \{(\bar{u}(t), \bar{v}(t)) : \bar{u}(t) \in R^p, \bar{v}(t) \in R^q \quad (9.4)$$

$$S_{\min}(t) \leq \langle B(t)\bar{u}(t) \rangle_n \leq S_{\max}(t), \ K_{\min}(t) \leq \langle C(t)\bar{v}(t) \rangle_n \leq K_{\max}(t)\} \quad (9.5)$$

where $S_{\min}(t) = (S_{\min 1}(t), S_{\min 2}(t), \ldots, S_{\min n}(t))' \in R^n$ is the vector of the minimum acceptable volume of production, in which each i-th coordinate $S_{\min i}(t)$ is the value of the minimum acceptable volume of production of the i-th type $(i \in \overline{1, \ n})$ (for example, the break-even point for each type of product);

$$S_{\max}(t) = (S_{\max 1}(t), S_{\max 2}(t), \ldots, S_{\max n}(t)) \in R^n \quad (9.6)$$

is the vector of the upper limit output, in which each i-coordinate is the value of the maximum acceptable volume of production of the i-th type $(i \in \overline{1, \ n})$ (for example, the maximum market capacity for each product name, the maximum production capacity, etc.).

$$K_{\min}(t) = (K_{\min 1}(t), K_{\min 2}(t), \ldots, K_{\min n}(t))$$

and

$$K_{\max}(t) = (K_{\max 1}(t), K_{\max 2}(t), \ldots, K_{\max n}(t))$$

are the influence of the risk vector on the output of each type of product [8]. The following constraints $t \in \overline{0, T - 1}$ must also be met for all:

$$\begin{cases} x_i(t) \geq 0 & (i \in \overline{1, \ n}), \\ u_j(t) \geq 0 & (j \in \overline{1, \ p}), \\ v_l(t) \geq 0 & (l \in \overline{1, \ q}). \end{cases} \quad (9.7)$$

It should be noted that in the process management of the enterprise's sole proprietorship of restrictions (9.6), (9.7) is a necessary condition that must satisfy the parameters of the system states generated by the implementation of optimal management actions in a discrete dynamic system (9.1).

9.4 Formation of Quality Criteria for Assessing Implementation of Enterprise Innovation Management Processes

The quality of the system management process (9.1) on the integer time interval $\overline{0,T}$, in particular, is estimated by the functional, the value $\Phi(u(\,\cdot\,))$, which for the fixed management of the innovation processes is calculated by the formula:

$$
\begin{aligned}
\Phi(u(\,\cdot\,)) &= \max_{v(\cdot)\in V(\overline{0,T})} \gamma(x_{\overline{0,T}}(T;\, x_0, I_0, u(\,\cdot\,), v(\,\cdot\,)) = \\
&= \max_{x(T)\in G^{+}_{\overline{0,T}}(T;\, x_0,\, I_0,\, u(\cdot),\, V(0,T))} \gamma(x(T)),
\end{aligned}
\tag{9.8}
$$

where $\gamma : R^n \to R^1$ is a functional defined on the final vectors of the system state (9.1), which evaluates the quality of innovation processes management.

It is advisable to consider the following specific types of functionality:

1. $\gamma(x(T))$ is a linear function $\forall x \in R^n$ that is the role of the optimization criterion we use in the linear functional;

2. $\gamma(x(T))$ is the convex function, that is, we use convex functional.

Consider the first case when $\gamma(x(T))$ is a linear function $\forall x \in R^n$. For example, $\gamma(x(T)) = <c, x(T)>_n$ is a scalar product of a vector $x(t) \in R^n$ corresponding to a fixed vector. Then, if the vector of prices for products of a single volume $c(t) = \{c_1(t), c_2(t), \ldots, c_n(t)\} \in R^n$ (unit of production) of each type is taken as a vector, then the optimization criterion will be the volume of gross profit from the sale products of the enterprise in the period of time t ($t \in \overline{0, T-1}$).

Consider the case when $\gamma(x(T))$ is the convex real function $\forall x \in R^n$. This case should be considered in planning tasks when a fixed order for the volume of production is set, and it is necessary to "approach," as much as possible, the specified volume. In this case, consider the distance from the possible final phase vector of the system to a given fixed vector in space R^n as a functional value (we perform the operation of calculating the Euclidean norm between these vectors in space R^n), which is a convex function.

9.5 Statement of Optimization Task of Implementation of Enterprise Innovation Management Processes Program

Adoption process in uncertain economic and environmental conditions, as well as the resulting risk, leads to the need to solve the problem with the best choice in terms of incomplete information about the system under consideration. A typical situation associated with decision-making in dynamic systems is the need to organize the procedure of program management in conditions of uncertainty and the resulting risk. Such a procedure, aimed at achieving a particular management goal, is often necessary to accompany the optimization process, allowing obtainment of a guaranteed, better or, in some sense, acceptable result; that is, to use a minimax approach [2].

Let us consider a variety of alternatives to possible management actions:

$$
U(\overline{0,T}) = \left\{ u(\cdot) : u(\cdot) = \{u(t)\}_{t\in\overline{0,T-1}}, \; \forall t \in \overline{0, T-1}, \; u(t) \in U_1 \right\}
\tag{9.9}
$$

There is a set of all possible innovation programs of management processes in a period of time $\overline{0, T}$,

$$V(\overline{0, T}) = \left\{ v(\cdot) : \ v(\cdot) = \{v(t)\}_{t \in \overline{0, T-1}}, \ \forall t \in \overline{0, T-1}, \ v(t) \in V_1 \right\} \qquad (9.10)$$

is the set of all valid implementation risks in the interval $\overline{0, T}$.

On the basis of the provisions of the formulated concept, to solve the optimization task of innovation management processes, for each fixed program management, we construct an appropriate area of reach, which is determined by sorting out all possible acceptable risk vectors [6]. The convex hull of each constructed reachability domain is a convex polyhedron (since they were defined for vectors that are vertices polyhedral constraints) [11], at the vertices of which the functions are optimized to take extreme values. For each domain of reach (corresponding polyhedron), we find a vertex (vector) that determines the maximum value of the objective function for the corresponding fixed program management and the available implementations of the risk vectors, which is generated by the corresponding worst implementation of this vector. Furthermore, from this set of sets and possible program management and the corresponding maximum values of the objective function, we choose such a pair that the maximum value of the objective function is the smallest (minimum) that is the guaranteed value of the objective function or minimax result. The program management included in this pair satisfies the minimax condition, that is, it is a minimax management of the innovation processes, or guaranteed management of the innovation processes.

Note that the minimax condition (principle) is applied in problems of canonical form when we investigate the target function for the minimum. In the real practical formulation of the task of optimization management of innovation processes there can be a situation when it is necessary to maximize the target function, that is, to solve the task maximinally (in this case, the worst risk vectors and minimize the target function). In order to bring such a task to the minimax task, it is necessary to turn the original target function into the opposite one by multiplying its values by (-1), thus forming a new target function. Then it is known that minimax management will coincide with maximin; therefore, it is sufficient to investigate only minimax problems.

For fixed possible implementations of program management of innovation processes $u(\cdot) \in U(\overline{0, T})$ and risk vector $v(\cdot) \in V(\overline{0, T})$, consider $x_{\overline{0, T}}(T; x_o, I_o, u(\cdot), v(\cdot))$ - the final state (state at time T) of the process trajectory generated by the system (9.1) [9] corresponding to the pair $(u(\cdot), v(\cdot))$. Develop plurality:

$$G_{\overline{0, T}}^+(T; x_o, I_o, u(\cdot), V(0, T)) = \{x(T) : x(T) \in R^n, \qquad (9.11)$$

$$x(T) = x_{\overline{0, T}}(T; x_o, I_o, u(\cdot), v(\cdot)), v(\cdot) \in V(0, T)\} \qquad (9.12)$$

The reachability range [9] of the system (9.1) is the set of all possible final states of this system at the initial $x(0) = \{0, I_0\}$ which corresponds to the fixed program management of the innovation processes $u(\cdot) \in U(\overline{0, T})$.

The quality of the system management process (9.1) on an integer period of time $\overline{0, \ T}$ is estimated by the functional $\Phi(u(\cdot))$, the value of which for the fixed program management of the innovation processes $u(\cdot) \in U(\overline{0, T})$ and the initial state of the process $x(0) = \{0, I_0\}$ is calculated by the formula:

$$\Phi(u(\cdot)) = \max_{v(\cdot) \in V(\overline{0, T})} \gamma(x_{\overline{0, T}}(T; x_0, I_0, u(\cdot), v(\cdot))) =$$

$$= \max_{x(T) \in G_{\overline{0, T}}^+(T; x_0, I_0, u(\cdot), V(0, T))} \gamma(x(T)) \qquad (9.13)$$

where $\gamma : R^n \to R$ is the functional defined on the final phase vectors of the equation (9.1), which evaluates the quality of innovation processes.

Then we can formulate the minimax program task of the innovation management processes; you need to find the optimal minimax program innovation management processes which satisfy the condition (minimax):

$$
\begin{aligned}
\Phi^{(e)} = \Phi(u^{(e)}(\,\cdot\,)) &= \max_{v(\cdot)\in V(\overline{0,T})} \gamma(x_{\overline{0,T}}(T; x_0, I_0, u^{(e)}(\,\cdot\,), v(\,\cdot\,)) = \\
&= \min_{u(\cdot)\in U(\overline{0,T})} \max_{v(\cdot)\in V(\overline{0,T})} \gamma(x_{\overline{0,T}}(T; x_0, I_0, u(\,\cdot\,), v(\,\cdot\,)) = \\
&= \max_{x(T)\in G^{+}_{\overline{0,T}}(T; x_0, I_0, u^{(e)}(\cdot), V(\overline{0,T}))} \gamma(x(T)) = \\
&= \min_{u(\cdot)\in U(\overline{0,T})} \max_{x(T)\in G^{+}_{\overline{0,T}}(T; x_0, I_0, u(\cdot), V(\overline{0,T}))} \gamma(x(T)),
\end{aligned}
\tag{9.14}
$$

where $\Phi^{(e)} = \Phi(u^{(e)}(\,\cdot\,))$ is the minimax result of solving this task [9].

Thus, the formed relations (9.1) to (9.14) are the economic-mathematical model of the task formulated above.

It should be noted that this system allows the user to simulate the dynamics of a multi-step process of EIPM depending on the given initial conditions and the choice of specific implementations of management actions.

9.6 Structural and Functional Model for Solving the Task of Dynamic

In this section, we consider the current economic and mathematical model of innovation management processes of agricultural enterprises. On a given integer time interval, $\overline{0,T} = \{0,1,\ldots,T\}\,(T>0)$, we consider a multistage dynamic management system of an innovation process, which consists of a single management object (enterprise for processing agricultural raw materials), the movement of which is described by a linear discrete recurrent vector equation (dynamic model) [5-16]. Here, for further simplification of mathematical calculations we will consider the following equation:

$$
x(t+1) = A(t)x(t) + B(t)u(t) + C(t)v(t), \quad x(0) = \{x_0, I_0\}
\tag{9.15}
$$

where

- $t \in \overline{0,T-1} = \{0,\,1,\,\ldots,\,T-1\}\,(T>0)$;

- $x(t) \in R^n$ is the phase vector (vector of phase variables), which is a set of basic parameters describing the state of the system of EIPM at time t;

- R^n is the dimensional Euclidean space of column vectors, and $n \in N$ is the set of natural numbers;

- $u(t) \in R^p$ is the vector of management (management action) that satisfies a given restriction:

$$
u(t) \in U_1 \subset R^p
\tag{9.16}
$$

where U_1 is a finite set of vectors (plurality alternatives to management actions), that is a finite set of vectors R^p, that determine all possible implementations of different management scenarios at time t; $p \in N$;

- $v(t) \in R^q$ is the vector of risks affecting the implementation process EIPM that meet the specified limit:

$$v(t) \in V_1 \subset R^q \tag{9.17}$$

- V_1 is a convex, closed and bounded polyhedron of space R^q; that is, a set that restricts the possible values of the realization of the risk vector at the time t; $q \in N$; and

- $A(t)$, $B(t)$ and $C(t)$ are matrices of dimensions $(n \times n)$, $(n \times p)$ and $(n \times q)$, respectively, determining the dynamics EIPM.

We describe the information capabilities the subject of management in the process management of innovation processes in a discrete dynamic system (9.13) to (9.15).

We assume that in the course of the implementation of EIPM and a fixed natural number $s >> T > 0$ each time $t \in \overline{1,T}$ the subject of management has such information capabilities corresponding to the implementation of the phase vector of the system, management influence and risk vector on the integer period of time $\overline{-s,t}$, preceding the considered process of the innovation management process:

1. The history of realization of the phase vector of the system is known

$$x_t(\cdot) = (x_1(\cdot)_t, x_2(\cdot)_t, \ldots, x_n(\cdot)_t) = \{(x_1(\tau), x_2(\tau), \ldots, x_n(\tau))\}_{\tau \in \overline{-s,t}};$$
$$= \{x(\tau)\}_{\tau \in \overline{-s,t}}$$

2. The known history of implementation influences the management of the system

$$u_t(\cdot) = (u_1(\cdot)_t, u_2(\cdot)_t, \ldots, u_p(\cdot)_t) = \{(u_1(\tau), u_2(\tau), \ldots, u_p(\tau))\}_{\tau \in \overline{-s,t-1}};$$
$$= \{u(\tau)\}_{\tau \in \overline{-s,t-1}}$$

3. The history of the implementation of the risk vector of the system is known

$$v_t(\cdot) = (v_1(\cdot)_t, v_2(\cdot)_t, \ldots, v_q(\cdot)_t) = \{(v_1(\tau), v_2(\tau), \ldots, v_q(\tau))\}_{\tau \in \overline{-s,t-1}}.$$
$$= \{v(\tau)\}_{\tau \in \overline{-s,t-1}}$$

Note that on the basis of these data it is possible to solve the task of *a posteriori* identification (discussed in the following sections) of all the main elements of a discrete dynamic system (9.1), i.e., to determine the elements of matrices $A(t)$, $B(t)$ and $C(t)$. We assume that the subject of management also known equations (9.15) and constraints (9.16) and (9.17).

The management process under consideration is estimated by the value of the convex functional $\gamma : R^n \to R^1$ defined on possible realizations of the phase vector $\chi(T) \in R^n$ of the system at the final time T.

Then, for the system (9.15) to (9.17) the purpose of minimax program management of innovation processes from the point of view of the subject management can be formulated as follows:

On a given period of time $\overline{0,T}$ it is necessary that the subject of management formed such management

$$u^{(e)}(\cdot) = \{u^{(e)}(t)\}_{t \in \overline{0,T-1}}$$

(for all $t \in \overline{0,T-1} : u(t) \in U_1$) that there was a minimum value of the convex functional defined on implementation of the vector $x(T) \in R^n$ (where $\chi(T)$ (where there is an implementation of the phase vector of the system at the time T, the corresponding management of innovation processes $u(\cdot))$ at the worst (that maximize the value of the functional γ) possible implementations of the risk vector

$$v(\cdot) = \{v(t)\}_{t \in \overline{0, T-1}}$$

(for all $t \in \overline{0, T-1}: \ v(t) \in V_1$).

9.7   Formulation of the Task of Minimax Program Management of Innovation Processes at Enterprises

Based on restrictions (9.14) and (9.15),

$$U(\overline{0, T}) = \left\{ u(\cdot) : u(\cdot) = \{u(t)\}_{t \in \overline{0, T-1}}, \forall t \in \overline{0, T-1}, \ u(t) \in U_1 \right\} \tag{9.18}$$

there are many alternatives to all possible implementations of innovation processes $u(\cdot)$ program managements (all possible scenarios of innovation management processes implementation) on the integer time interval $\overline{0, T}$, which is a set of finite:

$$V(\overline{0, T}) = \left\{ v(\cdot) : v(\cdot) = \{v(t)\}_{t \in \overline{0, T-1}}, \forall t \in \overline{0, T-1}, \ v(t) \in V_1 \right\} \tag{9.19}$$

where there is a set of all admissible implementations of the risk vector $v(\cdot)$ (all admissible scenarios of implementation of the risk vector) on the integer interval of time $v(\cdot)$.

Consider the following equations (9.19) for fixed and possible implementations of program management of the innovation processes and the risk vector

$$v(\cdot) \in V(\overline{0, T})$$

$$x_{\overline{0, T}}(T; x_0, I_0, u(\cdot), v(\cdot))$$

The final state (state at time T) of the process trajectories is generated by the systems (9.13) to (9.15) and corresponds to the set

$$(x_0, I_0, u(\cdot), v(\cdot))$$

Let's choose a specific program management

$$u^*(\cdot) = \{u^*(t)\}_{t \in \overline{0, T-1}} \in U(\overline{0, T})$$

with a finite set $U(\overline{0, T})$ of alternatives to all possible program innovation management processes $u(\cdot)$ over a period of time $\overline{0, T}$.

Then, during the implementation of the fixed program management

$$u^*(\cdot) = \{u^*(t)\}_{t \in \overline{0, T-1}}$$

and on the basis of the multistep equation (9.15), will be implemented such a trajectory of the system and (9.15) will go into a system of this type:

$$x^*(t+1) = A(t)^*(t+1) + B(t)u^*(t) + C(t)v(t), x^*(0) = \{x_0, I_0\}, \forall t \in \overline{0, T-1} \tag{9.20}$$

where the final state will be denoted by

$$x^*(T) = x_{\overline{0,T}}(T; x_0, I_0, u^*(\,\cdot\,), v(\,\cdot\,))$$

which is the state at the time t of the trajectory of the management process of the innovation processes generated by the systems (9.15) to (9.17) (with a fixed implementation of the risk vector $v(\cdot) \in V(\overline{0,T})$).

For all valid implementations of sets

$$(x_0, I_0, u(\,\cdot\,), v(\,\cdot\,))$$

$$x(0) = \{_0, I_0\}$$

$$u(\,\cdot\,) \in U(\overline{0,T})$$

and

$$v(\,\cdot\,) \in V(\overline{0,T})$$

For the quality management process in systems (9.13) to (9.15), describing the EIPM, we propose to evaluating the terminal functional $\Phi(u(\cdot))$, the value of which evaluates the quality of the management process of the innovation processes, determined by the following ratio:

$$\tilde{\Phi} = \tilde{\Phi}(x_0, I_0, u(\,\cdot\,), v(\,\cdot\,)) = \Phi(x(T)) = \Phi(x_{\overline{0,T}}(T; x_0, I_0, u(\,\cdot\,), v(\,\cdot\,))) \qquad (9.21)$$

where $\Phi : R^n \to R^1$ is functionality:

$$x(T) = x_{\overline{0,T}}(T; x_0, I_0, u_T(\,\cdot\,), v_T(\,\cdot\,))$$

It should be noted that with the help of the functional Φ based on the ratio (9.19), which determines its value, it is also possible to assess the impact of damage that is possible in the implementation of a specific risk vector $v_T(\,\cdot\,) \in V(\overline{0,T})$.

Then for each fixed program of the innovation management process $u(\cdot) \in U(\overline{0,T})$ from the solution of the optimization task we can find the value of the selected functional:

$$\tilde{\Phi}^{(e)}_{u(\cdot)} = \max_{v(\cdot) \in V(\overline{0,T})} \tilde{\Phi}(x_0, I_0, u(\,\cdot\,), v(\,\cdot\,)) \qquad (9.22)$$

where $v(\cdot) \in V(\overline{0,T})$ introduced above, is the set of all admissible realizations of the vector of risks on an integer interval.

Lets proceed to the formulation of the task of minimax program management of innovation processes with the presence of risks.

Next, we consider the task of minimax program EIPM.

Task 1. It is necessary to find the minimax program management $u^{(e)}(\,\cdot\,) \in U(\overline{0,T})$ satisfying the minimax condition:

$$\begin{aligned}
\tilde{\Phi}^{(e)} &= \max_{v(\cdot) \in V(\overline{0,T})} \tilde{\Phi}(x_0, I_0, u^{(e)}(\,\cdot\,), v(\,\cdot\,)) \\
&= \min_{u(\cdot) \in U(\overline{0,T})} \max_{v(\cdot) \in V(\overline{0,T})} \tilde{\Phi}(x_0, I_0, u(\,\cdot\,), v(\,\cdot\,)) \\
&= \min_{u(\cdot) \in U(\overline{0,T})} \tilde{\Phi}^{(e)}_{u(\cdot)} \\
&= \min_{u(\cdot) \in U(\overline{0,T})} \max_{v(\cdot) \in V(\overline{0,T})} (x_{\overline{0,T}}(T; x_0, I_0, u(\,\cdot\,), v(\,\cdot\,))) \\
&= \max_{v(\cdot) \in V(\overline{0,T})} (x_{\overline{0,T}}(T; x_0, I_0, u^{(e)}(\,\cdot\,), v(\,\cdot\,))) = \Phi^{(e)}
\end{aligned} \qquad (9.23)$$

Note that given the limitation and finiteness of the set of possible program managements $U(\overline{0,T})$ and (9.21), we show that the solution of this task is reduced to the solution of a finite number of optimization problems with a convex functional of the process quality [13].

9.8 General Scheme for Solving the Task of Minimax Program Management of Innovation Processes at the Enterprises

Consider a fixed time interval $(\overline{\tau,\vartheta} \subseteq \overline{0,T} (\tau < \vartheta)$ and a set where $(X(0) = \{x_0, I_0\})$ is a convex closed and bounded polyhedron (with a finite number of vertices) in space; 2^{R^n} is the set of all subsets of space R^n; $u_{\overline{\tau,\vartheta}}(\,\cdot\,) \in U(\overline{\tau,\vartheta})$ is possible program management on the time interval $\overline{\tau,\vartheta}$.

On the basis of (9.13) to (9.15) we introduce:

$$X^{(+)}_{u_{\overline{\tau,\vartheta}}(\cdot)}(\tau, X(\tau), \vartheta, V(\overline{\tau,\vartheta})) = \{x(\vartheta) : x(\vartheta) \in R^n \qquad (9.24)$$

$$x(t+1) = A(t)x(t) + B(t)u(t) + C(t)v(t), \forall t \in \overline{\tau,\vartheta-1}, \; v(t) \in V_1 \qquad (9.25)$$

$$u_{\overline{\tau,\vartheta}}(\,\cdot\,) = \{u(t)\}_{t\in\overline{\tau,\vartheta-1}}, v(\,\cdot\,) = \{v(t)\}_{t\in\overline{\tau,\vartheta-1}} \in V(\overline{\tau,\vartheta}))\} \qquad (9.26)$$

and will call the domain of reach or the predicted set of phase states of systems (9.15) to (9.17) at the time, which corresponds to the set $(X(\tau), u_{\overline{\tau,\vartheta}}(\,\cdot\,))$ [10].

Given the linearity of the recurrent dynamical system (9.15) and the introduced set condition V_1, which is a convex, closed and bounded polyhedron in space R^q, it can be shown that the following properties of the introduced set $u_{\overline{\tau,\vartheta}}(\,\cdot\,) = \{u(t)\}_{t\in\overline{\tau,\vartheta-1}} \in U(\overline{\tau,\vartheta})$ are valid for the fixed program management [8]:

1. $X^{(+)}_{u_{\overline{\tau,t}}(\cdot)}(\tau, X(\tau), t, V(\overline{\tau,t})) = X^{(+)}_{u_{\overline{\tau,t}}(\cdot)}(t)$ for all is $t \in \overline{\tau+1,\vartheta}$, a non-empty, convex, closed and bounded polyhedron (with a finite number of vertices) in space $R^n (u_{\overline{\tau,t}}(\,\cdot\,) = \{u(t)\}_{t\in\overline{\tau,t-1}})$ (see, for example, [9]);

2. for all $t \in \overline{\tau,\vartheta-1}$ and $X^{(+)}_{u_{\overline{0,\tau}}(\cdot)}(\tau) = X(\tau)$ fair recurrence ratio:

$$X^{(+)}_{u_{\overline{\tau,t+1}}(\cdot)}(\tau, X(\tau), t+1, V(\overline{\tau,t+1})) = X^{(+)}_{u_{\overline{t,t+1}}(\cdot)}(t, X^{(+)}_{u_{\overline{\tau,t}}(\cdot)}(t), t+1, V(\overline{t,t+1}))$$
$$= X^{(+)}_{u(t)}(t, X^{(+)}_{u_{\overline{\tau,t}}(\cdot)}(t), t+1, V_1) \qquad (9.27)$$

Then it follows from the relation (9.27) that the multistep task of constructing the reachability domain $X^{(+)}_{u_{\overline{\tau,\vartheta}}(\cdot)}(\tau, X(\tau), \vartheta, V(\overline{\tau,\vartheta}))$ is reduced to the solution of a finite recurrent sequence of only one-step problems of constructing the following reachability domains, respectively:

$$X^{(+)}_{u_{\overline{\tau,t+1}}(\cdot)}(t+1) = X^{(+)}_{u_{\overline{t,t+1}}(\cdot)}(t, X^{(+)}_{u_{\overline{\tau,t}}(\cdot)}(t), t+1, V(\overline{t,t+1}))$$
$$= X^{(+)}_{u(t)}(t, X^{(+)}_{u_{\overline{\tau,t}}(\cdot)}(t), t+1, V_1), t \in \overline{\tau,\vartheta-1}, X^{(+)}_{u_{\overline{\tau,\tau}}(\cdot)}(\tau) = X(\tau) \qquad (9.28)$$

Based on these properties, the general scheme of solving Task 1 for a dynamic system (9.15) to (9.17), (9.22) can be described as the implementation of the following sequence of actions [9]:

1. Let's sort by increasing the natural index j to a finite set $U(\overline{0,T})$ consisting of N_u possible program managements $u_T^{(j)}(\cdot) = \{u^{(j)}(t)\}_{t \in \overline{0,T-1}} \in U(\overline{0,T})$ over a period of time $\overline{0,T}$, that is, we have

$$U(\overline{0,T}) = \{u_T^{(j)}(\cdot)\}_{j \in \overline{1,N_u}}$$

2. For fixed and possible program management (i.e., from a set of alternatives of possible management actions $(u_T^{(j)}(\cdot) \in U(\overline{0,T}))$ $(j \in \overline{1,N_u})$, taking into account the above property, the area of reach $X_{u_T^{(j)}(\cdot)}^{(+)}(0,X(0),T,V(\overline{0,T}))$ considered dynamic system (9.15) to (9.17) at the final time t, which corresponds to fixed set $(\{x_0,I_0,\},u_{0,T}^{(j)}(\cdot))$ $)) = (X(0),u_{0,T}^{(j)}(\cdot)) \in 2^{R^n} \times U(\overline{0,T})$, are convex, closed and a bounded polyhedron (with a finite number of vertices) of the space R^n that we built on the basis of the recurrent formulas (9.27) and (9.28) by implementing the construction of T single-step domains of reach, namely:

$$X_{u_{t+1}^{(j)}(\cdot)}^{(+)}(0,X(0),t+1,V(\overline{0,t+1})) = X_{u_{t,t+1}^{(j)}(\cdot)}^{(+)}(t,X_{u_t^{(j)}(\cdot)}^{(+)}(t),t+1,V(\overline{t,t+1}))$$
$$= X_{u^{(j)}(t)}^{(+)}(t, X_{u_t^{(j)}(\cdot)}^{(+)}(t),t+1,V_1) \,\forall\, t \in \overline{0,T-1}$$

$$(9.29)$$

where $X(0) = \{x_0, I_0\}$; $X_{u_t^{(j)}(\cdot)}^{(+)}(t) = X_{u_t^{(j)}(\cdot)}^{(+)}(0,X(0),t,V(\overline{0,t}))$.

3. For the selected fixed program management $u_{0,T}^{(j)}(\cdot) \in U(\overline{0,T})$ $(j \in \overline{1,N_u})$ and the range of reach constructed in accordance with it $X_{u_{0,T}^{(j)}(\cdot)}^{(+)}(0,X(0),T,V(\overline{0,T}))$ which is a convex, closed and bounded polyhedron (with a finite number of vertices) of space R^n, with a solution of the convex mathematical program task with a convex terminal functional Φ and linear constraints, describes the area reach

$$X_{u_{0,T}^{(j)}(\cdot)}^{(+)}(0,X(0),T,V(\overline{0,T}))$$

(see, for example, [5]) in accordance with (9.20), (9.21), and (9.24) to (9.26), we find the following value of the quality functional Φ:

$$\Phi_{u_{0,T}^{(j)}(\cdot)}^{(e)} = \max_{x(T) \in X_{u_{0,T}^{(j)}(\cdot)}^{(+)}(0,\{x_0,I_0\},T,V(\overline{0,T}))} \Phi(x(T)) \qquad (9.30)$$

It should be noted that for solving the problem, one can use the Zeytendeik method [11].

4. With the decoupling of the following discrete optimization problem, we find the program management $\hat{u}_{0,T}^{(e)}(\cdot) \in U(\overline{0,T})$ and the numerical value $\hat{\Phi}^{(e)}$:

$$\min_{u_{0,T}(\cdot) \in U(\overline{0,T})} \Phi_{u_{0,T}(\cdot)}^{(e)} = \min_{i \in \overline{1,N_u}} \Phi_{u_{0,T}^{(j)}(\cdot)}^{(e)} = \Phi_{\hat{u}_{0,T}^{(j)}(\cdot)}^{(e)} = \hat{\Phi}^{(e)} \qquad (9.31)$$

Based on relations (9.21) to (9.23) and (9.24) to (9.30), it can be shown that the following equalities hold:

$$u^{(e)}(\cdot) = u_{0,T}^{(e)}(\cdot) = \hat{u}_{0,T}^{(e)}(\cdot) \in U(\overline{0,T}) \qquad (9.32)$$

$$\Phi^{(e)} = \hat{\Phi}^{(e)} \tag{9.33}$$

which shows that as a result of the implementation of the proposed general scheme, a complete solution to Task 1 was found [2].

Note that the procedure for constructing one-step reach $X^{(+)}_{u^{(i)}(t)}(t, X^{(+)}_{u^{(i)}_{\overline{0,t}}(\cdot)}(t), t+1, V_1)$, $\forall t \in \overline{0, T-1}$, areas appearing in formula (9.29) can be implemented similarly to a computational algorithm [4], which reduces the solutions of this task in the implementation of solutions of a finite number of tasks of linear mathematical programming.

9.9 Model of Multicriteria Optimization of Program Management of Innovation Processes at the Enterprises

Based on the restrictions (9.15) to (9.17) the set

$$U(\overline{0, T}) = \left\{ u_T(\,\cdot\,) : u_T(\,\cdot\,) = \{u(t)\}_{t \in \overline{0, T-1}} \in R^{(p \times T)}, \forall t \in \overline{0, T-1},\ u(t) \in U_1 \right\} \tag{9.34}$$

There are many alternatives to all possible implementations of program management of innovation processes $u_T(\,\cdot\,)$ (all possible scenarios of implementing management of innovation processes) on an integer time interval $\overline{0, T}$, which is a finite set.

Thus, summarizing the above, we note that the solution for Task 2 of minimax program management of innovation processes under the presence of risks is found by performing the proposed general scheme and reducing it to the implementation of solutions of a finite number of linear tasks and convex mathematical programming, as well as discrete optimization tasks.

$$V(\overline{0, T}) = \left\{ v_T(\,\cdot\,) : v_T(\,\cdot\,) = \{v(t)\}_{t \in \overline{0, T-1}} \in R^{(q \times T)}, \forall t \in \overline{0, T-1},\ v(t) \in V_1 \right\} \tag{9.35}$$

There is a set of all permissible realizations of the risk vector $v_T(\,\cdot\,)$ (all possible scenarios for the realization of the risk vector) at integer time intervals $\overline{0, T}$.

We choose a specific program management $u_T^*(\,\cdot\,) = \{u^*(t)\}_{t \in \overline{0, T-1}} \in U(\overline{0, T})$, $\forall t \in \overline{0, T-1}: u^*(t) \in U_1$ from a finite set of alternatives $U(\overline{0, T})$ of all possible program managements $u_T(\,\cdot\,)$ on a time interval $\overline{0, T}$.

Then, with a fixed program management $u_T^*(\,\cdot\,) \in U(\overline{0, T})$ and a risk vector $v_T^*(\,\cdot\,) \in V(\overline{0, T})$ based on the multistep equation (9.15), we realize the following trajectory of the system under consideration:

$$\forall t \in \overline{0, T-1}: \bar{x}^*(t+1) = A(t)\bar{x}^*(t+1) + B(t)\bar{u}^*(t) + C(t)\bar{v}^*(t), x^*(0) = \{x_0, I_0\} \tag{9.36}$$

where

- $\bar{x}^*(T) = x_{\overline{0, T}}(T; x_0, I_0, u_T^*(\,\cdot\,),;$

- $v_T^*(\cdot))$ there is a state at the moment of time T of the trajectory of the process of innovation processes management, generated by systems (9.15) to (9.17) and corresponds to the set $(x_0, I_0, u_T^*(\,\cdot\,), v_T^*(\,\cdot\,))$; that is, the final state of this system.

For all acceptable implementations of the sets, let $(x_0, I_0, u_T(\,\cdot\,), v_T(\,\cdot\,))$, $x(0) = \{x_0, I_0\}$, $u_T(\,\cdot\,) \in U(\overline{0, T})$ and $v_T(\,\cdot\,) \in V(\overline{0, T})$ be the quality of the management process in systems (9.15) to (9.17). For describing the innovation processes management, we suggest evaluating, for example, by the vector terminal functionality (an indicator of the quality of the process) $\Phi = \Phi(_1\Phi,_2, \ldots \Phi,_r)$; that is, a set of r convex functionals Φ_i, $i \in \overline{1,r}$, the values of which assess the quality of the innovation management processes, which are determined by such relations:

$$\Phi_i(x_0,I_0, u_T(\,\cdot\,),v_T(\,\cdot\,)) = F_i(x_{\overline{0,T}}(T; x_0, I_0, u_T(\,\cdot\,), v_T(\,\cdot\,))) = F_i(x(T)), i \in \overline{1,r}$$

(9.37)

where

- $F_i : R^n \to R^1$ is a convex functional for each $i \in \overline{1,r}$; $x(T) = x_{\overline{0,T}}(T; x_0,)$; and

- $I_0, u_T(\,\cdot\,), v_T(\,\cdot\,))$.

On the basis of the introduced relation (9.37) of the vector functional $\Phi = (\Phi_1, \Phi_2, \ldots, \Phi_r)$ for assessing the quality of the considered process of optimizing the innovation management processes, we introduce into consideration a scalar objective function $F(x_0,I_0, u_T(\,\cdot\,),v_T(\,\cdot\,))$, the value of which for all implementations of sets that are admissible over a period of time $\overline{0,}$ $(x_0,I_0, u_T(\,\cdot\,), v_T(\,\cdot\,))$, where $u_T(\cdot) = \{u(t)\}_{t\in \overline{0,T-1}} \in U(\overline{0,T})$ and $v_T(\cdot) = \{v(t)\}_{t\in \overline{0,T-1}} \in V(\overline{0,T})$ is determined according to:

$$\begin{aligned}
F(x_0,I_0, u_T(\,\cdot\,),v_T(\,\cdot\,)) &= \sum_{i=1}^{r} \mu_i \cdot \Phi_i(x_0,I_0, u_T(\,\cdot\,),v_T(\,\cdot\,)) \\
&= \sum_{i=1}^{r} \mu_i \cdot F_i(x_{\overline{0,T}}(T; x_0, I_0, u_T(\,\cdot\,), v_T(\,\cdot\,)) \\
&= \sum_{i=1}^{r} \mu_i \cdot F_i(x(T)) = \gamma(x(T)) \\
\forall i \in \overline{1,r} &: \mu_i \geq 0, \sum_{i=1}^{r} \mu_i = 1
\end{aligned}$$

(9.38)

where

- $x(T) = (x_{\overline{0,T}}(T;x_0,I_0, u_T(\,\cdot\,),v_T(\,\cdot\,))$; and

- y is a convex functional introduced earlier.

Note that the objective function $F(x_0,I_0, u_T(\,\cdot\,),v_T(\,\cdot\,))$ is a convex scalar convolution of a vector functional $\Phi = (\Phi_1, \Phi_2, \ldots, \Phi_r)$; that is, it is formed in accordance with the scalarization method of vector objective functions (see, for example, [4]) with inherent weights μ_i, $i \in \overline{1,r}$ that can be determined, for example, by expert or knowledge statistical information about the history of the implementation of the main parameters of the process.

Formulation of a multicriteria task is used to find a guaranteed result of a minimax program management of an innovation process. Then the meaningful multicriteria task of finding a guaranteed (minimax) result of program management of an innovation process with the presence of risks can be formulated as follows: consider for a given period of time $\overline{0,T}$ the process of optimizing the program management of an EIPM, described by the economic-mathematical model (9.15) to (9.17), (9.38) and a given initial phase vector of the system $x(0) = \{_0,I_0\}$. It is necessary to find such program management $u_T^{(e)}(\cdot) = \{u^{(e)}(t)\}_{t\in \overline{0,T-1}} \in U(\overline{0,T})$ on the time interval $\overline{0,T}$, which guarantees the result of the EIPM subject, which is estimated by the objective function of the form (9.38), which is the smallest compared to the results possible with the implementation of any other managements $u_T(\cdot) = \{u(t)\}_{t \in \overline{0,T-1}} \in U(\overline{0,T})$ and risks $v_T(\cdot) = \{v(t)\}_{t \in \overline{0,T-1}} \in V(\overline{0,T})$ in the same period of time; that is, for the objective function values that meet these program management and implementation risks, the following condition extremality:

$$F(x_0, I_0, u_T^{(e)}(\,\cdot\,), v_T(\,\cdot\,)) \leq \max_{v_T(\cdot) \in V(\overline{0,T})} F(x_0, I_0, u_\tau(\,\cdot\,), v_T(\,\cdot\,)) \tag{9.39}$$

Note that condition (9.39) is a guaranteed optimality condition or a minimax condition when implementing innovation management processes on the considered time interval $\overline{0,T}$. Based on the above-developed economic and mathematical model (9.15) to (9.17) and (9.38) describing the dynamics of the main innovation management process parameters on the considered time interval $\overline{0,T}$, and with the quality criteria for the implementation of the process in question, we can formulate the task of multicriteria optimization of the program minimax innovation management processes in the presence of risks.

Task 2. For a given time interval and the initial phase vector of the system $x(0) = \{_0, I_0\}$ it is necessary to find $U^{(e)}(\overline{0,T}) \subseteq U(\overline{0,T})$ a set of possible program managements $u_T^{(e)}(\cdot) = \{u^{(e)}(t)\}_{t \in \overline{0,T-1}} \in U(\overline{0,T})$ on the time interval $\overline{0,T}$ that satisfy such a minimax condition:

$$U^{(e)}(\overline{0,T}) = u_T^{(e)}(\cdot) : u_T^{(e)}(\cdot) = \{u^{(e)}(t)\}_{t \in \overline{0,T-1}} \in U(\overline{0,T}) \tag{9.40}$$

$$\begin{aligned} F^{(e)} &= \max_{v_T(\cdot) \in V(\overline{0,T})} F(x_0, I_0, u_T^{(e)}(\,\cdot\,), v_\tau(\,\cdot\,)) \\ &= \min_{u_T(\cdot) \in U(\overline{0,T})} \max_{v_T(\cdot) \in V(\overline{0,T})} F(x_0, I_0, u_T(\,\cdot\,), v_T(\,\cdot\,)) \end{aligned} \tag{9.41}$$

which we will call the set of minimax program managements for this problem, and the number $F^{(e)}$ will be called the guaranteed or minimax result for this task [3].

Note that the set of possible program management $U(\overline{0,T})$ is a finite set and, taking into account (9.39) and (9.40), it can be shown (see, for example, [4]) that there is a solution to Task 2 and we reduce it by solving a finite number of optimization problems with linear and convex functionals of the quality of the corresponding processes, as well as discrete optimization problems.

The general scheme for solving Task 2:

For any fixed time intervals $\overline{\tau, \vartheta} \subseteq \overline{0,T}$ ($\tau < \vartheta$) and a set, where $X(\tau) \subset R^n$ ($X(0) = \{_0, I_0\}$) is a convex closed and bounded polyhedron (with a finite number of vertices) in space R^n; 2^{R^n} is the set of all subsets of space R^n; $u_{\overline{\tau,\vartheta}}(\,\cdot\,) \in U(\overline{\tau,\vartheta})$, it is possible to program management on the time interval $\overline{\tau, \vartheta}$, on the basis of (9.15) to (9.17), we consider the range of reach (predictive set [4]) of the phase states of the systems (9.15) to (9.17) at the moment of time ϑ corresponding to the set $(X(\tau), u_{\overline{\tau,\vartheta}}(\,\cdot\,))$:

$$X_{u_{\overline{\tau,\vartheta}}(\cdot)}^{(+)}(\tau, X(\tau), \vartheta, V(\overline{\tau,\vartheta})) = \{x(\vartheta) : x(\vartheta) \in R^n \tag{9.42}$$

$$\bar{x}(t+1) = A(t)\bar{x}(t) + B(t)\bar{u}(t) + C(t)\bar{v}(t), \tag{9.43}$$

$$u_{\overline{\tau,\vartheta}}(\,\cdot\,) = \{u(t)\}_{t \in \overline{\tau,\vartheta-1}} \forall t \in \overline{\tau, \vartheta-1} : v(t) \in V_1\} \tag{9.44}$$

Taking into account that the linearity of the current dynamical system (9.15) and the introduced condition on the set V_1 is a convex, closed and bounded polyhedron in space R^q, it can be shown that for fixed program management $u_{\overline{\tau,\vartheta}}(\,\cdot\,) = \{u(t)\}_{t\in \overline{\tau,\vartheta-1}} \in U(\overline{\tau,\vartheta})$ the properties of the set are valid [4]:

1. $X^{(+)}_{u_{\tau,t}(\cdot)}(\tau,X(\tau),t,V(\overline{\tau,t})) = X^{(+)}_{u_{\tau,t}(\cdot)}(t)$ for all $t \in \overline{\tau+1,\vartheta}$ there is a non-empty, convex, closed and bounded polyhedron (with a finite number of vertices) in the space $R^n(u_{\overline{\tau,t}}(\,\cdot\,) = \{u(t)\}_{t\in \overline{\tau,t-1}})$;

2. For all $t \in \overline{\tau,\vartheta-1}$ and $X^{(+)}_{u_{0,\tau}(\cdot)}(\tau) = X(\tau)$ a fair recurrence relation:

$$
\begin{aligned}
X^{(+)}_{u_{\tau,t+1}(\cdot)}(\tau,X(\tau),t+1,V(\overline{\tau,t+1})) &= X^{(+)}_{u_{t,t+1}(\cdot)}(t,X^{(+)}_{u_{\tau,t}(\cdot)}(t),t+1,V(\overline{t,t+1})) \\
&= X^{(+)}_{u(t)}(t, X^{(+)}_{u_{\tau,t}(\cdot)}(t),t+1,V_1)
\end{aligned}
$$

$$(9.45)$$

With (9.45) it follows that the multistep task of constructing an attainable domain $X^{(+)}_{u_{\tau,\vartheta}(\cdot)}(\tau,X(\tau),\vartheta,V(\overline{\tau,\vartheta}))$ is reduced to solving a finite recurrent sequence of one:

$$
\begin{aligned}
X^{(+)}_{u_{\tau,t+1}(\cdot)}(t+1) &= X^{(+)}_{u_{t,t+1}(\cdot)}(t, X^{(+)}_{u_{\tau,t}(\cdot)}(t),t+1,V(\overline{t,t+1})) \\
&= X^{(+)}_{u(t)}(t, X^{(+)}_{u_{\tau,t}(\cdot)}(t),t+1,V_1), t \in \overline{\tau,\vartheta-1}, X^{(+)}_{u_{\tau,\tau}(\cdot)}(\tau) = X(\tau)
\end{aligned}
$$

$$(9.46)$$

Thus, based on these properties, the general scheme for solving Task 2 for the dynamic system (9.15) to (9.17), (9.38) can be described as the following sequence of steps:

(a) By increasing the natural index j, we put in order a finite set of alternatives $U(\overline{0,T})$, which consist of N_u possible program management

$$
u^{(j)}_T(\,\cdot\,) = \{u^{(j)}(t)\}_{t\in\overline{0,T-1}} \in U(\overline{0,T})
$$

at an interval of time $\overline{0,T}$; that is, we have $U(\overline{0,T}) = \{u^{(j)}_T(\,\cdot\,)\}_{j\in\overline{1,N_u}}$.

(b) Based on the above property for fixed and possible program management

$$
u^{(j)}_T(\,\cdot\,) \in U(\overline{0,T})(j \in \overline{1,N_u})
$$

the range of reach $X^{(+)}_{u^{(j)}_T(\cdot)}(0,X(0),T,V(\overline{0,T}))$ of the considered dynamic system (9.15) - (9.17) for the final time T, corresponds to a fixed set $(X(0),u^{(j)}_T(\,\cdot\,)) \in 2^{R^n} \times U(\overline{0,T})$ is a convex, closed and bounded polyhedron (with a finite number of vertices) spaces R^n, we build on the basis of recurrent formulas (9.45) and (9.46) by implementing the construction of T one-step reach areas, namely:

$$
\begin{aligned}
X^{(+)}_{u^{(j)}_{t+1}(\cdot)}(0,X(0),t+1,V(\overline{0,t+1})) &= X^{(+)}_{u^{(j)}_{t,t+1}(\cdot)}(t,X^{(+)}_{u^{(j)}_t(\cdot)}(t),t+1,V(\overline{t,t+1})) \\
&= X^{(+)}_{u^{(j)}(t)}(t, X^{(+)}_{u^{(j)}_t(\cdot)}(t),t+1,V_1)
\end{aligned}
$$

$$(9.47)$$

where

- $X(0) = \{x_0, I_0\}$;
- $X^{(+)}_{u^{(j)}_t(\cdot)}(t) = X^{(+)}_{u^{(j)}_t(\cdot)}(0,X(0),t,V(\overline{0,t}))$

3. For the constructed corresponding range $X^{(+)}_{u^{(j)}_T(\cdot)}(0,X(0),T,V(\overline{0,T}))$, which is a convex, closed and bounded polyhedron (with a finite number of vertices) of the space R^n and the selected fixed program management $u^{(j)}_T(\cdot) \in U(\overline{0,T})$ $(j \in \overline{1,N_u})$, to solve the task of convex mathematical programming with a convex terminal functional of the following form:

$$F(x_0,I_0,u_T(\,\cdot\,),v_T(\,\cdot\,)) = \sum_{i=1}^{r} \mu_i \cdot \Phi_i(x_0,I_0,u_T(\,\cdot\,),v_T(\,\cdot\,))$$

$$\forall i \in \overline{1,r} \; : \; \mu_i \geq 0, \; \sum_{i=1}^{r} \mu_i = 1 \tag{9.48}$$

formed from a functional $\Phi = (\Phi_1,\Phi_2,\ldots,\Phi_r)$ on the basis of (9.38), and a finite system of linear constraints, the solution set of which describes the range of reach $X^{(+)}_{u^{(j)}_T(\cdot)}(0,X(0),T,V(\overline{0,T}))$ [10], according to (9.37), (9.38), and (9.39) we find the value of this functional:

$$
\begin{aligned}
F_{u^{(j)}_T(\cdot)} &= F(x_0,I_0,u^{(j)}_T(\,\cdot\,),v^{(e)}_T(\,\cdot\,)) \\
&= \max_{v_T(\cdot)\in V(\overline{0,T})} F(x_0,I_0,u^{(j)}_T(\,\cdot\,),v_T(\,\cdot\,)) \\
&= \max_{x(T)\in X^{(+)}_{u^{(j)}_T(\cdot)}(0,X(0),T,V(\overline{0,T}))} \sum_{i=1}^{r} \mu_i \cdot F_i(x_{\overline{0,T}}(T;x_0,I_0,u^{(j)}_T(\,\cdot\,),v_T(\,\cdot\,))) \\
&= \max_{x(T)\in X^{(+)}_{u^{(j)}_T(\cdot)}(0,X(0),T,V(\overline{0,T}))} \sum_{i=1}^{r} \mu_i \cdot F_i(x(T)) \\
&= \max_{x(T)\in X^{(+)}_{u^{(j)}_T(\cdot)}(0,X(0),T,V(\overline{0,T}))} \gamma(x(T))
\end{aligned}
\tag{9.49}
$$

where

- $x(T) = (x_{\overline{0,T}}(T;x_0,I_0,u^{(j)}_T(\,\cdot\,),v_T(\,\cdot\,))$; and
- γ is a convex functional introduced earlier.

4. Based on (9.49) from the junction of the following finite discrete optimization problem, we find $\tilde{U}^{(e)}(\overline{0,T})$ the set of program managements $\tilde{u}^{(e)}_T(\,\cdot\,) \in U(\overline{0,T})$ and the numerical value $\tilde{F}^{(e)}$:

$$\tilde{U}^{(e)}(\overline{0,T}) = \tilde{u}^{(e)}_T(\cdot) : \tilde{u}^{(e)}_T(\cdot) = \{\tilde{u}^{(e)}(t)\}_{t\in \overline{0,T-1}} \in U(\overline{0,T}) \tag{9.50}$$

$$F(x_0,\tilde{u}^{(e)}_T(\,\cdot\,),v^{(e)}_T(\,\cdot\,)) = \min_{u_T(\cdot)\in U(\overline{0,T})} F_{u_T(\cdot)} = \min_{j\in \overline{1,N_u}} F_{u^{(j)}_T(\cdot)} = F_{\tilde{u}^{(e)}_T(\cdot)} = \tilde{F}^{(e)} \tag{9.51}$$

Taking into account (9.37) to (9.51), it can be shown that the following equalities hold:

$$U^{(e)}(\overline{0,T}) = \tilde{U}^{(e)}(\overline{0,T}) \tag{9.52}$$

$$F^{(e)} = \tilde{F}^{(e)} \tag{9.53}$$

The fulfillment of equalities (9.52) and (9.53) means that as a result of applying the proposed general scheme, we have a complete solution to Task 2.

One-step reach areas:

$$X^{(+)}_{u^{(j)}_{t,t+1}(\cdot)}(t, X^{(+)}_{u_{\overline{\tau,t}}(\cdot)}(t), t+1, V(\overline{t,t+1})) = X^{(+)}_{u^{(j)}(t)}(t, X^{(+)}_{u_{\overline{\tau,t}}(\cdot)}(t), t+1, V_1)$$
$$t \in \overline{\tau, \vartheta - 1}, (j \in \overline{1, N_u})$$
(9.54)

From formula (9.46), one can construct by constructing a solution to this task in the implementation of solutions of a finite number of tasks of linear mathematical programming [9].

Thus, summarizing the above, we note that the solution of Task 2 of minimax program management of innovation processes under the presence of risks is found by performing the proposed general scheme and reducing it to the implementation of solutions of a finite number of linear tasks and convex mathematical programming, as well as discrete optimization tasks.

It should be noted that the proposed general solution for developing a multicriteria task of finding a minimax program management of innovation processes with risks allows you to apply different types of convolutions for the objective function, which are limited by the information resources of the process under study.

9.10 Conclusion

1. The conceptual model of dynamic optimization of the EIPM program is constructed. To solve this problem, the program management procedure is organized taking into account the risks, for which a structural and functional model for solving the task of dynamic optimization of the EIPM program is developed.

2. On the basis of the provisions of the formulated concept, to solve the task of optimization of program management of innovation processes, for each fixed program management, we build the appropriate area of reach, which is determined by sorting out all possible acceptable risk vectors. The convex hull of each constructed reach region is a convex polyhedron (since they were defined for vectors that are vertices of polyhedral constraints), at the vertices of which the optimized functions take extreme values. For each domain of reach (corresponding polyhedron), we find a vertex (vector) that determines the maximum value of the objective function for the corresponding fixed program management and the available implementations of the risk vectors that are generated by the corresponding worst implementation of this vector. Furthermore, from this set of sets and possible program management and the corresponding maximum values of the objective function, we choose a pair such that the maximum value of the objective function is either the smallest (minimum); that is, the guaranteed value of the objective function or the minimum result. The program management included in this pair satisfies the minimax condition; that is, it is a minimax management of the innovation processes, or guaranteed management of the innovation processes, in the considered problem.

3. The minimax condition (principle) is applied in problems of canonical form when we investigate the target function for the minimum. In the real practical formulation of the task of optimization of innovation management processes, there can be a situation when it is necessary to maximize the target function; that is, to solve the task maximally (in this case, the worst risk vectors and minimize the target function). In order to bring such a task to the minimax task, it is necessary to turn the original target function into the opposite one by multiplying its values by (-1), thus forming a new target function. Then, it is known that

minimax management will coincide with maximin; therefore, it is sufficient to investigate only the minimax task.

4. The economic-mathematical model allows describing the dynamics of the multi-step process of EIPM depending on the given initial conditions of investment resources and other initial values of the parameters of the system state and the choice of specific management implementations influences. As a criterion of efficiency of optimization of management of innovation processes it is possible to consider various types of functionals of linear or convex cells.

5. Taking into account the multi-aspect criteria of optimization of the process under study, the study proposes a dynamic model of multicriteria optimization of the EIPM program. It is proposed to form a target function $F(x_0, I_0, u_T(\cdot), v_T(\cdot))$ in the form of a convex scalar convolution of the vector functional $\Phi = (\Phi_1, \Phi_2, \ldots \Phi_r)$. That is, it is formed in accordance with the method scalarize vector of the objective functions with integral weight coefficients μ_i, $i \in \overline{1, r}$ that can be determined; for example, the expert proposed by the general scheme of solving the task of multicriteria optimization of min-max EIPM in the presence of risks allows the use of different types of folds in the objective function, which is limited by the capabilities of information resources for the process under study.

REFERENCES

1. Babenko, V., & Salem, A. B. M. (2018). Modeling of the control of innovative processes of a production activity taking into account risks. *International Journal of Economics and Statistics*, 6, 99. URL: http://naun.org/cms.action?id=18790

2. Babenko, V., Alisejko, E., & Kochuyeva, Z. (2017). The task of minimax adaptive management of innovative processes at an enterprise with risk assessment. *Innovative Technologies and Scientific Solutions for Industries*, 1(1), 6-13. DOI: https://doi.org/10.30837/2522-9818.2017.1.006

3. Babenko, V., Chebanova, N., Ryzhikova, N., Rudenko, S., & Birchenko, N. (2018). Research into the process of multi-level management of enterprise production activities with taking risks into consideration. *Eastern-European Journal of Enterprise Technologies*, 1(3), 91. DOI: 10.15587/1729-4061.2018.123461

4. Babenko, V., Nazarenko, O., Nazarenko, I., Mandych, O., & Krutko, M. (2018). Aspects of program control over technological innovations with consideration of risks. *Eastern-European Journal of Enterprise Technologies*, 3(4), 93. DOI: 10.15587/1729-4061.2018.133603

5. Babenko, V., Romanenkov, Y., Yakymova, L., & Nakisko, A. (2017). Development of the model of minimax adaptive management of innovative processes at an enterprise with consideration of risks. *Eastern-European Journal of Enterprise Technologies*, 5(4), 49-56. DOI: https://doi.org/10.15587/1729-4061.2017.112076

6. Bulaev, V. V., & Shorikov, A. F. (2018). Discretization procedure for linear dynamical systems. *Journal of Mathematical Sciences*, 230(5), 664-667.. DOI: 10.1007/s10958-018-3765-5

7. Alatas, B. (2017). Performance comparisons of current metaheuristic algorithms on unconstrained optimization problems. *Periodicals of Engineering and Natural Sciences*, 5(3).

8. Shorikov, A. F., & Babenko, V. A. (2014). Optimization of assured result in dynamical model of management of innovation process in the enterprise of agricultural production complex. *Economy of Region/Ekonomika Regiona*, 37(1). DOI: 10.17059/2014-1-18

9. Shorikov, A. F. (2016, December). Algorithm for solving of two-level hierarchical minimax program control problem in discrete-time dynamical system with incomplete information. In *AIP Conference Proceedings* (Vol. 1789, No. 1, p. 060011). AIP Publishing. DOI: 10.1063/1.5007384

10. Shorikov, A. F. (2014). Minimax program control for the approach process in a two-level hierarchical discrete dynamical system. *Automation and Remote Control*, 75(3), 458-469. DOI: 10.1134/S0005117914030047

11. Tabak, D. (1970). Optimal control of nonlinear discrete time systems by mathematical programming. *Journal of the Franklin Institute*, 289(2), 111-119.

12. Sumesh, C. S., & Ramesh, A. (2018). Numerical modelling and optimization of dry orthogonal turning of Al6061 T6 alloy. *Periodica Polytechnica Mechanical Engineering*, 62(3), 196-202. DOI: 10.3311/PPme.11347.

13. Turai, B. M., & Satish, C. (2018, April). Mathematical modelling and numerical simulation of forces in milling process. In *AIP Conference Proceedings* (Vol. 1952, No. 1, p. 020068). AIP Publishing. DOI: 10.1063/1.5032030

14. Tyagi, K., & Tyagi, K. (2015). A comparative analysis of optimization techniques. *International Journal of Computer Applications*, 975, 8887.

15. Nayyar, A., Le, D. N., & Nguyen, N. G. (Eds.). (2018). *Advances in Swarm Intelligence for Optimizing Problems in Computer Science*. CRC Press. DOI: 10.1201/9780429445927

16. Le, D. N. (2017). A new ant algorithm for optimal service selection with end-to-end QoS constraints. *Journal of Internet Technology*, 18(5), 1017-1030. DOI: 10.6138/JIT.2017.18.5.20150103

CHAPTER 10

USING SIMULATION FOR DEVELOPMENT OF AUTOMOBILE GAS DIESEL ENGINE SYSTEMS AND THEIR OPERATIONAL CONTROL

Mikhail G. Shatrov, Vladimir V. Sinyavski, Andrey Yu. Dunin, Ivan G. Shishlov, Sergei D. Skorodelov, Andrey L. Yakovenko

DSc in Engineering Program, Moscow Automobile and Road Construction State Technical University (MADI), Moscow, Russia
Corresponding authors: dvs@Madi.ru

Abstract

The work in this chapter focuses on the development of gas supply, diesel fuel supply and electronic control systems for automobile gas diesel engines. Different ways of converting diesel engines to operate on natural gas were analyzed. A gas diesel process with minimized ignition portion of diesel fuel injected by the common rail (CR) system was selected. Electronic engine control and modular gas feed systems which can be used on high- and middle-speed gas diesel engines were developed. A diesel CR fuel supply system was developed in cooperation with the industrial partner. Simulation was used to obtain basic parameters and control methods of these systems. The base diesel engine was converted into gas diesel engine using the systems developed. Bench tests of the gas diesel engine demonstrated a high share of diesel fuel substitution with gas, high fuel efficiency and large decrease of NO_x and CO_2 emissions.

Keywords: Gas diesel engine, dual fuel engine, engine control system; gas feed system, diesel fuel system, injection rate shaping

10.1   Introduction

Conversion of diesel engines into gas and gas diesel engines (dual fuel engines) provides many benefits and it is widely used today for automobile, locomotive, stationary and marine engines.

The reserves of gas on our planet are much higher than that of oil. Natural gas is cheaper than oil and the price difference will grow as more oil is produced from hard-to-reach deposits. According to forecasts, by 2035, the amount of extracted natural gas will reach 5.1 billion tons and its proportion in fuel balance on Earth will grow up to 25% [1]. Engines fueled by natural gas have much cleaner exhaust emissions compared with diesel, especially particles and nitrogen oxides. Change-over to natural gas makes it possible to decrease emission of CO_2 up to 30% due to lower content of carbon in natural gas and its lower consumption compared with diesel fuel because of the higher caloric effect of natural gas (methane).

The most efficient way to develop gas and gas diesel engines is conversion of existing diesel engines for operation on natural gas.

There are several methods of conversion of diesel engines to be fed with natural gas. Spark ignition gas engines using a stoichiometric gas-air mixture. Stable combustion of gas is ensured and a three-way catalyst similar to that mounted on petrol engines may be mounted [2]. Stoichiometric gas-air mixture degrades fuel economy relative to diesel engine, but as natural gas is practically two times cheaper than diesel fuel in Russia, fuel costs decrease. Research of fuel consumption by buses in Serbia showed that buses with stoichiometric gas engines had up to 10−25% higher fuel consumption than buses with diesel engines. Still, as in Serbia, natural gas is 52% cheaper than diesel fuel, and the cost of gas fuel is significantly lower [3]. Stoichiometric gas engines have pretty high exhaust gas temperature, which may result in deterioration of the turbocharger and so limits engine boosting.

Spark ignition gas engines using a lean gas-air mixture have a low exhaust gas temperature and therefore may have much higher power. They also have high fuel efficiency and low emissions of NO_x, which allows the elimination of the reduction catalyzer in compliance with ecological standards. Prechamber with enriched gas-air mixture is often used for middle-speed gas engines to inflame and control the lean mixture combustion in the main combustion chamber. The FEV company developed a prechamber system for a gas engine operating on a lean gas-air mixture. To get the efficient combustion without knock and low NOx emissions, the prechamber dimensions, as well as the number and size of the prechamner holes, as well as their layout were optimized. The Miller cycle was used. Simulation was made using the charge motion design (CMD) package to investigate the influence of turbulence on the combustion process. Experiments were carried out on a one-cylinder diesel engine converted for operation on natural gas. After thorough calculation and experimental perfection, a very high mean indicated that effective pressure of 32 bars was attained, there was no knock and emissions of NO did not exceed the limits of the standard TA-Luft [4].

Jenbacher J624 (type 6) engines using lean gas-air mixture having D/S=190/210 mm operating at 1500 rpm are aimed for power generation. They have a gas enriched prechamber and attain a high brake mean effective pressure of 2.4 MPa. The advanced Miller cycle is used there to avoid knock, raise the thermal efficiency up to 48.7% and reduce emissions of NOx. The two-stage turbocharging system is mounted to compensate for filling efficiency degradation caused by the Miller cycle [5, 6]. This is a perfect solution for power generation because the engine operates constantly at a high speed, which prevents knock.

The worse fuel efficiency of gas diesel engines is compensated by lower gas price when the engine is connected directly to the gas pipe. In Russia, gas directly from the pipe may be up to four times cheaper than at the filling station [2]. The use of spark ignition lean mixture combustion on high boosted transport engines is limited by knock which appears at low speeds and transfer modes especially in engines having large cylinder size.

Gas diesel (dual-fuel) engines may have larger cylinder size and higher boosting as they do not have problems with knock. Gas diesel engines with a mechanical diesel fuel supply system have a comparatively low substitution of diesel fuel with gas. The percentage of diesel fuel is 20−30% at full loads, which grows when the load decreases and reaches 100% at idle [7]. The percentage of diesel fuel may be decreased and many engine parameters are significantly improved if the common rail (CR) system is used, which injects a small portion of diesel fuel to ignite the gas-air mixture.

The analyses conducted in the Bauman Moscow State Technical University [8] demonstrated that if the fuel sprays are larger, ignition stability of the gas is higher and the ignition portion of diesel fuel may be lower. If the injector nozzle holes do not change, the fuel spray size depends mainly on the diesel fuel injection pressure (if the pressure grows, the fuel drops become smaller and the fuel spray surface increases), speed and direction of gas movement during the compression stroke (if the speed increases, the mixture formation and combustion of the gas-air mixture improve), backpressure in the cylinder (if the backpressure increases, the diesel fuel atomization improves). At low engine speeds and loads, the pressure and speed of the working medium in the cylinder decrease; also, the backpressure drops due to lower boost pressure. Therefore, a very small diesel fuel ignition portion that can be less than 5% at high load has to be augmented at low loads. One can obtain larger fuel sprays by raising the injection pressure and using a special baffled piston to increase the tangential speed of the working medium.

The problems of combustion in gas diesel engines are reviewed in [9]: high percentage of HC and CO emissions caused by incomplete combustion in some areas, especially at low loads, and cycle-to-cycle instability at high loads. To solve these problems, a number of parameters should be thoroughly controlled: pilot dose of diesel fuel and its multistage injection, diesel fuel injection timing, the amount of gas, and the amount and temperature of air entering the cylinder taking into consideration engine speed and load. Using a fast and efficient control algorithm is the best way to solve these problems. Based on the complete analysis, gas diesel engine using a minimized portion of diesel fuel supplied by the CR system was chosen for automobile engine because it ensures high boosting, engine efficiency, ecological parameters and avoids knock.

10.2 Computer Modeling

A pretty simple and fast 0-dimensional model was used for calculation of gas diesel engine parameters [10]. The model uses Vibe formula for heat release and Woschni formula for heat losses calculation, and empirical formulas for determining cylinder walls temperature and mechanical losses. It takes into account composition of the working medium at any time of the engine cycle. Combustion of the natural gas is calculated based on one-step macro reactions of the mixture's main components. After the model was validated using the tests results of a four-cylinder 2.636 liter gas diesel engine, it showed a high agreement of calculated and experimental parameters.

Gas exchange is calculated based on the quasi-stationary method; compressor and turbine maps are utilized for calculation of parameters at the cylinder inlet and outlet. The model was used for the following aims:

- Calculation of the following basic parameters of gas diesel engines was required for development and adjustment of the gas feed, diesel fuel supply and electronic engine control systems:
  - Injection rate of gas and diesel fuel
  - Counterpressure in the cylinder at the time of diesel fuel injection start
  - Optimal diesel fuel injection advance angle in a wide range of engine speeds and loads

- Analysis of experimental parameters obtained during the engine tests of the gas diesel engine after the systems developed were manufactured, mounted on the engine and their final adjustment made.

10.3 Gas Diesel Engine Systems Developed

Research was carried out for the Cummins KAMA inline 6-cylinder gas diesel engine having D/S=107/124 mm, compression ratio 17.3:1, break mean effective pressure 1.73 MPa at rated speed 2300 rpm. For conversion of diesel engines into gas diesel engines, electronic engine control, modular gas feed and CR fuel supply systems were developed.

10.3.1 Electronic Engine Control System

A completely new electronic engine control system for 6-cylinder gas diesel engines was developed which controls the supply of gaseous and diesel fuel (Figure 10.1).

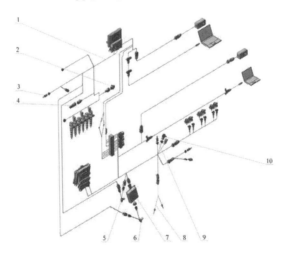

Figure 10.1 Components of the electronic engine control system for gas diesel engines: (1) information calculation block, (2, 10) intake manifold temperature and pressure sensors, (3, 9) cooling agent temperature sensors, (4) barometric correction sensor, (5) crankshaft position sensor, (6) camshaft position sensor, (7) crankshaft and camshaft position sensors adapter, (8) block of thermocouples.

The system generates electric control impulses to control actuators and carries out synchronization and distribution of impulses by the cylinders depending on the engine operation mode on the basis of information received from many sensors.

10.3.2 Modular Gas Feed System

The gas feed system [11] has a modular design which enables its use in engines of different sizes. Each module ensures reduction of pressure and supply of natural gas. One module is used on the automobile Cummins KAMA gas diesel engine and three modules, for example, on the middle-speed locomotive D200 six cylinder gas diesel engine having $\frac{D}{S} = \frac{200}{280}$ mm.

10.3.3 Common Rail Fuel System for Supply of the Ignition Portion of Diesel Fuel

In the course of applied research and experimental development, a domestic common rail fuel supply system for a truck diesel engine was developed (Figure 10.2).

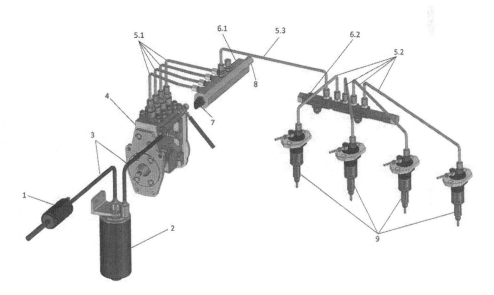

Figure 10.2 Common rail fuel supply system for a truck diesel engine: (1) fuel feed pump, (2) filter, (3) low pressure fuel lines, (4) high pressure fuel pump, (5.1, 5.2, 5.3) high pressure fuel lines, (6.1) coupler, (6.2) common rail, (7) pressure sensor, (8) emergency valve, (9) CR injector.

Domestic manufacturers of diesel engines, KAMAZ Public Company, MMZ Open Company and Avtodiesel (YaMZ) Public Company, aimed at developing engines with perspective energetic and ecological parameters, may become potential customers of the additional variant of fuel supply system being developed for other models of diesel engines. In this context, it is important to ensure injection pressure up to 200 MPa and higher [12], as well as injection rate front shape control [13, 14] and organization of traditional fuel distribution in the combustion chamber [15].

The low pressure line of the fuel supply system includes (Figure 10.2): fuel feed pump (1), fuel filter (2), and fuel lines (3) connecting these elements.

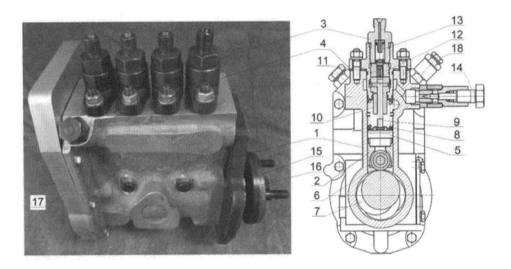

Figure 10.3   HP fuel pump: (1) HP fuel pump body, (2) tappet, (3) push fitting, (4) insert section body, (5) plunger support, (6)tappet roller, (7) camshaft, (8) plunger spring, (9) plunger, (10) plunger liner, (11) delivery valve, (12) delivery valve seat, (13) delivery valve spring, (14) control valve, (15) plate fastening the HP fuel pump to the engine, (16) HP fuel pump drive flange; (17) HP fuel pump rear cover, (18) bypass valve.

The high pressure line includes: High pressure fuel pump (HP pump) (4), coupler 6.1, common rail (6.2), CR injectors (9), fuel lines (5.1). The pressure sensor (7) and emergency valve (8) are mounted on the coupler.

The HP pump (4), fuel lines (5) and CR injectors (9) ensure fuel injection into the engine cylinder with pressure 30–200 MPa. Fuel used for injector control enters a common low pressure line (not shown in Figure 10.2) from each CR injector.

The fuel from each of the four sections of the HP pump (4) enters the coupler (6.1) which is equipped with the fuel pressure sensor (7) and emergency valve (8) via the fuel lines (5.1).

The coupler (6.1) is connected with the common rail (6.2) which supplies the CR injectors (9) with fuel.

The HP fuel pump has a traditional design (Figure 10.3) in line with closed case (1) (without hatch) and insert sections with bodies (4). The camshaft (7) has the eccentric shape cams. The delivery valve (11) has a traditional design with relief collar. Variation of the injection rate of the HP fuel pump is effected by the control valve (14).

In Figure 10.4, a scheme of the CR injector (CRI) and four laboratory prototypes is presented.

The use of the "floating bush" in the design may be considered as a modern approach enabling an increase in the service life of the CRI.

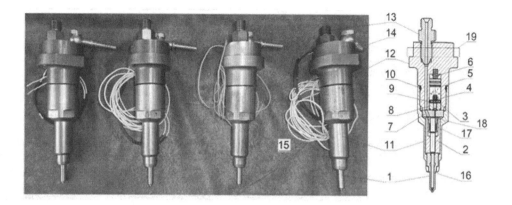

Figure 10.4 CR injectors: (1) injection nozzle, (2) spacer, (3) armature, (4) armature spring, (5) electromagnet, (6) magnet spring, (7) valve seat, (8) armature body, (9) spacer, (10) ring, (11) nozzle nut, (12) injector body, (13, 14) connectors, (15) electromagnet power wires, (16) needle valve, (17) needle valve spring, (18) control chamber, (19) clamp mounting point.

Figure 10.5 shows a possible design of a diesel injector nozzle which enables a uniform distribution of fuel in the combustion chamber zones and relative correction of the dynamics of injected sprays directed at the different zones of the combustion chamber [1].

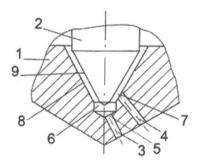

Figure 10.5 Injector nozzle diagram: (1) injector nozzle body, (2) needle valve, (3, 4) spray holes of the first (lower) and second (upper) groups, (5) intake edges of the first group of spray holes in the sack volume, (6) sack volume, (7) intake edges of the second group of spray holes on the locking cone, (8) locking cone of the injector nozzle body seat, (9) needle valve locking cone.

As shown in Figure 10.5, the injector nozzle consists of a body (1) and locking needle valve (2). It has two groups of spray holes (3 and 4). The inlet edges (5) of the holes of the first group (3) are located in the sack volume (6) and inlet edges (7) of the holes of the second group (4) on the locking conical surface (8) of the injector nozzle body.

Research carried out at MADI showed that coefficients of flow of the lower holes (3) μ_{hl} and of the upper holes (4) μ_{hu} differ considerably and depend on the position y of the locking needle valve (2). At $y > 0.2$ mm, μ_{hl} is larger than μ_{hu} by 10–20% and at < 0.1 mm, μ_{hl} is 2 to 3 times higher than μ_{hu}. This enables carrying out directional correction of the fuel supply by different zones of the diesel engine combustion chamber taking into account its operation conditions. At that, the holes of the first group are directed to the remote walls of the combustion chamber located in the piston, and the holes of the second group to the nearest zones. The design makes it possible to more efficiently use the air in the combustion chamber of the diesel engine, in which the injector is displaced in relation to the combustion chamber axis.

10.4 Results and Discussion

10.4.1 Results of Diesel Fuel Supply System Simulation

Computational adaptation of the injector nozzle design to a specific model of the diesel engine stipulates the use of a method and simulation program for calculation of the fuel equipment working process, making it possible to estimate the injection characteristics that it provides.

Following is the method of calculation of diesel engine fuel feed system using a correcting injector nozzle developed at MADI.

The method of calculation of the fuel feed system (FFS) operation is based on the theory of unsteady flow of real fluid in the fuel line. At that, it is assumed that the fuel motion is one-dimensional and isothermal and its density and speed of impulse (wave) distribution are constant.

The following assumptions are made when generating the equation of boundary conditions at the injector:

- At a certain time, the fuel pressure in any element of the FFS investigated is equal;

- Friction of the needle valve in the guide orifice is negligibly low;

- Yield of the injector elements is not taken into account;

- There are no wave propagation effects in the injector spring;

- Dynamic component of the force acting on the needle valve is not taken into account;

- Fuel properties are constant; and

- The gaseous phase is taken into account by way of a volume (not filled with fuel).

A computational scheme of the injector nozzle is shown in Figure 10.6.

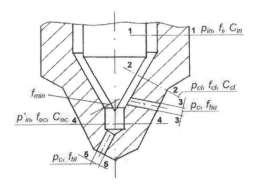

Figure 10.6   Computational scheme of the injector nozzle.

Under these assumptions, the equations of border conditions modeling hydrodynamic processes in the injector for the most common stages of the calculation are written as follows:

$$
\begin{cases}
\alpha_{in} V_{in} 6n \frac{dp_{in}}{d\phi} = \left(f_{fp} c' - \mu_{in} f_{in} \sqrt{\frac{2}{\rho}} \sqrt{p_{in} - p_c} - \sigma_3 f_{nv} c_{nv} - z_3 \right) \sigma_4; \\
6n \frac{dV_{hlin}}{d\phi} = -\left(f_{fp} c' - \sigma_3 f_{nv} c_{nv} \right) \sigma_4'; \\
M6n \frac{dc_{nv}}{d\phi} = \left[\left(f_{nv} - f_{nv}' \right)(p_{in} - p_{in0}) + \left(f_{nv}' - f_{ec} \right) p_{cl} + f_{ec} p_{in}' - \delta' y \right] \sigma_3; \\
6n \frac{dy}{d\phi} = n v \sigma_3;
\end{cases}
$$

$$(10.1)$$

$$
\begin{cases}
Q_{in} = \mu_{in} f_{in} \sqrt{\frac{2}{\rho}(p_{in} - p_c)}; \\
p_{cl} = p_{in} - \frac{\rho Q_{in}^2}{2(\mu_{cl} f_{cl})^2}; \\
p_{cll} = p_{cl} + \frac{\rho Q_{in}^2}{2 f_{cl}^2}; \\
Q_{hu} = \mu_{hu} f_{hu} \sqrt{\frac{2}{\rho}(p_{cll} - p_c)}; \\
Q_{hl} = Q_{in} - Q_{hu}; \\
p_{sv} = \frac{\rho Q_{hl}^2}{2(\mu_h f_h)^2} + p_c; \\
p_{in}' = p_{sv} - \frac{\rho Q_{hl}^2}{2(f_{ec} \varepsilon_{ec})^2}.
\end{cases}
$$

$$(10.2)$$

The following legend is used in systems (10.1) and (10.2) and further on:

- c_{nv} – injector nozzle valve speed;

- c, c' – fuel speed at the inlet to the fuel pipe and outlet from it;

- d_{fp} – diameter of the fuel pipe channel;

- f_{nv}, f_h – area of the needle valve along its axle and area of the injector nozzle spray holes;

- f_{nv}' – area limited by the locking edge of the needle valve;

- f_{fp} – cross section area of the fuel pipe channel;

- M – masses of injector moving parts;

- p_{in}, p_{in0} – fuel pressure in the injector: current value and at the time of needle valve motion start;

- p_{in}', cl – current pressure at the inlet to the spray holes of the injector nozzle in the clearance between the locking cones of the needle valve and injector nozzle body, as well as in the sack volume;

- p_{sv}, cl – delivery head upstream of the spray holes in the sack volume and in the clearance between the locking cones of the needle valve and injector;

- p_c – current pressure in the diesel engine cylinder;

- V_{in} – fuel volume contained in the injector;

- y, y – current and maximal needle valve lift;

- δ' – stiffness of the delivery valve spring and injector spring;

- α, ρ, ν – coefficients of fuel compressibility, density and kinematic viscosity;

- μ_{cl} – coefficient of flow in the clearance between the locking cones of the injector nozzle;

- μ_{hl}, μ_{hu} – coefficients of flow of the spray holes of the first (lower) and second (upper) groups of the injector nozzle correspondingly;

- $\mu_{hl}f_{hl}, \mu_{hu}f_{hu}, \mu_{in}f_{in}$ – equivalent flow areas of spray holes of the first and second groups and of the injector nozzle assembly;

- φ_c – fuel pump camshaft turning angle; and

- z_3 – flow rate through the clearance between the needle valve and the injector nozzle body.

The first equation of the system (10.1) is an equation of the volume balance in the injector nozzle cavity. This equation is solved if there is no rupture of integrity. If integrity was not restored, a second equation is used. The order of using these two equations is defined by step functions $\sigma_4 \to \sigma_4'$:

$$\sigma_4 = 0 \text{ and } \sigma_4' = 1 \text{ at } V_{hlin}' \geq 0 \text{ and } p_{in}' = 0; \tag{10.3}$$

$$\sigma_4 = 1 \text{ and } \sigma_4' = 0 \text{ at } V_{hlin}' = 0 \text{ and } p_{in}' > 0; \tag{10.4}$$

The third equation of the system (10.1) is the dynamic balance of the needle valve. The inertial force of the needle is set equal to the sum of fuel and spring forces applied to the needle. The step function $\sigma_3 = 0$ if the needle valve is on the seat (or on the rest) and the resulting force applied to the needle valve (the F_{nv} force) presses the needle valve to the seat (or to the rest), i.e., $\sigma_3 = 0$ at $y = 0$ and $F_{nv} < 0$ or at $y = m$ and $F_{nv} > 0$; $\sigma_3 = 1$ in all other cases.

Dependencies of flows Q_{in}, Q_{hl}, Q_{hu} through the injector on pressures $_{in}, p_{sv}, p_{in}'$, $p_{cl}, _{cll}$ are shown in the system (10.2). At that, it is taken into consideration that calculated dependencies of $\mu_{in}f_{in}\mu_{cl}, \epsilon_{ec}, \mu_{hl}, \mu_{hu}, f_{cl}, f_{min}, f_{ec}, f_{in}$ on the needle valve position y are known.

Calculation of $\mu_{in}f_{in}$ is carried out by the system of equations:

$$\begin{cases} \dfrac{1}{(\mu_{in}f_{in})^2} = \dfrac{1}{(\mu_{cl}f_{cl})^2} + \dfrac{1}{(\mu_{hu}f_{hu}+\mu_{mhl}f_{mhl})^2} - \dfrac{1}{f_{cl}^2}; \\ \dfrac{1}{(\mu_{mhl}f_{mhl})^2} = \dfrac{1}{(\mu_m f_m)^2} + \dfrac{1}{(\mu_{hl}f_{hl})^2} - \dfrac{1}{(\epsilon_{ec}f_{ec})^2}. \end{cases} \tag{10.5}$$

Calculation of $f_{min} = f(y)$ and $f_{cl} = f(y)$ is carried out by the method of MADI.

The minimal cross-section area f_{min} in the clearance between the locking cones of the needle valve and the seat is estimated as the area of the lateral surface of the truncated cone with the generating line S_{zh}. At that, the generating line S_{zh} is perpendicular to the bisector between angles β_{nv} and β_{in}, i.e., perpendicular to the flow line of the working fluid (Figure 10.7). Then

$$f_{min} = 0.5\pi(d_{sv} + d_{nvl})S_{zh} \tag{10.6}$$

where d_{sv} and d_{nvl} are the diameters indicated in Figure 10.7.

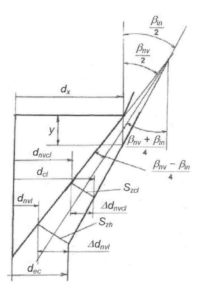

Figure 10.7   Scheme of clearance between the locking cones of the needle valve and the seat.

$$d_{nvl} = d_{ec} - 2\Delta d_{nvl},$$
$$\Delta d_{nvl} = S_{zh} \cos\left(\frac{\beta_{nv}+\beta_{in}}{4}\right),$$
$$S_{zh} = \left[\sin\left(\frac{\beta_{nv}}{2}\right)\Big/\cos\left(\frac{\beta_{nv}-\beta_{in}}{4}\right)\right]\left[y + \frac{d_x-d_{ec}}{2}\left(ctg\left(\frac{\beta_{in}}{2}\right) - ctg\left(\frac{\beta_{nv}}{2}\right)\right)\right].$$

$$(10.7)$$

Calculation of the dependence $f_{cl} = f(y)$ is carried out by indicated formulas (10.6) and (10.7) but on condition that d_{sv} is d_{cl}; d_{nvl} is d_{nvcl}; Δd_{nvl} is Δd_{dnvcl}. In this publication, d_{cl} − is an average value of d_x and d_{sv}.

Experiments show that coefficients μ_{cl}, μ_{min} and ϵ_{sv} have quite certain values and depend on the design of the injector nozzle, flow conditions and the needle valve position. In this way, for the needle valves of the Noginsk Fuel Equipment Factory, the following empiric formulas for determining μ_{mcl}, μ_{min}, ϵ_{sv} were obtained:

$$\mu_{cl} = 0,573\left(1 - \frac{f_{cl}}{f_i}\right)^{-1,53}\overline{Re}_{K\Phi}^{0,32};$$
$$\mu_{min} = 1,439\left(\frac{f_{min}}{f_{ec}}\right)^{0,25};$$
$$\varepsilon_{ec} = 0,815\left(\frac{f_{min}}{f_{ec}}\right)^{0,25}.$$

$$(10.8)$$

In (10.8) and further on, $\overline{Re}_{cl} = \frac{Re_{cl}}{2300}$.

The Reynolds numbers in the clearance between the locking cones of the needle valve and the seat are calculated by the formulas:

$$Re_{cl} = \frac{4R_g c_{cl}}{\nu};$$
$$R_g = \frac{f_{cl}}{\Pi};$$
$$\Pi = \pi\left(d_{cl} + d_{nvcl}\right).$$

$$(10.9)$$

The foregoing method of modeling was realized in the simulation model of hydrodynamic calculation of the FFS working process.

The model approbation was carried out on the base of the FFS of the V8 diesel engine having $\frac{D}{S} = \frac{110}{115}$. The FFS investigated was equipped with the A-size Bosch fuel pump and prototype injector nozzle (Figure 10.5) manufactured by the Noginsk Fuel Equipment Factory.

Experimental hydraulic characteristics of the injector are presented in Figure 10.8.

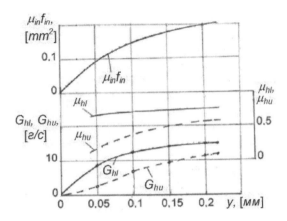

Figure 10.8   Hydraulic characteristics of the injector nozzle.

A specific feature of the hydraulic characteristics of the correcting injector (Figure 10.5) is that at partial lifts, the through capacity of the spray holes of the second group is $2 - 3$ times lower than that of the first group. When the needle valve lift (y) increases, the values of mhl and mhu become closer and differ by $20-25\%$.

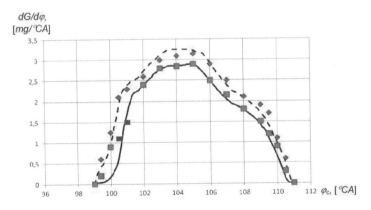

Figure 10.9   Injection characteristics of the FFS of the diesel engine V8 having $\frac{D}{S} = \frac{110}{115}$ with correcting injector nozzle ($n_c = 1400$ rpm,$q_i n_j = 58mm^3$): ● ■ experiment for the spray holes of the first and second groups correspondingly, - - - calculation for the spray holes of the first and second groups correspondingly.

Experimental research of the injection characteristics was carried out at the following conditions: high pressure fuel pump camshaft speed $n_c = 1400$ rpm, fuel rate $q_i n_j = 58mm^3$.

The results presented in Figure 10.9 demonstrate that the model developed assures close values of simulation results and experimental data.

Comparison of calculated and experimental data has also demonstrated that in the initial injection period, the rate of fuel supply rise in the combustion chamber of the diesel engine from the spray holes of the first group is 1.5 to 2 times higher than that from the holes of the second group. At that, fuel injection rates via the holes of the first group exceed the injection rates from the holes of the second group by 20%.

In such a way, prerequisites are created for a more efficient use of air in the diesel engines including those in which the injector is mounted non-symmetrically in respect to the combustion chamber axis. This promotes improvement of fuel efficiency, decrease of combustion process dynamics and the amount of toxic components in the exhaust gases.

The desired fuel injection law at any operation mode of the engine is formed by variation of the control impulse duration [13, 14] and pressure in the common rail (6.2) shown in Figure 10.2. It also depends on wave phenomenon originating in the high pressure line and having a considerable impact on the fuel injection process in case of a multistage injection [16].

To estimate the potential of injection rate control using this method, a series of calculations was carried out using the program complex developed at MADI (Figures 10.10 to 10.12).

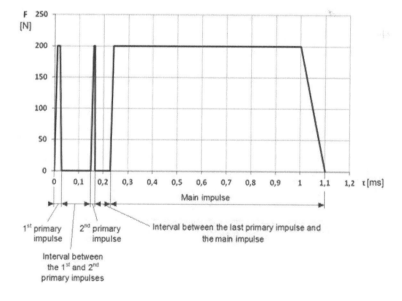

Figure 10.10 The force of an electric magnet formed by two primary and one basic control impulses.

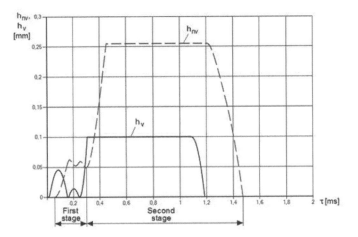

Figure 10.11   Results of calculation of the displacement of the needle valve h_{nv} and control valve h_v.

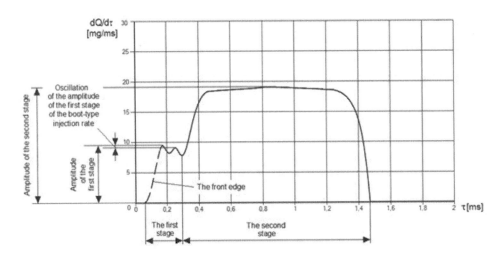

Figure 10.12   Calculated boot-type injection rate shape formed by two primary and one main control impulses.

The reviewed method of injection rate shaping is applicable in cases when the control impulse consists of:

- Primary and main impulses (Figures 10.3 and 10.4);

- Main and additional impulses, following the main impulse (Figure 10.15); and

- Primary, main and post impulses (Figure 10.16).

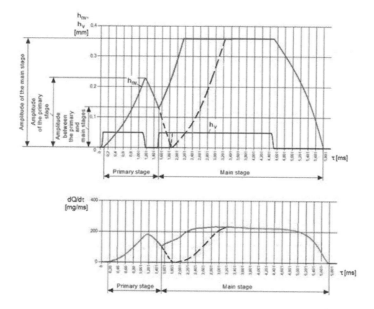

Figure 10.13 Results of computer modeling of the influence of the time of the main electric impulse start on the control valve lift h_v and needle valve lift h_{nv} of the common rail injector and on the injector rate shaping.

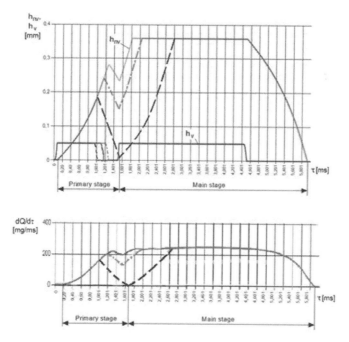

Figure 10.14 Results of computer modeling of the influence of variation of the duration of the primary electric impulse on the control valve lift h_v and needle valve lift h_{nv} of the common rail injector and on the injection rate shaping.

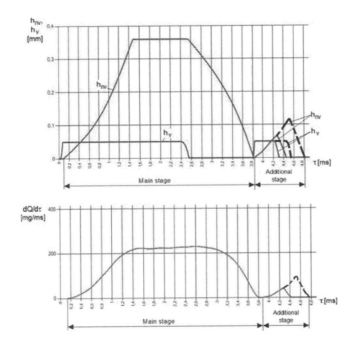

Figure 10.15   Results of computer modeling of the influence of the variation of duration of the additional electric impulse on the control valve lift h_v and needle valve lift h_{nv} of the common rail injector and on the injection rate shaping.

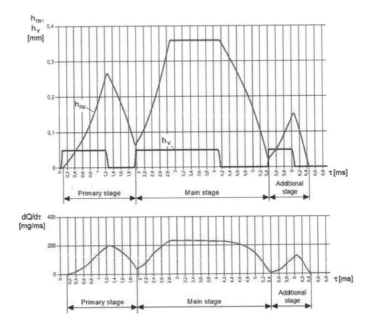

Figure 10.16   Results of computer modeling of the control valve lift h_v, needle valve lift h_{nv} and the injection rate shaping when applying a primary impulse followed by additional electric impulses.

10.4.2 Results of Engine Bed Tests

The results of the Cummins KAMA gas diesel engine tests by the load and speed characteristics are presented in Figures 10.17 and 10.18.

To check the accuracy of the computer model and analyze the experimental results, parameters of the engine at all operation modes were calculated and compared with the experimental data. During calculations, experimental values of gas consumption Gg and diesel fuel consumption Gd were used.

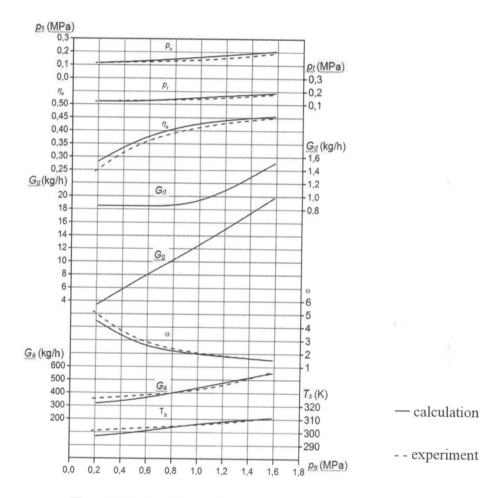

Figure 10.17 Load characteristic of the gas diesel engine at $n = 1420$ rpm.

Figures 10.17 and 10.18 show a high effective efficiency of $\eta = 0.43{-}0.45$ at full speed and load of the engine. The calculated and experimental values of the boost pressure $_s$, gas pressure before the turbine p_t, air consumption G_a, air access coefficient α, boost air temperature $_s$ and effective efficiency η at high load and high engine speed are close. The difference between parameters G_a, α and η is larger at low loads (Figure 10.17), which may be explained by not very accurate description of experimental compressor and turbine maps by polynomials at low engine loads.

As seen from Figure 10.18, the values of mean effective pressure pe are pretty low at low engine speed. This may be caused by a decrease in the amount of air in the cylinder and as a consequence, of the air access coefficient α, because the air is partially substituted by gas compared with the base diesel engine. The airflow in the gas diesel engine was almost 8% lower than in the base diesel engine.

Other reasons may be similar to those described in [8]. In a diesel engine, all the fuel is located in the combustion chamber. In a gas diesel engine, a part of gas fills the gaps between piston/cylinder head and piston/liner, where it burns incompletely or does not burn at all. This effect is stronger at low engine speed when the air turbulence in the cylinder is low. This phenomenon is indirectly confirmed by a higher calculated effective efficiency compared with its experimental value at low engine speed (Figure 10.18) because incomplete combustion of fuel in the gaps is not taken into consideration in the simulation model implemented.

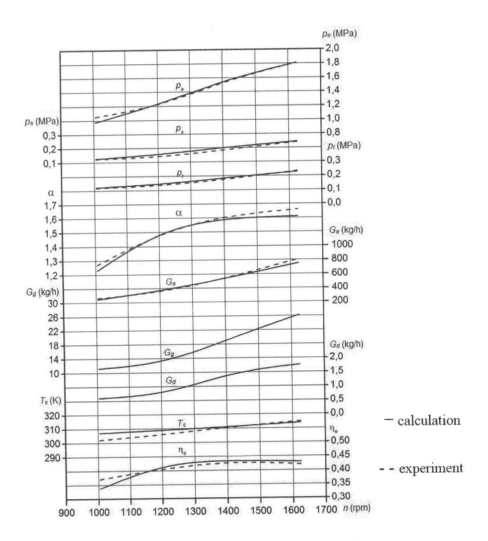

Figure 10.18 Speed characteristic of the gas diesel engine.

Tuning of the turbocharger may result in some increase of the brake mean effective pressure at low engine speeds. But to get the high values of pe as in the base diesel engine, the shape of the combustion chamber should be redesigned.

The comparison of parameters of the base Cummins KAMA diesel engine and its gas diesel version at three engine speeds and two loads, maximal and partial (30−40%), was carried out in [17]. At full loads, the percentage of diesel fuel was 4.5−6.2%, and at low loads was 8.7−8.9%. The percentage of diesel fuel at idle was 33%. The effective efficiency of the gas diesel engine was approximately 2% higher than that of the base diesel engine and its highest value was 0.45. On average, at full and partial loads, correspondingly, emissions of CO_2 decreased 1.47 and 1.15 times and amounted to 7.6% and 3.3% while emissions of NOx decreased 7.4 and 1.52 times and amounted to 1007 ppm and 140 ppm.

10.5   Conclusion

1. Analysis demonstrated that gas diesel working process with a minimized igniting portion of diesel fuel supplied by the CR system is the most reasonable way of converting an automobile diesel engine to operate on natural gas.

2. Calculations of a gas diesel engine using a model developed at MADI were carried out at different modes to get parameters required for the development and adjustment of gas feed, diesel fuel supply and engine electronic control systems. The base high-speed diesel engine was converted into a gas diesel engine and used for experimental perfection of these systems. Experimental engine test parameters showed good agreement with calculated parameters by the speed and load characteristics.

3. The method of hydrodynamic calculation of the working process of the fuel feed system with correcting injector nozzle demonstrated good agreement with the results of experimental investigations of the prototype injector nozzle.

4. Implementation of the calculation method developed for perfection of the working processes of diesel engines in which the injector is mounted non-symmetrically in respect to the combustion chamber axis enables a considerable decrease in the combustion duration and raises the efficiency of the diesel engine working process.

5. After conversion of the base diesel engine into gas diesel engine using the systems developed, a high degree of diesel fuel substitution by gas was achieved: the average diesel fuel portion amounted to 5.6, 8.8 and 33%, correspondingly, at full load, approximately 35% load and idle. On average, emissions of CO_2 decreased 1.47 and 1.15 times and emissions of NOx decreased 7.4 and 1.52 times correspondingly, at full and partial loads. Effective efficiency of the gas diesel was on average 2 percent higher than of the base diesel engine and its maximal value was 0.45.

Acknowledgments

Applied research and experimental development of diesel fuel feed systems were carried out with financial support of the state represented by the Ministry of Education and Science of the Russian Federation under Agreement No 14.580.21.0002 of 27.07.2015, the Unique Identifier PNIER: RFMEFI58015X0002.

REFERENCES

1. Markov V.A., Gaivoronski A.I., Grehov L.V., Ivaschenko N.A. *Operation of Diesel Engine on Non-Traditional Fuels. Legion-Avtodata*, Moscow, 2008, 464 p.

2. Luksho, V. A. (2015). *A Complex Method of Increasing Energy Efficiency of Gas Engines with High Compression Ratio and Shortened Intake and Exhaust Strokes* (Doctoral dissertation, PhD thesis, NAMI, Moscow).

3. Ivkovic I. S., Kaplanovic, S. M., & Milovanovic, B. M. M. (2017). Influence of road and traffic conditions on fuel consumption and fuel cost for different bus technologies. *Thermal Science*, 21(1B), 693-706. DOI: 10.2298/tsci160301135i

4. Geiger, J., Heuser, P., Lauer, S., Berthold Huchtebrock, B., & Sankhla, H. (2013). Combustion System Development for a Large Bore Gas Engine - Efficient Combination of Simulation and Experiment. Paper no 80, *27th SIMAC Congress*, Helsinki.

5. Klausner, J., Lang, J., & Trapp, C. (2011). J624-Der weltweit erste Gasmotor mit zweistufiger Aufladung. *MTZ-Motortechnische Zeitschrift*, 72(4), 284-289. DOI: 10.1365/s35146-011-0069-4

6. Grotz, M., Bowing, R., Lang, J., Thalhauser, J., Christiner, P., & Wimmer, A. (2015). Efficiency increase of a high performance gas engine for distributed power generation. *Proceedings of the CIMAC Cascades, Graz*, 26-25.

7. Kudryavtzev A., Lomashov V.Belaz (2010). Trucks of XXI Century with DM family gas diesel engines. *AvtoGasoZapravochniy komplex + Alternatvnoye toplivo/AutoGasFillingComplex + Alternative Fuel*, 3: 3-6.

8. Grehov, L. V., Ivsachenko, N. A., & Markov, V. A. (2010). On the way to improve the gas-diesel cycle. *AvtoGasoZapravochniy komplex+ Alternatvnoye toplivo/AutoGasFillingComplex+ Alternative Fuel*, 7(100), 10-14.

9. Mikulski, M., & Wierzbicki, S. (2017). Validation of a zero-dimensional and two-phase combustion model for dual-fuel compression ignition engine simulation. *Thermal Science*, 21, 387-399. DOI: 10.2298/tsci160127076m

10. Khatchijan, A. S., Sinyavskiy, V. V., Shishlov, I. G., & Karpov, D. M. (2010). Modeling of parameters and characteristics of natural gas powered engines. *Transport na Alternativnom Toplive/Transport on Alternative Fuel*, 3(15), 14-19.

11. Shatrov, M. G., Sinyavski, V. V., Dunin, A. Y., Shishlov, I. G., & Vakulenko, A. V. (2017). Method of conversion of high-and middle-speed diesel engines into gas diesel engines. *Facta Universitatis, Series: Mechanical Engineering*, 15(3), 383-395. DOI: 10.22190/fume171004023s

12. Shatrov, M. G., Golubkov, L. N., Dunin, A. U., Yakovenko, A. L., & Dushkin, P. V. (2015). Influence of high injection pressure on fuel injection perfomances and diesel engine worcking process. *Thermal Science*, 19, 192-192. DOI: 10.2298/tsci151109192s

13. Shatrov, M. G., Golubkov, L. N., Dunin, A. Y., Dushkin, P. V., & Yakovenko, A. L. (2017). A method of control of injection rate shape by acting upon electromagnetic control valve of common rail injector. *International Journal of Mechanical Engineering and Technology*, 8(11), 676-690.

14. Shatrov, M. G., Golubkov, L. N., Dunin, A. U., Dushkin, P. V., & Yakovenko, A. L. (2017). The new generation of common rail fuel injection system for Russian locomotive diesel engines. *Pollution Research*, 36(3), 678-684.

15. Shatrov, M. G., Malchuk, V. I., Dunin, A. U., & Yakovenko, A. L. (2016). The influence of location of input edges of injection holes on hydraulic characteristics of injector the diesel fuel system. *International Journal of Applied Engineering Research*, 11(20), 10267-10273.

16. Shatrov, M. G., Golubkov, L. N., Dunin, A. U., Yakovenko, A. L., & Dushkin, P. V. (2016). Experimental research of hydrodynamic effects in common rail fuel system in case of multiple injection. *International Journal of Applied Engineering Research*, 11(10), 6949-6953.

17. Sinyavski, V. V., Alekseev, I. V., Ivanov, I. Y., Bogdanov, S. N., & Trofimenko, Y. V. (2017). Physical simulation of high-and medium-speed engines powered by natural gas. *Pollution Research*, 36(3), 684-690.

PART VI

TOWARDS COGNITIVE COMPUTING

Datasets tend to be large, unstructured, and need to be manually adapted to fit into the Big Data Analysis software structure. This is a time-consuming and error-prone task for humans. With cognitive computing (CC) there is no need to pre-tag this type of data manually, as is currently the case. Cognitive computing platforms (APIs) use artificial intelligence for cognitive analytics, signal processing, machine learning (ML), reasoning, natural language processing, speech recognition, vision (object recognition), adaptive human-computer interface, dialog and narrative generation. Cognitive computing apps link data analysis and adaptive page displays to adjust content for a particular type of audience and person, as they learn, and change over time. Typical use cases are: speech recognition, sentiment analysis, face detection, risk assessment, fraud detection, and behavioral recommendations.

In combination with machine learning, cognitive computing has large adaptability; adapting the different contexts with minimal human supervision. Cognitive computing is capable of natural language interaction, and APIs can have a chatbot or search assistant that understands queries, explains data insights and interacts with humans in natural language. Chapter 11 presents a use case regarding a vital monitoring process, detecting, adjusting and preventing drift in classification of evolving data streams.

Cognitive computing holds the potential to affect almost every human task. It will give users, early adopters, a competitive edge in terms of improved decision-making to comprehend what the client wants, needs, and respond automatically. The human in the loop is in charge of supervising the machines managing other machines. It is our role as humans to steer the AI Industry into a proficient era for mankind. Chapters 12 and 13 present AI- and ML-driven traffic-decongestion applications which have already proven to change the pattern of traffic in cities and contribute to achieving global sustainability goals.

- Chapter 11: Classification of Concept Drift in Evolving Data Stream

- Chapter 12: Dynamical Systems of Mass Transfer in Buslaev Contour Networks with Conflicts

- Chapter 13: Parallel Simulation and Visualization of Traffic Flows Using Cellular Automata Theory and Quasigasdynamic Approach

CHAPTER 11

CLASSIFICATION OF CONCEPT DRIFT IN EVOLVING DATA STREAM

MASHAIL ALTHABITI, MANAL ABDULLAH

Faculty of Computing and Information Technology, King Abdulaziz University, Jeddah, Saudi Arabia
Corresponding authors: malthabiti@kau.edu.sa; maaabdullah@kau.edu.sa

Abstract

The concept of Data Stream has emerged as a result of the evolution of technologies in different domains such as banking, e-commerce, social media, and many others. It is defined as a sequence of data instances generated at very high speed, which can be hard to store in memory. Thus, it became hard to extract knowledge from the continuous data stream using traditional data mining. Data stream mining algorithms should fulfill some requirements such as limited memory, concept drift detection, and one scan processing. Concept drift must be tracked to avoid poor performance and inaccurate results of predictive models. It refers to changing data stream distributions due to several reasons, including the changes in the environment, individual preferences, or adversary activities. In this chapter, we will present the data stream mining components. The problem of concept drift in classification algorithms and several existing state-of-the-art handling methods are highlighted. Besides, the most used datasets, tools, applications, and evaluation methods will be presented.

Keywords: Data stream mining, concept drift, classification, data mining

11.1 Introduction

Nowadays, millions of people around the world share data anywhere and anytime. The emerging technologies in telecommunications, the entertainment industry, social media sites, banking services, and other applications have led to the massive growth of generated data stream. The data stream can be referred to as the sequence of data examples that are produced at a very high rate and arrive continuously in a potentially infinite stream. According to the "10 Key Marketing Trends For 2017," report 90% of the data in the world has been produced in the last two years, 2.5 quintillion bytes each day [1]. As a result, the massive amount of data cannot be stored for further processing and mining. So, the data stream mining concept has emerged to extract the knowledge from the data stream and provide real-time processing.

However, it has some constraints that we must cope with such as concept drift, limited memory, and one scan of the data. Concept drift refers to the changes in data concepts over time. This may result in wrong predictions and inaccurate results. In non-stationary environments, a learning model based on unstable data can result in inaccurate results and predictions. The underlying data distribution may change, so the model will not be consistent with the new data anymore. For example, predicting a customer's behavior toward shopping, where her/his preferences have changed. Thus, this will produce wrong results based on old data. So, concept drift must be handled and tracked using detecting methods that can cope with the data stream.

Data stream mining with concept drift handling was highly studied last decade. There have been many surveys and studies in the literature about data stream mining from different perspectives. Gama *et al.* in [2] have surveyed the state-of-the-art adaptive learning algorithms with concept drift detection. They have addressed the concept drift through various applications and highlighted several evaluation techniques. In [3], Khamassi *et al.* have presented general criteria to help researchers in designing their concept drift handling methods. They have categorized the existing concept drift algorithms according to these criteria. Also, 14 drift detectors have been evaluated, including six artificial datasets, and compared in terms of accuracy and detection. The authors have used Naive Bayes (NB) and Hoeffding tree classifiers to test the drift detectors.

11.2 Data Mining

Traditional data mining can be defined as the process of finding and extracting valuable knowledge and patterns from massive datasets [4]. It can be applied to different kinds of data such as database data, data warehouse data, text data, and multimedia data. The data mining process was done in an offline mode where the historical data were used to train the predictive model.

Data mining consists of the following steps, as shown in Figure 11.1 [5]:

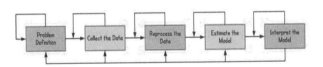

Figure 11.1   Traditional data mining process.

(1) *Defining the Problem*: This step is concerned with the understanding of the problem, objectives and formulating the hypothesis.

(2) *Collecting Data*: In this step, data can be generated under the expert's control or is collected without expert's influence.

(3) *Preprocessing Data*: This step is composed of several tasks such as detecting outliers or any abnormal values in the collected data. Also, variable scaling, encoding and selecting features.

(4) *Modeling*: In this step, an appropriate model is developed using a data mining technique.

(5) *Interpreting the Model*: In this step, the model will be interpreted to draw conclusions and make decision.

11.3 Data Stream Mining

Learning a model is considered an essential step in data mining and machine learning [6]. Previously, it was done in static environments where the whole datasets are available, stored and can be accessed many times. However, learning from massive datasets in non-stationary environments has become a challenging area. The huge generation of continuous data in everyday applications has engendered the concept of data stream.

The data stream is a sequence of potentially non-stop data instances that can be read and processed only once. As technologies continue to evolve, it is becoming harder to deal with the stream of data, such as web searches, banking, transactions, etc., on the Internet of Things (IoT) with traditional data mining [7]. Thus, data stream mining has become an attractive research area.

Data stream mining refers to the process of finding knowledge and valuable patterns in continuous, potentially infinite, high-volume data streams. It plays an essential role in predictive modeling and decision-making.

The main differences between traditional data mining and stream data mining are presented in Table 11.1 [8].

Table 11.1 Comparison of data mining and data stream mining

#	Parameter	Traditional Data Mining	Data Stream Mining
1.	Data Schema	Static	Dynamic
2.	Data Access	May or may not be Sequential	Sequential
3.	Data Scan	Flexible	Single Scan
4.	Memory	Flexible	Limited memory
5.	Algorithm	Processing time is not a constraint	Processing time is most important and must be as short as possible
6.	Data modeling	Persistent	Modeled as Transient Data streams
7.	Computation Results	Accurate	Approximate findings

11.3.1 Data Stream Challenges

Data stream mining has several challenges that must be taken into consideration when designing a data stream mining algorithm:

- *Resource Constraints*: The data stream is potentially infinite, huge and comes in high speed, so it is hard to store in a memory. Also, the processing time must be as short as possible [5].

- *One Scan*: Data stream cannot be accessed randomly or many times [5].

- *Data Preprocessing*: Since data is continuously arriving, it is not feasible to use manual data preprocessing methods. It should be fully automated and automatically updated as data evolves [9].

- *Privacy and Confidentiality*: The data stream is infinite and comes in portions, so the information will not be incomplete. In this case, it is hard to judge the privacy of a model that has a data stream as input [9].

- *Concept Drift*: Data instance may change over time.

- *Parameter Dependence*: Algorithms with a lot of parameters are impractical for data stream applications. So, it desirable for data stream algorithms to have few user-adjustable parameters [9].

- *Distinguishing between Correct Concept Drift and Noise*: Some algorithms interpret noise as concept drift, while data stream mining algorithms should be robust to noise and recognize it from concept drift [10].

Data stream mining research problems have been overcome using several approaches that are classified into data-based and task-based approaches, as described in Table 11.2 [13].

Table 11.2   Data-based and task-based approaches.

Methods	Approach	Description	Key points
Sampling.	Data-based method.	It is an old statistical method concerned with the probability of processing a data item or not.	The main obstacle with sampling is that it is not possible to determine the size of the dataset.
Load shedding.	Data-based method.	The process of dropping a series of examples in the streaming data.	It is not easy to be implemented in the data stream algorithms because the dropped data might be used in structuring the models.
Sketching.	Data-based method.	The method of sampling the stream vertically.	The main disadvantage of sketching is that of accuracy.
Synopsis data structures.	Data-based method.	The method of converting the summary of the streaming data into data structures and use it for analysis purposes.	The main synopsis data structures are frequency moments, wavelet analysis, quantiles, and histograms.
Aggregation.	Data-based method.	The process of summarizing the data stream using computing and statistical measures.	It is not recommended to be used with distributions that have high fluctuating data.
Approximation.	Task-based method.	The process of designing stream mining algorithms for computationally hard problems.	It considered a good solution for data stream mining problems.
Sliding window.	Task-based method.	The process of analyzing recent data streams and summarizing the old versions.	It emphasizes recent data and easily understood.
Algorithm output granularity.	Task-based method.	The process of mining the data stream, adapting resources, and merging the extracted knowledge when memory is full	It performs well with very high fluctuating data distribution.

11.3.2 Features of Data Stream Methods

Stream mining methods should include the following features [11]:

- The stream mining model should be incremental, so it updates itself for the new continuous incoming data stream.

- The stream mining model should be able to mine and process based on single access of incoming data stream.

- The stream mining model should have high processing and occupies a small space of memory.

- The stream mining model should track and handle concept drifts.

- The stream mining model should be able to generate results at any time because the data stream is potentially infinite.

11.4 Data Stream Sources

Nowadays, a massive data stream can be generated from social media applications such as Twitter, Facebook, Pinterest, and others [12]. The streaming of posts, likes, comments, and feeds have a significant role in social media analysis. The health industry is another source of data stream where a vast amount can be collected, including laboratory records, electronic medical records, doctor notes, and billing. Also, the financial industry can form an infinite data stream through credit and debit cards, loans, insurance, and other services. The presence of online banking service has increased the amount of generated data stream.

The data stream can be considered as one of the sources of big data [9]. Big data can be defined as a large volume of data that comes in various structures, including structured, semi-structured and unstructured, that is hard to be processed and analyzed using traditional techniques. It has four properties, including volume, variety, velocity, and value.

Every second, a massive amount of data is growing and generating continuously from different sources, including global positioning system (GPS), IoT, social media, health technologies and many more. It's generated in various formats such as text, audio, video, and others. The value of big data is found in the process of capturing the generated data and extracting the hidden knowledge. Big data streaming plays an essential role in predictive modeling; thus, it was highly studied over the last decade [9]. However, a change in the data stream may happen and be observed over time due to some reason; therefore, it will affect the accuracy of the predictive model results.

11.5 Data Stream Mining Components

The massive data stream can be generated from social media applications such as Twitter, Facebook, and Pinterest [12]; also, health, economic, and financial sectors, and many others. The process of data stream mining involves several components, as shown in Figure 11.2, including the streaming data as input, estimator, data mining algorithm, drift detection and the extracted knowledge as output.

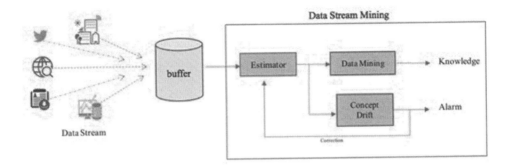

Figure 11.2   The main components of data stream mining.

11.5.1 Input

The data stream can be generated from different sources such as web searches, social media posts, real-time surveillance systems, banking activities, and other non-stationary environments.

11.5.2 Estimators

Estimators are used to estimate the statistics of certain parameters of the input data. They play an essential role in detecting the change of the distribution. For example, estimating the mean of the data in the memory, the standard deviation, weighted moving mean, and many others.

11.6 Data Stream Classification and Concept Drift

11.6.1 Data Stream Classification

Classification is a supervised machine learning algorithm. First, it uses the past data (training set) to build a model; then, it uses it to predict class labels (testing set) [4]. Classification algorithms in non-stationary environments must fulfill the data stream requirements regarding the processing time, limited memory and one-time scan. In the dynamic environment, some instances in streaming data may change over time because of the high velocity and limited memory, and this is called concept drift. It is the changes in data distribution of the output given the input, while the distribution of the input may stay unchanged [2]. For example, predicting a customer's behavior toward shopping, where her/his preferences have changed. Thus, this will produce the wrong results based on old data.

11.6.2 Concept Drift

Concept drift occurs between two points of time t_0 and t_1 when the joint distribution of x (independent variable) and y (target variable) at time t_0 is not equal to the joint distribution of (x, y) in t_1 [2].

It can be represented as:

$$pt_0(X, y) \neq pt_1(X, y) \tag{11.1}$$

Concept drifts may occur if there is a change in:

(1) The prior probabilities of classes $p(y)$;

(2) The class-conditional probability distributions $p(X, y)$; or

(3) The posterior probabilities $p(y|X)$.

It has been classified into two types: real concept drift and virtual concept drift, as shown in Figure 11.2. Real concept drift occurs in the case of changes in $p(y|X)$. Also, it's called concept shift. Virtual drift occurs if $p(X)$ changes without affecting $p(y|X)$.

Concept drift in the data stream may happen due to different reasons such as the changes in environment, individual preferences, or adversary activities [14]. It may happen in different forms [2], as shown in Figure 11.3:

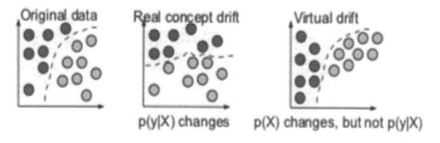

Figure 11.3   Types of concept drift.

a) *Sudden Drift*: When a concept changes to another abruptly.

b) *Incremental Drift*: When there are many intermediate concepts in between.

c) *Gradual Drift*: When the concepts emerge in a gradual way over time.

d) *Reoccurring Drift*: When old concepts reappear after some time.

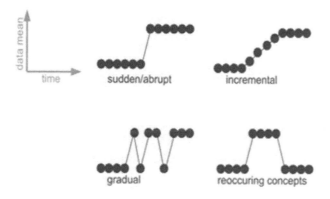

Figure 11.4   Forms of concept drift.

Data stream classification algorithms can be categorized into single classifiers and ensemble algorithms. Regarding concept drift adaptation, some algorithms update their classifiers continuously in the occurrence of drift or not. Other algorithms trigger changes in the classifier whenever a drift is detected [2].

11.6.3　Data Stream Classification Algorithms with Concept Drift

Data stream classification algorithms with concept drift can be classified into single classifier algorithms and ensemble algorithms.

11.6.4　Single Classifier

Some single classifier algorithms observe and detect the drift in the data distribution by using statistical methods and keep track of the base classifier performance [6]. In cases where drift is discovered, it will alarm the base classifier to update it or rebuild it using the following methods:

- Gama *et al.* [15] have designed the Drift Detection Method (DDM) that monitors the classifier error-rate. If the error rate reaches the warning and drift level, then we can observe that a data distribution has been changed [15].

- The DDM detector has been modified into an improved version named Early Drift Detection Method (EDDM) [16]. EDDM is used to detect gradual drift that emerges slowly by considering the distances between the classification errors.

- The Reactive Drift Detection Method (RDDM) is another modified version of DDM [17]. The proposed algorithm has overcome the problem of performance loss of DDM by discarding the older examples. It periodically recalculates the DMM calculations that determine the alarm and drift levels. Also, the drift occurs whenever the number of examples in the alarm level reached the threshold.

Other algorithms detect concept drift using windowing techniques by comparing the distributions in the windows such as:

- ADWIN [18] detects the different types of changes using sliding windows with the most recent examples. Concept drift can be observed if the means between two sub-windows is greater than the threshold. As the window grows, the processing time becomes longer. Thus, authors have proposed a developed version called ADWEN2 to satisfy the memory and time requirements.

- Similarly, the SEED algorithm uses a sliding window to detect change within the data stream. If the mean between two sub-windows exceeds a certain threshold, it suggests a drift and drops the old sub-window. The authors have evaluated and fed the proposed algorithm with a stream generated from a Bernoulli distribution generator to run the experiments. They found that SEED is faster and uses less memory compared to ADWEN2 [19].

- Concept-Adapting Very Fast Decision Tree is another algorithm that uses a single classifier [20]. It extends the VFDT algorithm with the ability to detect the concept drift. It also employs a sliding window to keep the classifier updated with the recent instances.

- Du *et al.* [21] have proposed a window-based algorithm called ADDM where the size of the window is dynamically determined. It detects the concept drift by keeping track of the entropy of the window. It reports a concept drift when the entropy is equal to one. ADDM has been evaluated using seven datasets containing different types of concept drift. It showed good performance in detecting drift compared to other methods. Also, it obtained high accuracy.

- Liu *et al.* [22] have proposed a fuzzy windowing method to adapt concept drift named FW-DA. The proposed algorithm reports a drift when there is a significant difference between the test statistics of the current window and the old window.

- Nishida and Yamauchi [23] have proposed a Statistical Test of Equal Proportions (STEPD) algorithm that considers the accuracy of two windows, recent and old. Drift is discovered if there is a significant difference between the two windows, which was calculated through a statistical test.

- Similarly to STEPD, de Lima Cabral and de Barros [24] proposed three detection methods named Fisher Proportions Drift Detector (FPDD), Fisher Square Drift Detector (FSDD), and Fisher Test Drift Detector (FTDD). The proposed methods adopted Fisher's exact statistical test and sliding windows (old and recent) as in STEPD. FPDD is a variation of STEPD that is used when the number of correct predictions over the two windows is small. While the FSDD adopted Fisher's exact test with the chi-square statistical test for homogeneity of proportions. FTDD is the simplest when it uses Fisher's exact test to detect drifts. The authors have run several experiments to compare the proposed methods against well-known detectors. Also, they have used two base learners, Naive Bayes (NB) and Hoeffding Trees, with synthesis and real-world datasets. The results showed that the accuracies of the proposed methods are better than the other compared detectors.

- Pesaranghader and Viktor [25] have proposed Fast Hoeffding Drift Detection Method (FHDDM). The proposed method monitors the probabilities of correct predictions over the sliding window. It compares the maximum and the most recent probabilities and observes the change if the differences between these probabilities equal or exceed the threshold.

- McDiarmid Drift Detection Method (MDDM) employs McDiarmid's inequality to detect concept drift [26]. It uses a sliding window over the prediction results and weighting approaches to give higher weights to the recent instances. While instances are processed, MDDM calculates the weighted mean over the sliding window, and the maximum mean observed so far during the process. It detects a concept drift if there is a significant difference between the two means, the significance determined by McDiarmid inequality. Tatashev and Yashina have tested the proposed algorithm using MOA against different methods, including DDM, EDDM, RDDM, ADWIN and many others. MDDM outperforms other algorithms in its shorter detection delays with high accuracy.

11.6.5 Ensemble Classifiers

In this approach, the algorithms use a set of classifiers where each classifier is assigned a weight and adapt to the changes by updating its components and its associated weights [6] such as:

- Dynamic Weighted Majority (DWM) [27] maintains a set of experts, each of them assigned to a weight. When an instance arrives, it is passed to an expert and then returned with a local prediction. DWM determines the global prediction using the local predictions and expert weights.

- The Accuracy Updated Ensemble (AUE2) algorithm [28] is another method that partitions the data stream into chunks, each chunk containing a set of examples. For every arriving chunk, a classifier associated with a weight will be created. Each classifier performance is evaluated by calculating the error rate on data chunk to determine the worst performing classifiers.

- In addition, two classifiers can be ensembled to form a detection system to detect both sudden and gradual drift [29]. They are composed of two classifiers: online classifier and block-based classifier. Whenever a data instance arrives, the online classifier updates itself, so any occurrence of sudden changes can be detected. While block-based classifiers work on blocks of data instances, which can observe the gradual changes. The classifiers error rate will be calculated to detect the changes. The drift can be observed if the value of the error rate is the same for the next blocks of the data stream.

- Double-Window-Based Classification (DWCDS) is another window-based method used to detect changes in data stream [30]. It detects the concept drift by checking the data distributions periodically. The proposed algorithm starts with generating decision trees using the data in the sliding window. If a concept drift is observed, then the DWCDS model will be updated.

- Bach and Maloof [31] have proposed a paired learner (PL) algorithm that ensembles two classifiers: stable and reactive. The stable classifier is used to predict based on its overall experience, while the reactive classifier predicts based on recent window. PL observes the distributional changes by comparing the performance of these two classifiers.

All the mentioned algorithms are summarized in Table 11.3.

Table 11.3   Classification of algorithms for concept drift detection.

Ord	Algorithm	Classifier	Type	Dataset	Key points
1.	FHDDM [25]	Naive Bayes (NV) and Hoeffding Tree	Single classifier	Sine1, Mixed, Circles, Airlines, Poker Hand, and Electricity.	The detection delay is shorter than other detectors.
2.	EDDM [16]	Decision tree and two nearest-neighbourhood learning algorithm	Single classifier	4 Artificial Datasets (SINE1, CIRCLES, GAUSS, MIXED and SINE1G) and 1 real dataset.	It can detect slow gradual drift and deal with noisy datasets.
3.	DDM [15]	Neural network, decision tree and perceptron.	Single classifier	8 Artificial Datasets and 1 real dataset.	It detects sudden changes and gradual changes (changes that do not emerge very slowly).
4.	DWM [27]	Incremental Tree Inducer (ITI) and NV	Ensemble classifiers	Stagger and Sea.	According to the performance changes, the classifiers are added and removed dynamically.
5.	PL [31]	Naive Bayes	Ensemble classifiers	Malware detection dataset, meeting scheduling dataset, electricity prediction dataset, and two synthesis dataset including Stagger and Sea.	The number of the trained learners used are less than other ensemble methods.
6.	DWCDS [30]	Random Decision Trees	Ensemble classifiers	SEA, HyperPlane, DDCup99, Yahoo shopping data and LED.	It detects drift better then single window-based algorithms.
7.	AUE2 [28]	Hoeffding Tree	Ensemble classifiers	Synthetic datasets generated by the MOA tool and 4-real datasets (Elec, Poker, Airline, and COV).	It consumes less memory comparing to other ensemble approaches. It detects different types of drift including sudden, gradual, recurring.
8.	ADWIN [18]	Naive Bayes	Single classifier	Electricity Market dataset and synthetic dataset.	ADWIN works only for one-dimensional data.
9.	Ensemble classificatio n system [29]	J48, Naive Bayes, and Random Forest	Ensemble classifiers	Census income and Spam email datasets.	It detects both sudden and gradual drift. It handles missing values.
10.	CVFDT [20]	Hoeffding Tree	Single classifier	hyperplane and web data.	CVFDT can keep its model up-to-date with streaming data that contains concept drift.
11.	ADDM [21]	IB1, j48, NNge, and SVM	Single classifier	Five artificial datasets (Gauss, Mixed, Stagger, Sine1, and Sine1g) and two real (Elist and Elec2).	ADDM used Hoeffding bound to determine the sliding window. In the evaluation, ADDM has lost upon one out of seven datasets.
12.	STEPD [23]	IB1 classifier and Naive Bayes	Single classifier	Five artificial datasets (STAGGER, GAUSS, MIXED2, CIRCLES, and HYPERP)	It can discover sudden and gradual drift with the presence of noise.
13.	FW-DA [22]	DDM and ECDD	Single classifier	SEA, Elec, Airline, and Spam.	FW_DA performed well in detecting and adapting concept drift.
14.	RDDM [16]	Naive Bayes	Single classifier	Agrawal, Mixed, Sin, Led, Airlines, pokerhand, and Electricity	RDDM has the higher accuracy among the others methods in detecting concept drift.
15.	MDDM [26]	Hoeffding Tree and Naive Bayes	Single classifier	SINE1 and MIXED, Led, CIRCLES pokerhand, FOREST COVERTYPE, and Electricity	MDDM outperforms other algorithms in its shorter detection delays with high accuracy.
16.	FPDD [24]	Naive Bayes (NB) and Hoeffding Tree	Single classifier	LED generator, Mixed generator, RandomRBF generator, Sine generator, Airlines, Covertype, Pokerhand.	FPDD is used when the number of errors or the number of correct predictions over the window is small.
17.	FSDD [24]	Naive Bayes (NB) and Hoeffding Tree	Single classifier	LED generator, Mixed generator, RandomRBF generator, Sine generator, Airlines, Covertype, Pokerhand.	FSDD adopts the chi-square statistical test.
18.	FTDD [24]	Naive Bayes (NB) and Hoeffding Tree	Single classifier	LED generator, Mixed generator, RandomRBF generator, Sine generator, Airlines, Covertype, Pokerhand.	FTDD uses Fisher's Exact test to detect concept drift exclusively.
19.	SEED [19]	Not available	Single classifier	Bernoulli distribution generator	It addresses the problem of volatility in data stream.

11.6.6 Output

This component represents the knowledge and valuable patterns extracted from the data stream.

11.7 Datasets

Several well-known datasets have been used to evaluate the effectiveness of the classification algorithms in detecting concept drift. Datasets can be real or artificial where contains one type of drift or various types. Table 11.4 shows the most used datasets in data stream mining studies with the presence of concept drift.

Table 11.4 Datasets for DSM with concept drift.

	Dataset Name	Type	# instants	# Attribute	Key points
1	Census Income [32]	Real	48842	14	• It has different independent variables including name, marital status, education, occupation, and many others. These variables are used to predict the person's income which represents the dependent variable. • it includes only gradual drifts.
2	Sine1 [15]	Artificial	-	2	• It involves sudden concept drift • it has two features x and y, each feature distributed in zero and one. • It uses [y = sin(x)] to draw the curve. The data is labeled to positive and negative according to its position to the curve.
3	Elec 2 [15]	Real	45,312	8	• It consists of five features used to predict target variable whether it's up or down. • It is collected from the Australian Electricity Market of Australia at 30-minute intervals from 1996 to 1998.
4	Airline [33]	Real	539,383	7	• It includes the flight information such as the departure date, time of flight, destination, distance, and many others. • It used to predict if a given flight will delay.
5	Cover Type [34]	Real	581,012	54	• It includes information of four wilderness areas in Colorado including Elevation, Aspect, Slope, Soil Type, and others variables. • it used to predict the forest cover type.
6	Stagger Generator [21]	Artificial	240	3	• The three features are shape, size, and color. • it contains sudden drift.
7	Sine 2 [15]	Artificial	-	2	• It involves two features x and y, each feature distributed in zero and one. • It uses [y < 0.5 + 0.3 sin(3πx)] to draw the curve. The data is labeled to positive and negative according to its position to the curve.
8	SEA Generator [35]	Artificial	-	3	• It is used to generate data stream containing sudden drift.
9	LED[28]	Artificial	-	24	• The 24 attributes used to predict the seven-digit showed over the LED display.
10	Mixed [15]	Artificial	-	4	• It contains sudden concept drift. • The example is labeled as positive if two of the three conditions are fulfilled: v, w, y < 0.5 0.3 * sin(3πx). If not, it will be labeled as negative.
11	Waveform generator[36]	Artificial	5000	40	• It composed of three classes. • It generates waveform by combining two from the three base waves.
12	Spam Filtering Data [22]	Real	9324	39916	• The dataset is derived from the Spam Assassin collection. • It contains 20% spam emails. • It has been considered as a typical dataset for gradual drift.
13	Poker Hand [25]	Real	1,000,000	11	• Each instance represents an example of five cards drawn from a standard 52 cards deck. Each card is described by two attributes (suit and rank). • It used to predict the poker hand.
14	Agrawal generator [17]	Artificial	-	9	• Contains the people information who intending to receive a loan of a given amount. • People classified into two groups, A and B.

11.8 Evaluation Measures

The following list presents the well-known evaluation measures for classification of data stream algorithms:

- *Accuracy Score*: It is calculated by dividing the number of correct predictions by the total classifier's predictions [4].

- *Recall*: It is also known as the true positive rate [4].

- *CPU Time*: It measures the total runtime of the CPU in training and testing the classifier [37].

- *Memory*: It measures the total memory consumed to run the classifier and store the running statistics [37].

- *Kappa Statistic*: It measures the homogeneity among the classifiers [37].

The concept drift detection can be assessed through different measures such as:

- *Probability of True Change Detection*: It measures the algorithm's ability to discover drifts when they occur [2].

- *Delay Time of Detection*: It measures the time that has passed before the change is detected [2].

11.9 Data Stream Mining Tools

The most popular tools used in data stream environments are listed below:

- Weka[1] provides a set of data mining and machine learning algorithms. These algorithms can be implemented directly on datasets through Weka GUI or Import Weka Java library [38].

- Massive Online Analysis (MOA)[2] is a project developed at the University of Waikato, New Zealand [39]. It provides an environment to deal with data stream, run experiments, and implement data stream mining algorithms. Besides, users can create new data stream algorithms and simulate different types of concept drifts, including abrupt, gradual, incremental and mixed drifts on synthetic and real data streams.

- Scalable Advanced Massive Online Analysis (SAMOA)[3] is an open source tool that provides the well-known data stream and machine learning algorithms [40].

- Apache Storm[4] is an open source platform for processing infinite streams of data. It is scalable and fast, which makes it suitable to produce immediate analytics, and perform online machine learning [41].

- RapidMiner[5] is an open source environment written in Java that is used for traditional data mining, text mining and data stream mining. Also, machine learning and predictive analysis are provided [11].

[1] https://www.cs.waikato.ac.nz/weka
[2] https://moa.cms.waikato.ac.nz
[3] https://moa.cms.waikato.ac.nz
[4] https://storm.apache.org
[5] https://rapidminer.com

11.10 Data Stream Mining Applications

Classification with concept drift can be used in several areas such as:

- *Monitoring Systems*: The monitoring system is used to distinguish normal behavior from abnormal behavior [42]. It processes a large amount of data that must be analyzed in real time. For example, intrusion detection systems that search for suspicious behavior in network traffic. Another example is fraud detectors that track adversary behavior and prevent online banking fraud. Also, transportation travel time and traffic prediction are monitored using data stream mining techniques.

- *Personal Assistance*: Data stream mining methods have been employed in different personal assistance applications. For example, in news feeds where it classifies user news feeds and categorizes the articles [42]. Besides, customer information and preferences are aggregated to segment customers based on their interests or to predict their needs [43]. Concept drift happens due to changing individual interests and behavior over time. Moreover, personal assistance applications address the spam filtering and recommendation systems.

- *Decision Support*: Decision support and diagnostics applications includes the evaluation of creditworthiness [42]. The results should have high accuracy because the cost of mistakes is high. For example, to predict bankruptcy the system makes the decision according to different bankruptcy prediction models under various economic conditions.

- *Artificial Intelligence*: These applications include navigation systems, smart homes, virtual reality, and vehicle monitoring [42]. Learning algorithms in this category should be adaptive and take concept drift into account.

11.11 Conclusion

Concept drift is one of the main challenges of data stream mining. It must be detected and handled to avoid inaccurate results of learning models. In this chapter, we have discussed the concept of the data stream. The data stream mining components, including the input/output, estimation methods, and classification algorithms with concept drift, have been presented. Also, we have highlighted the most used data stream mining tools, datasets, applications, and evaluation measures in data stream experiments.

REFERENCES

1. Cloud, I. M. (2017). *10 Key Marketing Trends for 2017 and Ideas for Exceeding Customer Expectations*. [Online]. Available: http://comsense.consulting/wpcontent/uploads/2017/03/10_Key_Marketing_Trends_for_2017_and_Ideas_for_Exceeding_Customer_Expectations.pdf. [Accessed: 23-Dec-2018].

2. Gama, J., Zliobait, I., Bifet, A., Pechenizkiy, M., & Bouchachia, A. (2014). A survey on concept drift adaptation. *ACM computing surveys* (CSUR), 46(4), 44. https://doi.org/10.1145/2523813

3. Khamassi, I., Sayed-Mouchaweh, M., Hammami, M., & Ghedira, K. (2018). Discussion and review on evolving data streams and concept drift adapting. *Evolving Systems*, 9(1), 1-23. https://doi.org/10.1007/s12530-016-9168-2

4. Han, J., Pei, J., & Kamber, M. (2011). *Data Mining: Concepts and Techniques*. Elsevier.

5. Kantardzic, M. (2011). *Data Mining: Concepts, Models, Methods, and Algorithms*. John Wiley & Sons.

6. Mittal, V., & Kashyap, I. (2016). Empirical study of impact of various concept drifts in data stream mining methods. *International Journal of Intelligent Systems and Applications*, 8(12), 65.

7. Gaber, M. M. (2012). Advances in data stream mining. *Wiley Interdisciplinary Reviews: Data Mining and Knowledge Discovery*, 2(1), 79-85.

8. PhridviRaj, M. S. B., & GuruRao, C. V. (2014). Data mining - past, present and future – a typical survey on data streams. *Procedia Technology*, 12, 255-263.

9. Krempl, G., Zliobaite, I., Brzezinski, D., Hullermeier, E., Last, M., Lemaire, V., ... & Stefanowski, J. (2014). Open challenges for data stream mining research. *ACM SIGKDD Explorations Newsletter*, 16(1), 1-10.

10. Tsymbal, A. (2004). The problem of concept drift: definitions and related work. *Computer Science Department, Trinity College Dublin*, 106(2), 58.

11. Kumar, A., & Singh, A. (2017, April). Stream mining a review: Tool and techniques. In *2017 International Conference of Electronics, Communication and Aerospace Technology (ICECA)* (Vol. 2, pp. 27-32). IEEE.

12. Warren, J. J. (2017). A big data primer. In *Big Data-Enabled Nursing* (pp. 33-59). Springer, Cham.

13. Gaber, M. M., Zaslavsky, A., & Krishnaswamy, S. (2005). Mining data streams: a review. *ACM Sigmod Record*, 34(2), 18-26.

14. Zliobait, I., Pechenizkiy, M., & Gama, J. (2016). An overview of concept drift applications. In *Big Data Analysis: New Algorithms for a New Society* (pp. 91-114). Springer, Cham.

15. JGama, J., Medas, P., Castillo, G., & Rodrigues, P. (2004, September). Learning with drift detection. In *Brazilian Symposium on Artificial Intelligence* (pp. 286-295). Springer, Berlin, Heidelberg.

16. Baena-Garcia, M., del Campo-Avila, J., Fidalgo-Merino, R., Bifet, A., Gavalda, R., & Morales-Bueno, R. (2006, September). Early drift detection method. In *Fourth International Workshop on Knowledge Discovery from Data Streams* (Vol. 6, pp. 77-86).

17. Barros, R. S., Cabral, D. R., Goncalves Jr, P. M., & Santos, S. G. (2017). RDDM: Reactive drift detection method. *Expert Systems with Applications*, 90, 344-355. DOI: 10.1016/j.eswa.2017.08.023

18. Bifet, A., & Gavalda, R. (2007, April). Learning from time-changing data with adaptive windowing. In *Proceedings of the 2007 SIAM International Conference on Data Mining* (pp. 443-448). Society for Industrial and Applied Mathematics.

19. Huang, D. T. J., Koh, Y. S., Dobbie, G., & Pears, R. (2014, December). Detecting volatility shift in data streams. In *2014 IEEE International Conference on Data Mining* (pp. 863-868). IEEE.

20. Hulten, G., Spencer, L., & Domingos, P. (2001, August). Mining time-changing data streams. In *Proceedings of the Seventh ACM SIGKDD International Conference on Knowledge Discovery and Data Mining* (pp. 97-106). ACM.

21. Du, L., Song, Q., & Jia, X. (2014). Detecting concept drift: an information entropy based method using an adaptive sliding window. *Intelligent Data Analysis*, 18(3), 337-364. https://doi.org/10.3233/ida-140645

22. Liu, A., Zhang, G., & Lu, J. (2017, July). Fuzzy time windowing for gradual concept drift adaptation. In *2017 IEEE International Conference on Fuzzy Systems (FUZZ-IEEE)* (pp. 1-6). IEEE.

23. Nishida, K., & Yamauchi, K. (2007, October). Detecting concept drift using statistical testing. In *International Conference on Discovery Science* (pp. 264-269). Springer, Berlin, Heidelberg. https://doi.org/10.1007/978-3-540-75488-6_27

24. de Lima Cabral, D. R., & de Barros, R. S. M. (2018). Concept drift detection based on Fisher's exact test. *Information Sciences*, 442, 220-234.

25. Pesaranghader, A., & Viktor, H. L. (2016, September). Fast hoeffding drift detection method for evolving data streams. In *Joint European Conference on Machine Learning and Knowledge Discovery in Databases* (pp. 96-111). Springer, Cham.

26. Pesaranghader, A., Viktor, H. L., & Paquet, E. (2018, July). McDiarmid drift detection methods for evolving data streams. In *2018 International Joint Conference on Neural Networks (IJCNN)* (pp. 1-9). IEEE.

27. Kolter, J. Z., & Maloof, M. A. (2003, November). Dynamic weighted majority: A new ensemble method for tracking concept drift. In *Third IEEE International Conference on Data Mining* (pp. 123-130). IEEE.

28. Brzezinski, D., & Stefanowski, J. (2013). Reacting to different types of concept drift: The accuracy updated ensemble algorithm. *IEEE Transactions on Neural Networks and Learning Systems*, 25(1), 81-94.

29. Jadhav, A., & Deshpande, L. (2017, January). An efficient approach to detect concept drifts in data streams. In *2017 IEEE 7th International Advance Computing Conference (IACC)* (pp. 28-32). IEEE.

30. Zhu, Q., Hu, X., Zhang, Y., Li, P., & Wu, X. (2010, August). A double-window-based classification algorithm for concept drifting data streams. In *2010 IEEE International Conference on Granular Computing* (pp. 639-644). IEEE.

31. Bach, S. H., & Maloof, M. A. (2008, December). Paired learners for concept drift. In *2008 Eighth IEEE International Conference on Data Mining* (pp. 23-32). IEEE.

32. "Census Income Data Set." [Online]. Available: https://archive.ics.uci.edu/ml/datasets/census+income. [Accessed: 21-Dec-2018].

33. "Elena Ikonomovska's Web page." [Online]. Available: https://kt.ijs.si/elena_ikonomovska/data.html. [Accessed: 03-Nov-2018].

34. "Covertype Data Set." [Online]. Available: https://archive.ics.uci.edu/ml/datasets/covertype. [Accessed: 28-Nov-2018].

35. Street, W. N., & Kim, Y. (2001, August). A streaming ensemble algorithm (SEA) for large-scale classification. In *Proceedings of the Seventh ACM SIGKDD International Conference on Knowledge Discovery and Data Mining* (pp. 377-382). ACM.

36. Barros, R. S. M., & Santos, S. G. T. C. (2018). A large-scale comparison of concept drift detectors. *Information Sciences*, 451, 348-370.

37. Dhaliwal, P., & Bhatia, M. P. S. (2017). Effective handling of recurring concept drifts in data streams. *Indian Journal of Science and Technology*, 10(30), 1-6.

38. Weka, W. E. K. A. (2012). Weka 3-Data Mining with Open Source Machine Learning Software in Java. Disponvel em http://www. cs. waikato. ac. nz/ml/weka.

39. Bifet, A., Holmes, G., Kirkby, R., & Pfahringer, B. (2010). MOA:: Massive online analysis. *Journal of Machine Learning Research*, 11(May), 1601-1604.

40. Morales, G. D. F., & Bifet, A. (2015). SAMOA: scalable advanced massive online analysis. *Journal of Machine Learning Research*, 16(1), 149-153.

41. Apache Storm. [Online]. Available: http://storm.apache.org/index.html. [Accessed: 03-Nov-2018]. https://storm.apache.org

42. Brzezinski, D. (2010). *Mining Data Streams with Concept Drift*. Master's thesis Computing Science. Poznan University of Technology. Poznan. Polan.

43. Zliobaite, I., Pechenizkiy, M., & Gama, J. (2016). An overview of concept drift applications. In *Big Data Analysis: New Algorithms for a New Society* (pp. 91-114). Springer, Cham. https://doi.org/10.1007/978-3-319-26989-4_4

CHAPTER 12

DYNAMICAL MASS TRANSFER SYSTEMS IN BUSLAEV CONTOUR NETWORKS WITH CONFLICTS

MARINA YASHINA,[1,*] ALEXANDER TATASHEV,[2] IVAN KUTEYNIKOV[2]

[1] Department of Higher Mathematics, Moscow Automobile and Road Construction State Technical University (MADI), Moscow, Russia
[2] Department of Mathematical Cybernetics and Information Technology, Moscow Technical University of Communications and Informatics (MTUCI), Moscow, Russia
*Corresponding author: yash-marina@yandex.ru

Abstract

Traffic flow models are relevant because of the exponential growth of road transport in megalopolises worldwide. In modern complex socio-technical systems the main processes of mass transfer are characterized by periodicity in space and time with natural boundaries on space location. However, there are not enough adequate approaches to describe such processes in terms of dynamical systems. In this chapter, we give a concise overview of our results obtained for Buslaev contour networks with regular, periodical structures; in particular, for contour chains and chainmails.

Keywords: Dynamical systems, traffic models, cellular atomata, mass transfer, Buslaev contour networks

12.1 Introduction

Traffic flow models are relevant because of the exponential growth of road transport in megalopolises worldwide. However, there are not enough adequate approaches to describe such processes. Currently it is clear that classical models of the mid-20th century have exhausted their possibilities for modeling of a large number of subjects (agents) on complex networks. Agent-based approach models are unstable with respect to approximation errors and if the set of data is large, then errors increase uncontrollably. Therefore, mid-level model development is relevant. The set of parameters of these models is limited. These models can be studied by simulation, and an analytical study of these models is also is possible.

In modern complex socio-technical systems, the main processes of mass transfer are characterized by periodicity in space and time with natural boundaries on space location, i.e., in a point in fixed time there is no more than one particle.

Buslaev *et al.* introduced the concept of contour networks as dynamical systems. These models reduce the number of parameters and get accurate results regarding the mass transfer and qualitative behavior of systems. Results for dynamical systems of Buslaev contour type have been obtained in [12-43]. These results are related to values of average velocities of particles, conditions of free movement (all particles move at any step after a moment) and collapse (no particle moves after a moment). The main characteristic of a Buslaev contour system is the average velocities of particles. These dynamical systems are a network of contours with common modes and the movement of particles in a given direction. Different applications of Buslaev networks are possible. Messages or network packets correspond to particles in models of communication or computer networks. The Ising model is applied in the study of experimental computers based on principles of quantum mechanics. Buslaev contour networks can be applied in the study of Ising model. We give a concise overview of known results.

The initial example is the particles' movement on a circle. This study is related to the cellular automata [1], dynamical systems [2-5], and simulation [6]. In [2-5], analytical results have been obtained regarding stationary probabilities of the system, the average velocity of particles, and conditions of self-organization (the system results in the state of free movement from any initial state).

Another type of traffic model is the two-dimensional Biham–Middleton–Levine (BML) traffic model [7]. Two types of particles move on a toroidal lattice in perpendicular directions. As noted in [7], the rule of particles' movement is the two-dimensional analogue of the movement on the one-dimensional rule relative to the cellular automaton CA 184 in the classification of Wolfram [1]. Some analytical results are also obtained for this model. These results give conditions of the system self-organization (all particles move at any step after a moment) or the collapse (no particle moves after a moment) [8-10].

It is noted in [11] that the models, equivalent to the elementary cellular automata CA 252 and CA 136, model a road section before the red light or after the red light respectively. In these papers, special cases are considered and there are no estimates of qualitative properties of the system in general.

The concept of a contour network has been introduced in [12]. The supporter of a contour network is a system of contours with common points (nodes). In the discrete version, a contour is a closed sequence of cells. There are particles on any contour. The particles move in accordance with given rules. We consider the individual movement such that the particles do not form clusters and the cluster movement such that the particles of the same cluster move simultaneously. The concept of the cluster movement has been introduced in

[13]. Particles (clusters) of different contours cannot pass through the same node simultaneously. In the case of individual movement, a delay occurs if a particle tries to move to a cell, occupied by another particle, or a delay can occur when a particle moves through a node. In the case of cluster movement, the particles of any cluster move simultaneously in accordance with the rule CA 240. Particles (clusters) move on their contours. In more general case, particles can go to another contour. In the case of continuous system, a cluster is a moving segment, and its velocity is constant. The delays of a cluster occur if clusters try to pass through the same node simultaneously. In [14], a generalized contour network with continuous state space and time was considered (Figure 12.1).

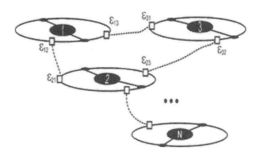

Figure 12.1   Contour network with continuous state space and time.

Analytical results have been obtained for types of contour networks such as multi-contours systems with contours of the same length under the assumption that there is a unique point of these contours and the rules of movement are different [15-18]; two-contours system with one common point and the contours of unequal lengths [19]; closed and open chains of contours [20-27]; two-dimensional contour systems with toroidal or rectangular structures called chainmails [28-32]; and systems with honeycomb structure and non-symmetrical chains [33]. Alexander P. Buslaev introduced the concept of the generalized transport-logistic model. Different versions of this model were studied in [30, 34-39].

In [20], the concept of the spectrum of a deterministic contour network is presented. The spectrum of the Wolfram cellular automata is defined in [44].

Alexander P. Buslaev has developed the following approach to traffic modeling. The velocity of a car is represented as the sum of the deterministic component and the stochastic component [41]. The deterministic component is the velocity of the cellular field movement, and the stochastic component is due to the movement of particles on the cellular field. The stochastic component models the individual maneuvers of cars. In [42, 43], on the basis of the deterministic-stochastic approach, mathematical models have been developed such that these models describe the segregation of transport flows.

This study develops approaches to study dynamical systems of Buslaev contour type. Analytical results have been obtained for contour networks such as closed binary chain of two-dimensional contour networks of the chainmail type, an isolated contour with movement of particles in two directions. Section 12.2 describes the construction of Buslaev contours networks. Section 12.3 considers a concepts of the spectrum, spectral cycle, eigenvalue of spectral cycle. Section 12.4 presents results regarding the spectrum of closed chains with different competition resolution rules. Section 12.5 presents results regarding the spectrum of the two-dimensional contour spectrum chainmail. Section 12.6 presents results regarding an exclusive process on a closed contour, and we note the relation the problem with the deterministic-stochastic approach to traffic modeling.

12.2 Construction of Buslaev Contour Networks

Professor Buslaev and his coworkers introduced contour networks with common nodes and competition rules in them. Models on contour networks can be used to study spectral quantization.

We consider a discrete graph consisting of cells and connections between neighbors and agents (particles) moving on this graph according to a given plan and according to a discrete chronometer. The characteristic properties of the dynamical system are:

- Rules for moving in accordance with the standard classification of cellular automata [1];

- The principle of a small-sized cell; the discretization is such that there is not more than one particle in one cell; and

- Special rules for the movement of particle flows at nodes when competition takes place.

The behavior of such systems has been poorly studied. Exact *a priori* results are available only for simple contours [3, 4]. Most of the papers in this area have experimental results presenting the model formulation and exclusive calculation. As network models have large dimension, their simulation requires an exponential number of computations, which is impossible in the near future.

We consider networks from contours with arbitrary links. The subject of the study is traffic delays depending on the network load, traffic rules on the contours and rules for competition resolving at nodes. We consider either deterministic rules of competition resolution, or the probability rules. In the case of deterministic rules, the priorities of particles participating in the competition are one-to-one correspondence identified. An example of a probability rule is a fair rule, in accordance with which all the particles win the competition with equal probability.

Thus, depending on system architecture, we initially have either a dynamical system with totally deterministic rules, or a Markov process. Stationary states of the systems are studied, in particular, steady fields of competitions, the reachability of free movement, self-organization and stopping the system. But the problem of describing network flows is not solved and attempts to do it influence the development of new mathematical branches.

Buslaev contour networks consist of the following items:

(A) Geometry: Contours, coordinates system, common nodes, matrix codes;

(B) Particles movement: Direction, movement mode (individual and connected movement);

(C) Competition in nodes: Resolution rules (deterministic or stochastic);

(D) Boundary conditions: System lattice can be open or closed.

In this work we study the Buslaev networks with the following competition resolution rules (C):

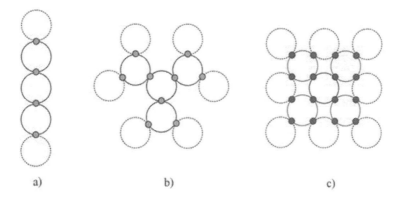

Figure 12.2   Closed contour: (a) chain, (b) honeycomb, (c) chainmail.

- *Left Resolution Rule*: In the case of competition only the particle on the left contour moves, e.g., the lazy rule. No competing particle moves.

- *Even-Odd Rule*: In the case of competition only the particle on the contour with even index moves.

- *Probablistic Rule*: Each competing particle moves with a given positive probability and the other particle does not move. The special case of the probabilistic rule is the egalitarian rule. In accordance with this rule, competing particles win the competition equiprobably.

One of the main characteristics of the contour system is the average velocity of particles. The definition of this concept is given in Section 12.3.

12.3 Concept of Spectrum

In the discrete version, the system state space is finite, and a sequence of states is repeated periodically from a moment (a spectral cycle). In the continuous version, a sequence of states is also repeated periodically from a moment. A value of the average velocity of movement corresponds to each spectral cycle. What spectral cycle is realized depends on the initial state. A spectral cycle and the related value of the average velocity form a spectral pair. The spectrum is the set of spectral pairs corresponding to different initial states of the system.

Let X be the state space. Then the dynamical system defines a mapping $A : X \to X$ Let the state space be finite. For any element $x \in X$; we have a trajectory in the space X:

$$x \to A(x) \to A(A(x)), \cdots, A(A \cdots A(x)). \tag{12.1}$$

We have $X(t_0) = X(t_0 + T^*)$, where T^* is the period. Then the cyclic sequence $X(t_0), X(t_0 + 1), \cdots, X(t_0 + T^* - 1)$ is a spectral cycle. The set of initial states is such that, for a finite time, the system results in a state belonging to this cycle, which is called the tail of the spectral cycle.

The value

$$\Lambda = \frac{V(T^*)}{MT^*} \qquad (12.2)$$

Where

- $V(T^*)$ is the average total distance that particles pass;

- T^* is the period; and

- M is called the eigenvalue of the spectral cycle (the average velocity).

Concepts of a spectral cycle and an eigenvalue of the spectral cycle are similar to concepts of an eigen function and an eigenvalue for the Sturm-Liouville problem.

The purpose of the study is to find the spectrum, in particular, the dependability of the average velocities of particles on the initial state of the system, the condition of the self-organization (the system results in the state of free movement, i.e., all particles move from any initial state) and collapse (no particle moves after a finite moment).

12.4   One-Dimensional Contour Network Binary Chain of Contours

A closed chain of N contours was studied in [4]. Each contour has common points (nodes) with two neighboring contours (Figure 12.3). There are two cells (the lower cell; cell 0, and the upper cell; cell 1) and a particle on each contour. In every discrete moment, the particle is located in upper (lower) cell and, if this is allowed, moves counterclockwise to the lower (upper) cell.

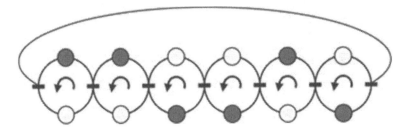

Figure 12.3   Binary closed contour chain with N=8 with state $(1, 1, 0, 0, 1, 0)$.

Particles cannot move through the common node simultaneously. If the particle, located to the right of the node, tries to move from the upper cell to the lower cell, and the particle, located to the left of the node, tries to move from the lower cell to the upper cell, then a competition occurs.

Let us consider the binary chain with left-priority rule.

The state of the system is the vector $(x_0, \cdots, x_{N-1})$, where $x_i = j$ if the particle of the ith contour is in the cell $j, j = 1, 2, i = 0, 1, \cdots, N - 1$.

The variation of the state $(x_0, x_1, \cdots, x_{N-1})$ equals

$$Var(x_0, x_1 \cdots, x_{N-1}) = \frac{1}{2} \sum_{i=1}^{N} |x_{i+1} - x| \qquad (12.3)$$

(the addition in indexes by modulo N):

Theorem 12.1 *Let the competition rule be left-priority.*

1) The dynamical system is equivalent to elementary cellular automaton CA 063 in terms of Wolfram classification, [5]. States of the system are cyclic vectors with N coordinates. The ith coordinate of vector equals 0 if the particle is in the cell 0, and equals 1 if the particle is in the cell 1. At any discrete moment, the value of each coordinate is changed except in the case in which the value of this coordinate equals 1, and the value of the neighboring coordinate on the left equals 0.

2) The space of states is divided into the set of recurrent states and the set of non-recurrent states. A state is non-recurrent if and only if the vector of this state contains at least one coordinate such that the value of this coordinate is equal to 1, and the values of neighboring coordinates on the left and on the right are equal to 0. The system can be in a non-recurrent state only at the initial moment.

3) Each recurrent state is repeated after no more than $2N$ steps, Figure 12.4.

4) The vector of state is shifted onto one position to the right for every two steps.

5) The spectrum of the system contains the values

$$V = 1 - \frac{k}{N}, k = 0, 1, , [\frac{N}{3}] \tag{12.4}$$

6) If the system is in a recurrent state at initial moment and the variation of the vector of the state is equal to k, then the average velocity of particles is equal to $(N - k)/N$.

7) If the system is in a recurrent state, then the variation is not more than $[\frac{N}{3}]$ – the integer part of $N/3$.

8) If the initial state is non-recurrent, then the average velocity of particles is equal to $(N - k)/N$; where k is the variation of the initial state vector.

If k is an integer value and satisfies the condition $0 \leq k \leq \frac{N}{3}$, then there exists an initial state such that the average velocity equals $(N - k)/N$.

Theorem 12.2 *Assume that the competition rule is odd-even, and N is an even number. Then the following is true.*

1) The state is recurrent if and only if there is a state vector, consider no configuration 101, 010, 110, where the utmost left and the utmost right positions are odd (non-priority).

2) All priority particles move at any step.

3) The velocity of any priority particle equals 1 if two neighboring cells are in the same state, and the velocity equals 1/2 if the neighboring particles are in the different states.

4) The spectrum velocities contain the values

$$V = 1 - \frac{k}{2N}, k = 0, 1, \cdots, [N/2] \tag{12.5}$$

Theorem 12.3 *Let the competition rule be lazy. Then the following is true.*

1) *The system is equivalent to cellular automaton CA 029.*

2) *The system over one step results in the state belonging to the spectral cycle. On each spectral cycle, each particle does not move at any moment or moves at any moment.*

3) *The spectrum of the system contains the values*

$$V = 1 - \frac{2k}{N}, k = 0, 1, \cdots, [N/2] \qquad (12.6)$$

Theorem 12.4 *Let the competition rule be probabilistic. Then the system results in a state of free movement from any initial state.*

12.5 Two-Dimensional Contour Network - Chainmail

Chainmail is a type of contour networks. We have obtained results regarding this type of system.

A contour network called chainmail was studied in [28-32]. The contours of this system form two-dimensional toroidal structure. There are common points (nodes) of each contour and four neighboring contours (Figure 12.4). These nodes are also the cells of this contour.

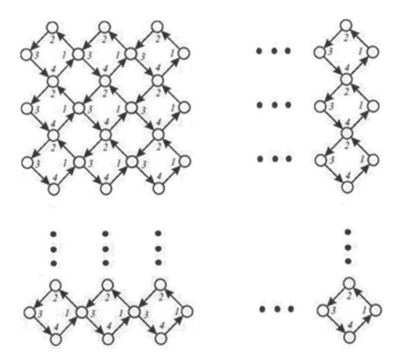

Figure 12.4   Open chainmail of size $2m \times 2n$

At any discrete moment the particle, moving on the contour in a given direction, is located at one of these cells. The movement on the contour is deterministic. However, the resolution rule for the particles trying to occupy the same vacant cell is stochastic.

Generally, the stationary state of the process depends on the initial state of the system and the realization of the random process. In [28, 29], a closed chainmail was considered. It was assumed that the system of contours forms a toroidal surface (Figure 12.5).

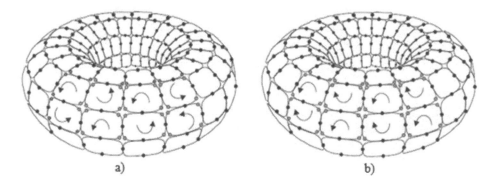

Figure 12.5   (a) Closed chainmail with one-directional movement. (b) Closed chainmail with co-directional movement.

The direction of movement is such that if, on a contour, the particle moves counter-clockwise, then, on four neighboring contours, particles move clockwise; and, if, on a contour, the particle moves clockwise, then, on four neighboring contours, particles move counterclockwise. This type of movement is called co-directional movement. In accordance with given rules of movement, each particle moves onto a cell in the direction of movement if there is no delay. Delay occurs in the case of a particle trying to move to the cell that is occupied by the particle of a neighboring contour. In [30], both the co-directional chainmail and one-directional one (all particles move counterclockwise) are presented. The types of the spectrum on these two versions of the chainmail are different. In [31], when the chainmail has a rectangular structure (open chainmail), the movement on a contour is deterministic. However, the competition resolution rule is stochastic. Generally, the stationary state of the process depends on the initial state and the realization of the process.

We formulate a hypothesis for theorems on the basis of simulation for chainmails considered in [28-30].

Theorem 12.5 *For any closed chainmail with co-directional movement, the following is true. For any set of integer numbers $s_1, \cdots, s_k$, $0 \le s_i \le \frac{mn}{k}$, there exists an initial state such that the velocity of particles on each contour of the ith diagonal is equal to $\frac{s_i k}{mn}$, $i = 1, \cdots, k$.*

Hypothesis 12.5. For any spectral cycle of closed chainmail with co-directional movement, average velocities are such as described in condition of Theorem 12.5.

Theorem 12.6 *For an open chainmail with co-directional movement, there are states of free movement.*

Hypothesis 12.6 [2]. Open chainmail with co-dimensional movement has the property of self-organization, i.e., the systems come to the state of free movement from any initial state (all particles move at every step from some moment).

Theorem 12.7 *The following statements are true for a closed chainmail with one-directional movement.*

1) *Suppose the number* k *and* $i_1, \cdots, i_k, j_1, \cdots, j_k$, *satisfy the following conditions. The set of all contours is divided into* k *sets* $G_{i_1 j_1}, \cdots, G_{i_k j_k}$ *and complement G of union of* $G_{i_1 j_1}, \cdots G_{i_k j_k}$. *Then there exists an initial state such that sets* $G_{i_1 j_1}, \cdots, G_{i_k j_k}$ *are in the state of collapse, and every particle of the set G moves at each step.*

2) *For any number* $s = 0, 1, \cdots, [n/3]$ *there exist initial states of the system such that the average velocity of the particle of each contour is equal to* $\frac{n-s}{n}$.

3) *For any number* $s = 0, 1, \cdots, [m/3]$ *there exist initial states of the system such that the average velocity of the particle of each contour is equal to* $\frac{m-s}{m}$.

Hypothesis 12.7. Any spectral cycle of a closed chainmail with one-directional movement satisfies the condition of Theorem 12.7.

Theorem 12.8 *The following statement is true for an open chainmail with one-directional movement. Assume that the number* k *and indexes* $i_1, \cdots, i_k, j_1, \cdots, j_k$, *satisfy the following. The set of all contours is divided into* k *sets of* $G_{i_1 j_1}, \cdots, G_{i_k j_k}$ *and complement G of union of* $G_{i_1 j_1}, \cdots, G_{i_k j_k}$. *Then there exists an initial state such that sets of* $G_{i_1 j_1}, \cdots, G_{i_k j_k}$ *are in the state of collapse, and every particle of the set G moves at each step.*

Hypothesis 12.8. Any spectral cycle of an open chainmail with one-directional movement that corresponds to the first satisfies the condition of Theorem 12.8.

All hypotheses were confirmed using computer modeling.

The competition resolution rule is stochastic. In accordance with the hypothesis, over a time interval with a finite average value, the system results in the state such that no competitions occur and therefore the process is deterministic after a moment. The analogous statement regarding the deterministic behavior of the system after some moment has been proved for closed chains considered in [23, 24]. In this sense, this system is deterministic-stochastic. We generalize the concept of the spectrum for these systems. Assume that the set of system states D contains the states such that, if the system is in a state belonging to set D, then the process of system work is deterministic in the current time and in the future. A periodical sequence of repeating states of the system is called a spectral cycle.

In [28, 29], a closed chainmail with the co-directional movement is considered such that each of two competing particles wins the competition equiprobably. A particle is called "green" if, at current time, this particle moves and does not compete. Competing particles are called "yellow." If, at current time, a particle does not move because the cell ahead is occupied, then this particle is called "red." Over a finite time, interval, there are no "yellow" particles, and no particle can be "yellow" in the future. Let us describe the spectral cycles of the system. We consider a chainmail of the dimension $(2m) \times (2n)$, and k is the greatest common divisor of the numbers m and n. The set of all contours is divided into k subsets called diagonals (Figure 12.6).

Any diagonal contains $\frac{4mn}{k}$ contours. Contours of a diagonal are ordered cyclically, and two contours have consecutive indexes if there is a common node of these contours. For example, the chainmail of the dimension 4×4 is divided into two diagonals. Each diagonal contains 8 contours, Figure 12.6. In the matrix of the system state, elements $a_{11}, a_{12}, a_{42}, a_{43}, a_{33}, a_{34}, a_{42}, a_{31}$, belong to one of these diagonals, and the other elements of the matrix belong to the other diagonals. Assume that diagonals are numbered

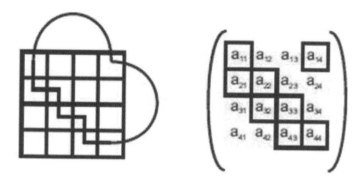

Figure 12.6 Diagonal on 4×4 chainmail

arbitrarily. For any set of integer numbers $0 \le s_i \le \frac{mn}{k}$, the state of the system can be set in such a way that at each step s_i, the quadruples of particles of the neighboring contours of the i-th diagonal are "green," and the remaining $\frac{mn}{k}$ quadruples of the particles of the diagonal contours are "red." At the same time at each step the configuration of the particles is shifted by one position. Through $\frac{4mn}{k}$ cycles, i.e., through the number of cycles equal to the number of contours located on the diagonal, the state of the system is repeated. Therefore, the smallest period of the spectral cycle does not exceed $\frac{4mn}{k}$. The average particle velocity on the i-th diagonal is equal to

$$V_i = \frac{s_i k}{mn}, i = 1, \cdots, k. \tag{12.7}$$

The period of the spectral cycle can be less than $\frac{4mn}{k}$. If, for example, all particles move at each step, then the period of the spectral cycle is 4.

Based on the results of simulation modeling, it is possible to formulate a hypothesis stating that all spectral cycles of a closed chain armor with a co-directional movement have the described form.

In [30], along with a closed chainmail with a co-directional movement, a closed chainmail with a one-directional movement was considered. It turned out that the behavior of these two variants of chainmail differ significantly. In the chainmail with a one-directional movement, on any spectral cycle, any particle either moves at each step (free movement) or does not move at all, i.e., the speed of each particle is 0 or 1. In this case, the contours on which the particles do not move form blocks of size 2×2.

Considered in [31, 32] were two variants of open chainmail with a co-directional and one-directional movement with a deterministic rule of conflict resolution. For chainmail with co-directional movement, no initial states were found, due to which the system would not fall into a state of free movement in a finite time. In the case of one-directional movement, the spectral cycles of an open/closed chainmail have a similar appearance. For the closed chainmail considered in [32] with a deterministic competition resolution for spectral cycles, and for the stochastic competition resolution rule, there are also spectral cycles with an average speed between 0 and 1. On these spectral cycles, the behavior of the chainmail sections is similar to the behavior of closed chainmail of contours with a deterministic conflict resolution rule. Such a chain of contours was considered in [21].

12.6   Random Process with Restrictions on the Contour with the Possibility of Particle Movement in Both Directions

Known traffic patterns have drawbacks and their application areas are limited. Therefore, the development of new models is relevant.

When modeling a traffic flow using a deterministic stochastic approach, the deterministic velocity component is assumed to be equal to the velocity of the main mass of the flow. In the model, the deterministic component of the flow rate is the speed of movement of the cell field. If the vehicle performs individual maneuvers, moving faster than the main mass of the flow, then in the model this corresponds to the movement of particles in the cell field forward. Similarly, it can be considered that the slow motion of a car is modeled by moving particles in the opposite direction. This leads to the relevance of the study of a model in which particles move in a cell field and, at the same time, particles can move in both directions.

We researched the stochastic motion of particles on a circle. We investigated a closed discrete contour, on which there are N particles and M particles. At each time moment, the particle is in one of the cells. At any time, $t = 0, 1, 2,...$ each particle tends to move one cell forward with probability p. A particle tends to move backward with probability q.

With probability $s, p+q+s = 1$, the particle makes no attempt to move. The movement of a particle is carried out if the cell into which the particle tends to move is free. If two particles tend to move to the same cell, then not one of the particles does not move. In the case $q = 0$, the results of [5] imply that the process of the system is reversible in time, i.e., the probabilistic law of the behavior of the system operation process in the stationary mode will not change when the direction of the time axis is reversed. The ergodic properties of a random prohibition process for which particles can move in both directions were studied in [4], but no general formula was obtained for the average speed of movement. Assuming that $M = 2$, $s = 0$, N is an even number, the stationary probabilities of the states of the system are found, and a formula is obtained for the average velocity of the particles and the intensity of their movements. It is proved that in these assumptions the process is reversible in time. It is established that, in general, the process is irreversible.

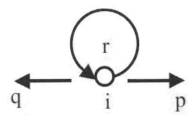

Figure 12.7   Particle movement rule.

12.7   Conclusion

A class of dynamical systems called contour networks has been introduced by Alexander P. Buslaev in order to overcome the shortcomings of known traffic models. The contour networks were studied by Buslaev *et al.* in [12-44]. We have given a concise overview of the scope and obtained new analytical results regarding the contour networks.

REFERENCES

1. Wolfram, Stephen (1983). Statistical mechanics of cellular automata. *Reviews of Modern Physics,* 55(3), 601. https:/dx.doi.org.10.1003/RevModPhys.55.601

2. Belitsky, V., & Ferrari, P. A. (2005). Invariant measures and convergence properties for cellular automaton 184 and related processes. *Journal of Statistical Physics,* 118(3-4), 589-623. doi:10/007/s10955-044-8822-4

3. Gray, L., & Griffeath, D. (2001). The ergodic theory of traffic jams. *Journal of Statistical Physics,* 105(3-4), 413-452. DOI: 10.1023/A:1012202706850

4. Blank, M. (2010). Metric properties of discrete time exclusion type processes in continuum. *Journal of Statistical Physics,* 140(1), 170-197.

5. Kanai, M., Nishinari, K., & Tokihiro, T. (2006). Exact solution and asymptotic behaviour of the asymmetric simple exclusion process on a ring. *Journal of Physics A: Mathematical and General,* 39(29), 9071.

6. Nagel, K., & Schreckenberg, M. (1992). A cellular automaton model for freeway traffic. *Journal de Physique I,* 2(12), 2221-2229.

7. Biham, O., Middleton, A. A., & Levine, D. (1992). Self-organization and a dynamical transition in traffic-flow models. *Physical Review A,* 46(10), R6124.

8. D'Souza, R. M. (2005). Coexisting phases and lattice dependence of a cellular automaton model for traffic flow. *Physical Review E,* 71(6), 066112.

9. Angel, O., Holroyd, A., & Martin, J. (2005). The jammed phase of the Biham-Middleton-Levine traffic model. *Electronic Communications in Probability,* 10, 167-178.

10. Austin, T. D., & Benjamini, I. (2006). For what number of cars must self organization occur in the Biham-Middleton-Levine traffic model from any possible starting configuration?. arXiv preprint math/0607759.

11. Zubillaga, D., Cruz, G., Aguilar, L., Zapotcatl, J., Fernndez, N., Aguilar, J., ... & Gershenson, C. (2014). Measuring the complexity of self-organizing traffic lights. *Entropy,* 16(5), 2384-2407.

12. Kozlov, V. V., Buslaev, A. P., & Tatashev, A. G. (2013, June). On synergy of totally connected flows on chainmails. In *Proc. of the 13 International Conference on Computational and Mathematical Methods in Science and Engineering,* Almeria, Spain (Vol. 3, pp. 861-874).

13. Bugaev, A. S., Buslaev, A. P., Kozlov, V. V., & Yashina, M. V. (2011, October). Distributed problems of monitoring and modern approaches to traffic modeling. In *2011 14th International IEEE Conference on Intelligent Transportation Systems* (ITSC) (pp. 477-481). IEEE.

14. Buslaev, A. P., & Yashina, M. V. (2016). Mathematical aspects on traffic of incompressible worms on simple circular structures. In *Proceedings of the 16th International Conference on Computational and Mathematical Methods on Science and Engineering,* CMMSE (pp. 4-8).

15. Buslaev, A., & Yashina, M. V. (2009). About Flows on a Traffic Flower with Control. In *Proceeding of the 2009 International Conference on Modelling Simulation and Visualization,* CSREAS Press, 2009, pp. 254-257.

16. Buslaev, A. P., Tatashev, A. G., & Yashina, M. V. (2016, June). About synergy of flows on flower. In *Proceedings of the Eleventh International Conference on Dependability and Complex Systems DepCos REL COMEX.* June 27-July 1, 2016, Brunow, Poland, Springer (pp. 75-84).

17. Buslaev, A. P., & Tatashev, A. G. (2017). Flows on discrete traffic flower. *Journal of Mathematics Research*, 9(1), 98-108. http://dx.doi.org.10.5539/jmr.v9n1p98

18. Buslaev, A. P., & Tatashev, A. G. (2018). Exact results for discrete dynamical systems on a pair of contours. *Mathematical Methods in the Applied Sciences*, 41(17), 7283-7294. http://dx.doi.org.10.1002/mma.4822.

19. Tatashev, A. G., & Yashina, M. V. (2019). Spectrum of continuous two-contours system. In *ITM Web of Conferences* (Vol. 24, p. 01014). EDP Sciences. DOI: 10.1051/itm-conf/20192401014

20. Kozlov, V. V., Buslaev, A. P., & Tatashev, A. G. (2015). Monotonic walks on a necklace and a coloured dynamic vector. *International Journal of Computer Mathematics*, 92(9), 1910-1920. http://dx.doi.org/1080/00207160.2014/915964

21. Kozlov, V. V., Buslaev, A. P., & Tatashev, A. G. (2014). Behavior of pendulums on a regular polygon. *Journal of Communication and Computer*, 11, 30-38.

22. Buslaev, A. P., Fomina, M. J., Tatashev, A. G., & Yashina, M. V. (2018, July). On discrete flow networks model spectra: statements, simulation, hypotheses. In *Journal of Physics: Conference Series* (Vol. 1053, No. 1, p. 012034). IOP Publishing.

23. Buslaev, A. P., Tatashev, A. G., & Yashina, M. V. (2018). On flows spectrum on closed trio of contours with uniform load. *European Journal of Pure and Applied Mathematics*, 11(1), 260-283. http://dx.doi.org.10.29020/nybg.ejpam.v11i1.3201

24. Buslaev, A. P., & Tatashev, A. G. (2018). Spectra of local cluster flows on open chain of contours. *European Journal of Pure and Applied Mathematics*, 11(3), 628-644. http://dx.doi.org.10.29020/ny/by.ejpam.v.Mi3.3292

25. Buslaev, A. P., Fomina, M. J., Tatashev, A. G., & Yashina, M. V. (2018, July). On discrete flow networks model spectra: statements, simulation, hypotheses. In *Journal of Physics: Conference Series* (Vol. 1053, No. 1, p. 012034). IOP Publishing.

26. Tatashev, A., & Yashina, M. (2019). Spectrum of elementary cellular automata and closed chains of contours. *Machines*, 7(2), 28. https:/doi.org/10.3390/machines7020028

27. Kozlov, V. V., Buslaev, A. P., & Tatashev, A. G. (2015). A dynamical communication system on a network. *Journal of Computational and Applied Mathematics*, 275, 247-261.

28. Buslaev, A. P., Tatashev, A. G., & Yashina, M. V. (2013, October). Qualitative properties of dynamical system on toroidal chainmail. In *AIP Conference Proceedings* (Vol. 1558, No. 1, pp. 1144-1147). AIP.

29. Kozlov, V. V., Buslaev, A. P., Tatashev, A. G., & Yashina, M. V. (2014). Monotonic walks of particles on a chainmail and coloured matrices. In *Proceedings of the 14th International Conference on Computational and Mathematical Methods in Science and Engineering*, CMSSE (Vol. 3, pp. 801-805).

30. A.S. Bugaev, A.P. Buslaev, V.V. Kozlov, A.G. Tatashev, M.V. Yashina (2015). The generalized transport and logistics model as a class of dynamic systems, *Mathematical Modeling*, 27(12), 65-87.

31. Fomina, M. J., Tolkachov, A. G., Tatashev, D. A., & Yashina, M. V. (2018, September). Cellular automata as traffic models and spectrum of two-dimensional contour networks open chainmails. In *2018 IEEE International Conference Quality Management, Transport and Information Security, Information Technologies* (IT&QM&IS) (pp. 435-440). IEEE. DOI: 10.1109/IT-MQIS.2018.8525079.

32. Tatashev A.G., Tolkachev D.A., Fomina M.Yu., Yashina M.V (2018). Closed chainmail and parallel CANT packets for traffic modeling. *Quality, Innovation, Education. European Center for Quality (Moscow)*, 5(156), 111-125.33.

33. Kozlov, V. V., Buslaev, A. P., Tatashev, A. G., & Yashina, M. V. (2015). Dynamical systems on honeycombs. In *Traffic and Granular Flow'13* (pp. 441-452). Springer, Cham.

34. Kozlov, V. V., Buslaev, A. P., & Tatashev, A. G. (2015). On real-valued oscillations of a bipendulum. *Applied Mathematics Letters*, 46, 44-49. http://dx.doi.org/10.1016/j.aml.2015.02.003

35. Buslaev A.P., Tatashev A.G., Yashina M.V (2015). On irrational oscillations oscillation of a bipendulum. *10th International Conference on Dependability and Complex Systems, DepCos-RELCOMEX 2015*, Brunow, Poland, 29 June- 3 July 2015: Code 154069, vol. 365, pp. 57-63.

36. Buslaev A.P., Yashina M.V (2016). On holonomic mathematical F-bipendulum, *Math. Meth. App. Sci.*, vol. 39, pp.4820-4828.

37. Buslaev, A. P., & Tatashev, A. G. (2016). On dynamical systems for transport logistic and communications. *Journal of Mathematics Research*, 8(8), 195-210. http://dx.doi.org/10.5539/jmr.v8n4p195

38. Buslaev, A. P., & Tatashev, A. G. (2016). Bernoulli algebra on common fractions and generalized oscillations. *Journal of Mathematics Research*, 8(3), 82-93. http://dx.doi.org/10.5539/

39. Buslaev, A. P., & Tatashev, A. G. (2016). On dynamical systems for transport logistic and communications. *Journal of Mathematics Research*, 8(8), 195-210. http://dx.doi.org/10.5539/jmr.v8n4p195

40. Arun, A., Velmurugan, S., & Errampalli, M. (2013). Methodological framework towards roadway capacity estimation for Indian multi-lane highways. *Procedia-Social and Behavioral Sciences*, 104, 477-486.

41. Buslaev, A. P., Prikhodko, V. M., Tatashev, A. G., & Yashina, M. V. (2005). The deterministic-stochastic flow model. *arXiv preprint physics/0504139*.

42. Bugaev A.S., Buslaev A.P., Tatashev A.G (2006). Monotonic random motion of particles on an integer strip and LYuMEN problem. *Mathematical Modeling*, vol. 18, no. 12, pp.19-34.

43. Bugaev A.S., Buslaev A.P., Tatashev A.G (2006). Simulation of segregation of a two-band particle stream. *Mathematical Modeling*, 20(9), pp.111-119.

44. Tatashev, A., & Yashina, M. (2019). Spectrum of elementary cellular automata and closed chains of contours. *Machines*, 7(2), 28. https:/doi.org/10.3390/machines7020028.

CHAPTER 13

PARALLEL SIMULATION AND VISUALIZATION OF TRAFFIC FLOWS USING CELLULAR AUTOMATA THEORY AND QUASIGASDYNAMIC APPROACH

ANTONINA CHECHINA,[1,*] NATALIA CHURBANOVA,[1,2] PAVEL SOKOLOV,[2,3] MARINA TRAPEZNIKOVA,[1,2] MIKHAIL GERMAN,[1] ALEXEY ERMAKOV,[1] OBIDZHON BOZOROV[4]

[1] Keldysh Institute of Applied Mathematics RAS, Moscow, Russia
[2] Moscow Automobile and Road Construction State Technical University (MADI), Moscow, Russia
[3] Moscow Technical University of Communications and Informatics, Moscow, Russia
[4] National University of Uzbekistan named after Mirzo Ulugbek, Tashkent, Uzbekistan
*Corresponding author: chechina.antonina@yandex.ru

Abstract

Research dealing with mathematical modeling of vehicular traffic flows on complex urban transport networks using modern supercomputers is presented in this chapter. The micro- and macroscopic models previously created by the authors were further developed in this work. The proposed 2D microscopic model is based on the cellular automata theory and includes various driving strategies. The "slow-to-start" version of the model is developed. The model is implemented as a program package that includes user interface and visualization module. The macroscopic model uses the continuous medium approximation: it is constructed by analogy with the quasigasdynamic system of equations. The one-dimensional version is proposed in the study; nevertheless, it allows reproducing changes in the number of lanes as well as possible road entrances and exits. Parallel algorithms adapted to high-performance computing systems have been created for both models, ensuring rapid computations on city road networks.

Keywords: Mathematical modeling of traffic flows, cellular automata, quasigasdynamic system of equations, parallel computing

13.1   Introduction

This work deals with two approaches to the vehicular traffic flow simulation: A 2D microscopic model based on the cellular automata theory, as well as a macroscopic quasigasdynamic traffic model are developed and verified.

The cellular automata theory (CA), first proposed by John von Neumann in the mid-twentieth century, has found its application in many fields of science. With its help, economic, social, technical, biological and other processes are modeled. Since 1992, when Kai Nagel and Michael Schreckenberg [10] applied the theory of cellular automata to transport modeling, scientists from around the world have created many variants of traffic flow models based on it (see, for example, Buslaev *et al.* [1], Maerivoet and De Moor [9]). Previously, this approach seemed to be the most promising for a detailed description of local road situations at short distances, since the models are quite flexible due to the ability to implement any driver strategy without significant algorithmic costs. However, in connection with the capacity of modern ultra-high-performance computing equipment, models of this type can also be successfully used to simulate traffic on large road networks.

To describe the basic regularities of dense traffic flow, it is convenient to use macroscopic models [13] based on the continuous medium approximation. In contrast to microscopic models, the main objects of study in such models are fields of the average vehicle speed and the density of flow of vehicles. In the paper by Sukhinova *et al.*[12], a 2D macroscopic model was proposed by the analogy with the quasigasdynamic (QGD) system of equations designed to describe a wide class of compressible gas flows, including low Mach number flows (see Chetverushkin [5]). The QGD traffic model included the concept of variable lateral velocity as the speed of changing lanes at multilane traffic. However, when modeling traffic at complex junctions and interchanges, and especially in numerical implementation, such a description can introduce additional difficulties. At the same time, in many practically important situations a one-dimensional description may be sufficient to study the peculiarities of vehicular flow and to obtain qualitatively correct results.

13.2   The Original CA Model

The original cellular automata model created by the authors presents a generalization of the classic Nagel-Schreckenberg model [10] for a multilane case with various driver behavior algorithms included.

The road is divided into equal cells. As is usual for traffic CA models, a cell is 7.5 meters long and one lane wide, and the time step is 1 second. The cell can be either empty or occupied by a single vehicle. Each car has a set of parameters: unique ID, maximum speed, current speed and final destination; its driver can be "cautious" or "aggressive," "cooperative" or not.

Each time step cell state update is carried out according to the following rules:

- A vehicle changes a lane if it is necessary (to reach the desired destination or to drive around an obstacle), it is advantageous for a driver (leads to speed increase and/or density decrease) and it is possible (i.e., if the lane change is allowed and the target cell is empty);

- A vehicle moves along the road according to the classic rules for the one-lane traffic [10].

Improved algorithms of lane changing, crossroad overcoming, queue forming, moving on the road with complex geometry, and driving around obstacles were created. Algorithms depicting different driving strategies were included.

13.3   The Slow-to-Start Version of the CA Model

According to the classic one-lane Nagel-Schreckenberg rules, the driver checks if the next cell is empty, and if it is, he starts moving. But there is another class of models – "slow-to-start" – where vehicles begin their movement only on condition that there is more than one free cell in front of them (see Maerivoet and De Moor [9]). This rule was included in the model so that cars did not disperse too quickly from the place of the traffic jam. It allows reproducing the effect of hysteresis that is observed during the transition from the free flow phase to the synchronized flow phase, depending on random processes in the traffic flow.

According to the three-phase theory by Kerner [6], there are three phases in the traffic flow: F is the phase of free flow, S is the phase of synchronized flow and J is the phase of wide moving jams. Due to the instability of the flow, for example, due to the effect of over-acceleration (see Kerner *et al.* [7]), phase transitions can occur spontaneously. As experimental data shows, models of the "slow-to-start" class reproduce such phase transitions more successfully.

To include the "slow-to-start" rule, the set of appropriate conditions was added to the created model. The results obtained using this model can be found in the paper by Chechina *et al.* [2].

13.4   Numerical Realization

The created program package consists of two modules: the computational module that carries out calculations and the user interface and visualization module that serves the purpose of getting the initial data from a user, transferring it to the computational module, getting results back and providing their visual interpretation. The architecture of the software system for the visualization of vehicle flows is based on three basic elements (Figure 13.1):

- Computing server;

- Storage server;

- Browser.

Files with the results have their own internal vector coordinate format. The browser uses HTML5 canvas technology to reproduce the results. Therefore, it is necessary to transform the results into a Cartesian coordinate system. Data is converted in a separate thread named "Thread 2." This is necessary so that the main thread can simultaneously transmit data to the browser ("Thread 1").

On the browser side, multithreading is also used:

- "Thread 0" - The main javascript thread responsible for the operation of the web page;

- "Thread 1" - Requests data from the server (if data become scarce);

- "Thread 2" - Draws the results frame by frame.

Such a system allows starting the playback of the results even before the computations end.

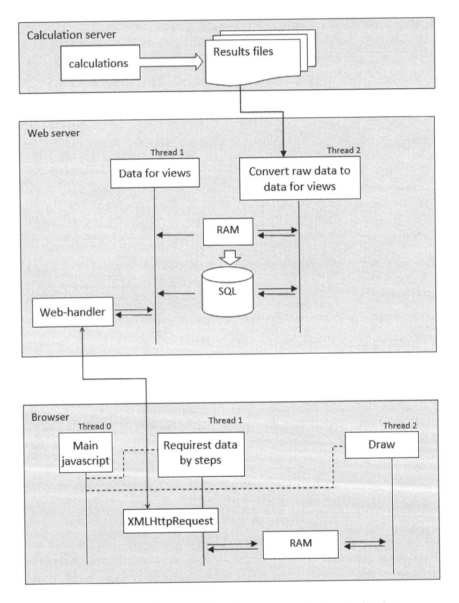

Figure 13.1   Architecture of the software system for the visualization.

The software package has the ability to define a network using a visual designer. A network of any size and configuration can be constructed from standard elements. An example of the road fragment design is shown in Figure 13.2.

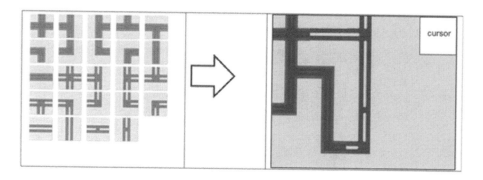

Figure 13.2　An example of complex road network created using basic road elements.

Results can be visualized using the visualization module (see Chechina *et al.* [3]). The example of visualization of a small network is shown in Figure 13.3.

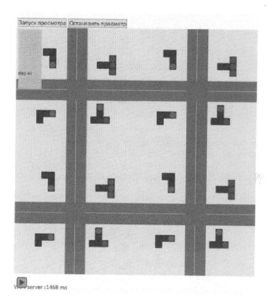

Figure 13.3　Visualization of traffic on small road network.

The code is written in C/C++ and uses the MPI library for parallel calculations. Separate subprograms simulate traffic on different types of road elements in parallel, with data exchange on the boundaries.

The results of computations for some standard road elements are shown in Figure 13.4. Different colors of cars represent different destinations attributed to them. Figure 13.4(a) and Figure 13.4(c) represent signalized intersections (T-cross and X-cross respectively). In Figure 13.4(b) a U-turn on a road with a wide median is shown. In Figure 13.4(d), where the road with an accident is presented, the black circle represents an unmoving car that experienced the accident. In Figure 13.4(e) an on-ramp is shown.

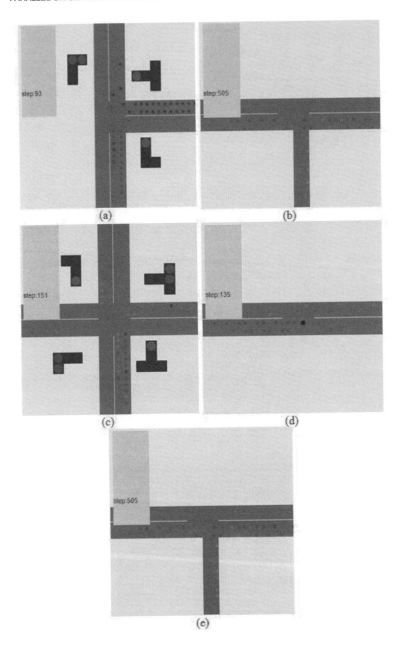

Figure 13.4   Basic road fragments.

At each time step processors exchange information on whether any vehicles are crossing the boundaries during this step. If the answer is positive, the data regarding those vehicles is packed and sent/received, and the cars appear on the next road fragment. In order to avoid a situation where the target cell is already occupied, the information about all vehicles that stopped near the beginning of the road fragment is collected. If there is a traffic jam on the road, the drivers from the previous (upstream) fragment that are nearing its end can see it and slow down or stop if necessary.

13.5 Test Predictions for the CA Model

The models have been verified by various numerical experiments (see, for example, Chechina *et al.* [2, 3], including the comparison with experimental data (Chechina *et al.* [4]).

One of the investigated test problems is traffic flow modeling on a small network composed of two intersections, which is a part of Moscow road network (Figure 13.5).

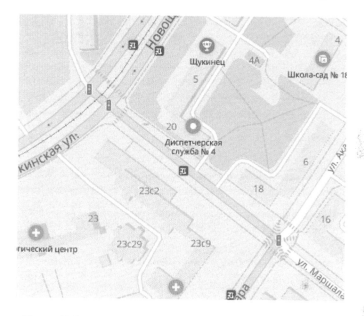

Figure 13.5   Two neighboring intersections on a map of Moscow.

These intersections are situated close enough in the network and therefore affect each other significantly, while other obstacles are farther away and have less of an impact. That is why it makes sense to simulate traffic on these two crossroads combined.

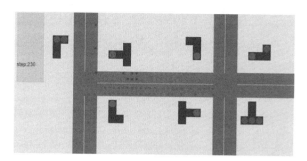

Figure 13.6   Simulating traffic on two neighboring intersections: T-Crossroad + X-Crossroad.

The result of modeling is shown in Figures 13.6 and 13.7. Along with visual representation of what's happening with traffic on this part of the network, various average characteristics can be obtained.

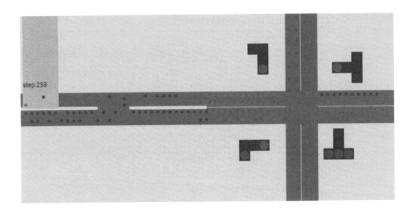

Figure 13.7   Simulating traffic on two neighboring intersections: U-Turn + X-Crossroad.

13.6   The QGD Approach to Traffic Flow Modeling

The one-dimensional variant of the quasigasdynamic (QGD) system of equations for the description of vehicular traffic flow can be written as follows:

$$\frac{\partial \rho}{\partial t} + \frac{\partial \rho V}{\partial x} = \frac{\partial}{\partial x}\frac{\tau}{2}\frac{\partial(\rho V^2 + P)}{\partial x} + F_\rho \tag{13.1}$$

$$\frac{\partial \rho V}{\partial t} + \frac{\partial \rho V^2}{\partial x} = f - \mathrm{grad}P + \frac{\partial}{\partial x}\frac{\tau}{2}\frac{\partial(\rho V^3 + PV)}{\partial x} + F_V \tag{13.2}$$

Here $\rho \left[\frac{\mathrm{veh}}{\mathrm{km \cdot lane}}\right]$ is the traffic density, and $V \left[\frac{\mathrm{km}}{\mathrm{h}}\right]$ is the spatial average speed of vehicles.

The above system belongs to macroscopic models of the second order [13]. It includes two equations in the form of conservation laws for obtaining the density (13.1) and the speed (13.2). These equations employ the additional functions listed below, which are related specifically to transport problems.

The analogue of pressure: $P(\rho) = \frac{\alpha \rho^\beta}{\beta}$. Phenomenological constants are taken from works by other authors as $\alpha = 60\frac{\mathrm{km}^2}{\mathrm{h}^2}$, $\beta = 2$.

The accelerating/decelerating force: $f = a\rho$. Here a is the relaxation term reflecting adaptation of the speed to the equilibrium speed: $a = \frac{V_{eq}(\rho) - V}{T}$.

The involved equilibrium speed $V_{eq}(\rho)$ has the sense of the optimal speed under the given conditions. It is a function that depends only on the density and is obtained from the fundamental diagram. In the current investigation the following parabolic fundamental diagram is used:

$$Q_{eq}(\rho) = \rho V_0 \left(1 - \frac{\rho}{\rho_{jam}}\right) \tag{13.3}$$

Taking into account the relation $Q_{eq} = \rho V_{eq}$ we get the next dependence of the equilibrium speed on the density:

$$V_{eq}(\rho) = V_0(1 - \frac{\rho}{\rho_{jam}}) \qquad (13.4)$$

Here V_0 is the free traffic speed, and ρ_{jam} is the density at which vehicles stop moving ("traffic jam"). In computations the next values are used: $V_0 = 90 \frac{km}{h}$, $\rho_{jam} = 120 \frac{veh}{km \cdot lane}$.

The function T depends on the density:

$$T(\rho) = t_0(1 + \frac{r\rho}{\rho_{jam} - r\rho}) \qquad (13.5)$$

where $t_0 = 50$ and $r = 0.95$ are the model parameters.

The source functions on the right-hand sides of equations (13.1) and (13.2) are equal to zero if the road is homogeneous, that is, the number of lanes does not change and there are no entrances/exits. If there is a change in the number of lanes, then the concept of the real function I, which has the meaning of the number of lanes, is introduced [13]. If there are entries/exits, then the concept of the effective source density v_{rmp} is introduced also by analogy with [13], and the source terms on the right-hand sides of (13.1) and (13.2) take the following form:

$$F_\rho(x, t) = -\frac{\rho V}{I}\frac{dI}{dx} + v_{rmp}(x) \qquad (13.6)$$

where

$$v_{rmp}(x, t) = \begin{cases} \frac{Q_{rmp}(t)}{IL_{rmp}} & \text{if } x \text{ is insidetheentry/exitzone,} \\ 0 & \text{otherwise,} \end{cases} \qquad (13.7)$$

$$F_V(x, t) = -\frac{\rho V^2}{I}\frac{dI}{dx} + V v_{rmp}(x) + \rho A_{rmp} \qquad (13.8)$$

where $A_{rmp} = \frac{(V_{rmp} - V)|Q_{rmp}|}{\rho I L_{rmp}}$

Here Q_{rmp} denotes the incoming (from the entry) or outgoing (from the exit) traffic flow, L_{rmp} is the acceleration band length - the length of the on-ramp or off-ramp, and V_{rmp} is the speed of on-ramp vehicles merging with or diverging from the main road, $V_{rmp} < V$.

One of the basic assumptions for the QGD system is the existence of additional mass flux that ensures a smooth solution at the reference scale of the medium [5]. The right-hand sides of equations (13.1) and (13.2) include such fluxes. By the analogy with gas dynamics, minimal reference time and space scales are introduced for traffic flows in order to satisfy the approximation of a continuous medium. The small parameter τ is interpreted as a reference time, which means the time interval in which several vehicles cross a given point of the road. As a reference length, the distance between vehicles for the given speed can be considered.

For numerical implementation of systems (13.1) and (13.2), an explicit finite-difference method is used. Convective terms are approximated by central differences [11]. The conditional stability of schemes is ensured by the presence of diffusion terms on the right-hand sides. As the numerical implementation is based on explicit computational algorithms, its parallelization can be performed with high efficiency. The parallel algorithm is focused on the use of distributed memory supercomputers.

13.7   Parallel Implementation of the QGD Traffic Model

For the interaction of parallel processes in the code, the technology MPI (message passing interface) is used. This technology is designed to transfer information between multiple processes that perform the same task. The main mechanism of MPI is the transmission and reception of messages. The message contains information and a sign indicating the type of message for selective reception.

Parallelization is based on the principle of geometrical parallelism. For traffic flow computations it is natural to use partitioning of the computational domain (the road network) into subdomains, each representing one segment of the network connecting two neighboring nodes (intersections). In network nodes the data exchange between adjacent segments occurs. The splitting is carried out in such a way that two neighboring sections have two common points for the correct implementation of boundary conditions at bordering points of subdomains. Thus, each section of the road is calculated on a separate processor, transmitting and synchronizing data using the MPI_Send function (for sending data), MPI_Recv (for receiving data) and MPI_Barrier (for synchronizing calculations). To work effectively, it is necessary that the number of calculated areas is less than or equal to the number of available processors of the computing system.

Further calculations were carried out at Keldysh Institute of Applied Mathematics RAS on the MVS-Express supercomputer, which has a distributed memory architecture (see KIAM official site [8]).

13.8   Test Predictions for the QGD Traffic Model

As in the case of the CA model, the QGD traffic model verification was performed by test problems on signalized and non-signalized intersections. In test predictions the intersection is represented as a graph, at parallelization each subdomain corresponds to a graph edge.

In the signalized intersection test problem a traffic light is placed in the graph node, allowing one or another entrance flow to alternately pass through the intersection in accordance with the traffic light phase.

For the flow for which the green light is on, conditions of matching are set on the boundary between neighboring subdomains – a simple exchange of the boundary values of densities and velocities takes place. For the flow for which a red light is on, boundary conditions change as follows.

For flow entering the node on the right boundary of the subdomain before the traffic light:

$$\rho_N^{n+1} = \rho_N^n + \frac{\Delta t}{h} (\rho V)_{N-1}^n \tag{13.9}$$

$$V_N^{n+1} = 0 \tag{13.10}$$

For flow exiting the node on the left boundary of the subdomain after the traffic light:

$$\rho_0^{n+1} = \rho_0^n - \frac{\Delta t}{h} (\rho V)_1^n \tag{13.11}$$

$$(\rho V)_0^{n+1} = (\rho V)_0^n - \frac{\Delta t}{h} (\rho V^2)_1^n \tag{13.12}$$

Here superscripts correspond to the time levels and subscripts correspond to the points of computational subdomains.

One of the problems solved with the use of the QGD model is traffic movement on the clover leaf intersection, a type of intersection that can be commonly seen on highways. The scheme of the intersection is shown in Figure 13.8.

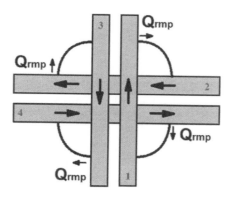

Figure 13.8   Clover leaf intersection (scheme).

It is a two-level road intersection where roads are connected via on-ramps and off-ramps only. The problem allows verifying the adequacy of functions (13.6) to (13.8). Entering flows Q_{in} at the beginning of the considered roads' segments are constant and are derived from initial densities of 20, 40, 25 and 45 $\frac{veh}{km \cdot lane}$ respectively for roads with numbers 1, 2, 3 and 4.

On off-ramps flows Q_{rmp} are defined by the formula:

$$Q_{rmp} = -\left(C - Q_{in}\right)/2 \tag{13.13}$$

where C is the corresponding road capacity.

The results of computation for different time moments are shown in Figure 13.9(a,b). The clover leaves are shown schematically because calculations along them are not carried out.

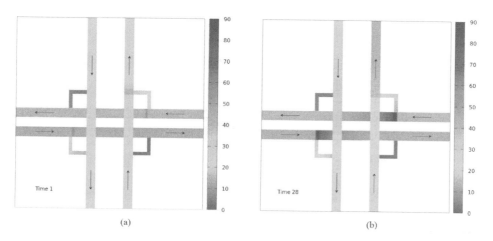

Figure 13.9   Clover leaf intersection (results of the simulation).

The influence of bottlenecks formed by entrances and exits can be clearly seen. Higher density regions resulted from these bottlenecks spreading upstream with time. Therefore, by using varying entering flows and on-ramp/off-ramp flows in this simple computation based on the one-dimensional model, one can obtain valid results for two-level clover leaf intersections.

The next problem is traffic flow simulation on a real fragment of Moscow city road network (Figure 13.10), including two nodes with traffic lights and two non-signalized nodes. In Figure 13.10(a), the map of the area is shown. In Figure 13.10(b), the traffic scheme is presented; black arrows show permitted driving directions. Traffic flows in all nodes are distributed equally in all directions.

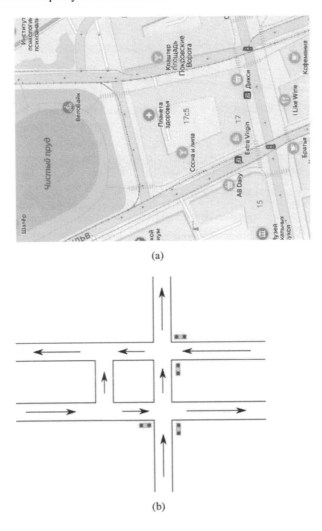

(a)

(b)

Figure 13.10   Modeling on neighboring intersections (map (a) and scheme (b)).

The obtained density fields for four subsequent time moments are presented in Figure 13.11. Green and red circles represent traffic lights. Arrows show driving directions. At the initial time moment traffic flow density is the same on all roads. It can be noticed that traffic becomes denser before the red traffic light and, after the light turns green, the density decreases again.

One can conclude that numerical simulation with the use of the proposed QGD traffic model and the developed parallel software led to correct results. In the calculations, a parallelization efficiency of almost 100 percent was achieved.

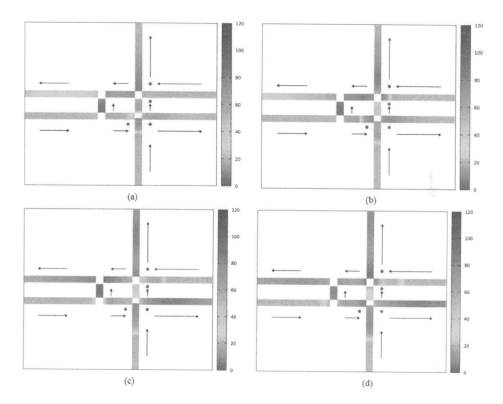

Figure 13.11   Modeling of neighboring intersections (results of simulation at different time moments).

13.9 Conclusion

The proposed models, namely, the CA model and the QGD traffic model, were verified on various test problems. Obtained results showed that the created software can be used for traffic modeling on real city road networks. Moreover, the CA model allows taking into consideration different driving strategies. The developed modeling tools make it possible to solve numerous traffic management tasks, both short term and long term, such as choosing traffic lights regimes, signs and road marking, rebuilding or reorganizing the roads and so on.

Acknowledgments

This work was supported by the Russian Foundation for Basic Research (grants 18-51-41001 and 18-01-00405) and by the Agency for Science and Technology of the Republic of Uzbekistan (grant MRU-OT-30/2017).

REFERENCES

1. Buslaev, A.P., Tatashev, A.G. and Yashina, M.V. (2018). On cellular automata, traffic and dynamical systems in graphs. *International Journal of Engineering & Technology*, 7(2.28), 351356.

2. Chechina, A., Churbanova, N. and Trapeznikova, M. (2018a). Multilane traffic flow modeling using cellular automata theory. *EPJ Web of Conferences*, 173, 06003.

3. Chechina, A., Churbanova, N., Trapeznikova, M., Ermakov, A. and German, M. (2018b). Traffic flow modeling on road networks using cellular automata theory. *International Journal of Engineering & Technology*, 7(2.28), 225-227.

4. Chechina, A., Churbanova, N. and Trapeznikova, M. (2019). Reproduction of experimental spatio-temporal structures in traffic flows using mathematical model based on cellular automata theory. *Periodicals of Engineering and Natural Sciences*, 7: 1, 76-81.

5. Chetverushkin, B.N. (2008). *Kinetic Schemes and Quasi-Gas Dynamic System of Equations*. CIMNE, Barcelona.

6. Kerner, B. (2004). *The Physics of Traffic*. Springer, Berlin.

7. Kerner, B., Klenov, S., Hermanns, G. and Schreckenberg, M. (2013). Effect of driver overacceleration on traffic breakdown in three-phase cellular automaton traffic flow models. *Physica A: Statistical Mechanics and its Applications*, 392, 4083-4105.

8. KIAM - The official site of Keldysh Institute of Applied Mathematics, Hybrid computational cluster MVS-Express available at: http://www.kiam.ru/MVS/resourses/mvse.html.

9. Maerivoet, S. and De Moor, B. (2005). Cellular automata models of road traffic. *Physics Reports*, 419(1), 1-64.

10. Nagel, K. and Schreckenberg, M. (1992). A cellular automaton model for freeway traffic. *J. Phys. I France*, 2, 2221-2229.

11. Samarskii, A.A. (2001). *The Theory of Difference Schemes*. CRC Press.

12. Sukhinova, A.B., Trapeznikova, M.A., Chetverushkin, B.N. and Churbanova, N.G. (2009). Two-dimensional macroscopic model of traffic flows. *Mathematical Models and Computer Simulation*, 1(6), 669-676.

13. Treiber, M. and Kesting, A. (2013). *Traffic Flow Dynamics. Data, Models and Simulation*. Springer, Berlin-Heidelberg.

Also of Interest

Check out these other similar books by the editor published by Scrivener Publishing

Emerging Extended Reality Technologies for Industry 4.0
Early Experiences with Conception, Design, Implementation, Evaluation and Deployment
Edited by Jolanda G. Tromp, Dac-Nhuong Le and Chung Van Le
Published 2020. ISBN 978-1-119-65463-6

Security Designs for the Cloud, IoT and Social Networking
Edited by Dac-Nhuong Le, Chintan Bhatt and Mani Madhukar
Published 2019. ISBN 978-1-119-59226-6

Network Modeling, Simulation and Analysis in MATLAB
Theory and Practices
Edited by Dac-Nhuong Le, Abhishek Kumar Pandey, Sairam Tadepalli, Pramod Singh Rathore and Jyotir Moy Chatterjee
Published 2019. ISBN 978-1-119-63143-9

Cyber Security in Parallel and Distributed Computing
Concepts, Techniques, Applications and Case Studies
Edited by Dac-Nhuong Le, Raghvendra Kumar, Brojo Kishore Mishra, Manju Khari and Jyotir Moy Chatterjee
Published 2019. ISBN 978-1-119-48805-7

Emerging Technologies for Health and Medicine
Virtual Reality, Augmented Reality, Artificial Intelligence, Internet of Things, Robotics, Industry 4.0
Edited by Dac-Nhuong Le, Chung Van Le, Jolanda G. Tromp and Gia Nhu Nguyen
Published 2018. ISBN 978-119-50981-3

Cloud Computing and Virtualization
Edited by Dac-Nhuong Le, Raghvendra Kumar, Gia Nhu Nguyen and Jyotir Moy Chatterjee
Published 2018. ISBN 978-119-48790-6

Printed and bound by CPI Group (UK) Ltd, Croydon, CR0 4YY